Counterinsurgency ....d

Counterinsurgency and Collusion in Northern Ireland

Mark McGovern

First published 2019 by Pluto Press
345 Archway Road, London N6 5AA

www.plutobooks.com

Copyright © Mark McGovern 2019

The right of Mark McGovern to be identified as the author of this work has been asserted by him in accordance with the Copyright, Designs and Patents Act 1988.

British Library Cataloguing in Publication Data
A catalogue record for this book is available from the British Library

ISBN 978 0 7453 3898 9   Hardback
ISBN 978 0 7453 3899 6   Paperback
ISBN 978 1 7868 0435 8   PDF eBook
ISBN 978 1 7868 0437 2   Kindle eBook
ISBN 978 1 7868 0436 5   EPUB eBook

This book is printed on paper suitable for recycling and made from fully managed and sustained forest sources. Logging, pulping and manufacturing processes are expected to conform to the environmental standards of the country of origin.

Typeset by Stanford DTP Services, Northampton, England

Simultaneously printed in the United Kingdom and United States of America

For Nicola, Oisín and Séimí

And in memory of my Dad

Contents

Acknowledgements ix
List of Abbreviations xii

Introduction: What is Collusion? 1
  Collusion and Mid-Ulster 1
  What is Collusion? 3
  Loyalism, Counterinsurgency and Collusion 4

1. British Counterinsurgency and the Roots of Collusion 7
  Collusion and British Counterinsurgency 7
  What is Counterinsurgency? 9
  Small Wars and Imperial Policing 11
  The Rule of Law and 'Counter-Gangs' 16

2. Northern Ireland and the Roots of Collusion 21
  McGurk's Bar and the MRF 21
  Revolution, 'Reprisal' and Partition 22
  Policing the State 24
  Collusion, Bombings and Sectarian Killings 28
  Eliminating Enemies 31

3. An Intelligence War 36
  Phases of Counterinsurgency 36
  Counterinsurgency, Informers and Policing 38
  Handling Informers, Changing the Rules 40
  Intelligence 'Leaks' 42
  The FRU and Brian Nelson 43
  Agents, Informers and a Void of Law 45
  Informers, Collusion and Deniability 48
  Covering Up Collusion 51
  The Liberal Ideology of Collusion 53

4. Arming Loyalism 57
  Providing Weapons 57
  Arms, Ulster Resistance and the Mid-Ulster UVF 59
  Seizures, Police 'Failures' and Loyalism Rearmed 61

5. Shooting to Kill: Targeting Republican Combatants 66
War and Mid-Ulster 66
'Set-Piece' Operations and Shooting to Kill 67
'Set-Piece' Shoot-to-Kill and Mid-Ulster 74
Collusion and the Case of Gerard Casey 78
Shootings at the Battery Bar 83
Killings in Cappagh 87

6. Stopping Sinn Fein: Collusion as Political Force 96
Targeting Sinn Fein 96
Endgame Politics 98
Local, Personal and Political 102
Targeting John Davey 104
The Killing of Bernard O'Hagan 107
The Shootings of Tommy Casey and Sean Anderson 110
The Killing of Patrick Shanaghan 114
The Killings of Tommy Donaghy and Malachy Carey 119
The Shooting of Danny Cassidy 123
Collusion and the Case of Eddie Fullerton 124

7. Instilling Fear: Targeting Republican Families and Communities 128
'See No Evil' and 'Breakfast Table' Collusion 128
Wars of Attrition 131
The Shooting of Phelim McNally 135
The Killing of Frank Hughes 138
Killings in the Moy 142
The Killing of Charlie and Teresa Fox 147
The Castlerock Massacre 151
The Killing of Roseann Mallon 155

Conclusion: Collusion, Truth and Justice 161
Dealing With the Past 161
Investigating Collusion 164
Postscript: What Proves Collusion? 168

Notes 171
Further Reading 225
Index 229

Acknowledgements

From the outset I would like to thank and pay tribute to the victims' relatives whose testimonies lie at the core of this book. Their efforts to preserve the memory of their loved ones and search for truth over many years are what have ensured that collusion remains such an important issue to be addressed in dealing with the past of the conflict in and about Northern Ireland. I hugely appreciate the time they took to invite me into their homes and I was humbled by their willingness to talk to me about some of the worst memories of their lives. The book could not have happened without their help, understanding and perseverance. I would therefore like to thank Michael Armstrong, Siobhan Nugent, Briege O'Donnell and Poilin Quinn, Martin Bogues, Mary Bogues and Anna Shanaghan, Suzanne Bunting, Danny Carey, Colette Casey, Fran Casey and Janet McGrail, Una and Geraldine Casey, Pauline Davey Kennedy, Johnny Donaghy, Paddy Fox, Bernadette McKearney and Tommy McKearney, Eileen Hughes, Martin Mallon, Donna and Oonagh Martin, Gerry McEldowney, Henry McNally, Kevin McNally and Lawrence McNally, Sean and Charity McPeake, John O'Hagan, Suzanne Bunting and the family of Liam Ryan. A special note, too, in memory of those family members who have passed away since the start of this project, including Neecie Kelly, Eamonn Hughes, Bridget Mallon, Peggy Quinn and Maura McKearney. There were some occasions, given the information already in the public realm, when it felt better to limit the pain of putting someone through remembering and retelling their story again, but I want to thank all those relatives who had already made those memories available via newspapers, news programmes and testimonies, particularly the families of Danny Cassidy and Eddie Fullerton.

I would like to thank the families and friends of other victims who I met and talked to and who provided invaluable insight into the workings of collusion in the killing of their own loved ones, including the family of Rory and Gerard Cairns, the family of Pat Finucane, the family and friends of Sam Marshall, the families of the victims of the McGurk's pub bombing, those of the Ormeau Road massacre and the relatives of the victims of the Loughinisland massacre.

A great many people helped make this book possible, but none more so than Mark Thompson, CEO of the human rights and victims' organisation Relatives for Justice. From the inception of the research and throughout its course, Mark and Relatives for Justice were partners in this work, providing support, access, information and insight. No one knows more about collusion than Mark – aside, perhaps, from those who were involved in it. I am grateful to Mark and to all the victims' families and staff at Relatives for Justice, particularly Andrée Murphy, Pauline Fitzpatrick, Mark Sykes and Mike Ritchie.

I want to thank a number of legal figures, political representatives and human rights and community activists who gave up their time to talk to me and whose knowledge and perspectives helped guide the work. They include Dr Michael Maguire (Police Ombudsman for Northern Ireland), Barra McGrory (former Director of Public Prosecutions for Northern Ireland), Niall Murphy (KRW Law), John Finucane (Finucane and Toner), Bernadette McAliskey, Denis Bradley (former Co-Chair of the Consultative Group on the Past), Mitchell McLaughlin (former Speaker of the Northern Ireland Assembly), Jefffrey Donaldson MP, Mark Durkan (former Deputy First Minister for Northern Ireland and MP), Patricia McBride, Barry Monteith, Breandán Mac Cionnaith, Jim Hasson, Johnny Rush and members of the Pat Finucane Centre, Bloody Sunday Trust, Bloody Sunday March for Justice, Coiste and the Committee on the Administration of Justice. A big thank you to Peter Heathwood who provided access to (and copies from) his unique archive of troubles-related television programmes. I am also very grateful to everyone at the Institute of Race Relations (IRR) and Race and Class, particularly IRR's director Liz Fekete, for their unstinting support for the work.

The book would not have happened without funding support from several bodies, so I am very grateful to Edge Hill University, the British Academy and the European Union under the Peace III Special Programme for Peace and Reconciliation Fund, via the 'Harms to Rights' strand of the Relatives for Justice 'Transitional Legacies' programme. I am thankful for the support and help of colleagues at Edge Hill and other universities, including Allison Moore, Paul Reynolds, Sally Hester, Victor Merriman, Bob Brecher, Cathy Bergin, Fionnuala Ní Aoláin, Kieran McEvoy and John Newsinger. I would also like to thank family and friends including my mum, brothers, sister and the wider McGovern, Gallagher, Foster and McPhee clans, Robbee, Tracey and the kids, Mark, Bobby, Roy (and Tommy) and all in the Park End and the Winslow.

Finally I would like to thank my wife Nicola and our two sons Oisín and Séimí. Nicola provided an invaluable contribution to the project itself, transcribing interviews and reviewing drafts, and throughout the love, support and forbearance of my family has been an irreplaceable source of strength and inspiration.

List of Abbreviations

COIN	Counterinsurgency Doctrine
DMSU	Divisional Mobile Support Unit
DUP	Democratic Unionist Party
FRU	Force Research Unit
GAA	Gaelic Athletics Association
HET	Historical Enquiries Team
INLA	Irish National Liberation Army
IRA	Irish Republican Army
IRSP	Irish Republican Socialist Party
LVF	Loyalist Volunteer Force
MRF	Military Reaction Force
NIO	Northern Ireland Office
PSNI	Police Service of Northern Ireland
RUC	Royal Ulster Constabulary
SAS	Special Air Service
SB	Special Branch
SDLP	Social Democratic and Labour Party
SPA	Special Powers Act
SRU	Special Reconnaissance Unit
TCG	Tasking and Co-ordinating Group
UDA	Ulster Defence Association
UDR	Ulster Defence Regiment
UFF	Ulster Freedom Fighters
USC	Ulster Special Constabulary
UVF	Ulster Volunteer Force

Introduction: What is Collusion?

Collusion and Mid-Ulster

On the evening of 8 May 1994, 76-year-old Roseann Mallon was shot dead by members of a loyalist paramilitary organisation, the Ulster Volunteer Force (UVF), as she sat in her sister-in-law's home in a remote rural part of East Tyrone. Roseann was the aged aunt of Martin and Christie Mallon, well-known republicans in the area. At the moment she was killed the house Roseann was in was under close, indeed constant, surveillance by covert units of the British Army. It included cameras able to relay live images to a nearby military command centre, home to British Army specialist units such as the Special Air Service (SAS). Whether the cameras were operational after dark remains the subject of dispute. In any case, six covert British soldiers were dug into hidden observation posts around the Mallon home. They were part of a much larger, sophisticated long-term surveillance operation, something that would require very senior military and political approval. The soldiers were also in constant, direct contact with an officer at their base who was overseeing matters. This British Army covert unit witnessed the shooting of Roseann Mallon and immediately relayed that information to their commanding officer. Yet the UVF gunmen were not only able to drive up to the house, run to and fire in through a window, kill Roseann (and wound her elderly sister-in-law Bridget), but also drive away again and make good their escape. The soldiers had been ordered to take no action. No one was ever found guilty for killing Roseann.

There is much more in the death of Roseann Mallon that makes it one of the 'most controversial' killings of the three decades of the Northern Ireland conflict.[1] It is an important part of a broader, darker story of the 'dirty war' that took place which resonates up to the present. Not least in the ongoing difficult, often politically divisive debates about how to deal with the legacy of the past and outstanding issues of truth and justice left in its wake. An inquest into Roseann Mallon's death has been 20 years in the making and remains unresolved. Roseann was one of several dozen people killed by loyalist paramilitaries in an area of Mid-Ulster encompassing East Tyrone and South Derry in the last years of the conflict, from 1988 to 1994. Many of these deaths, as with Roseann's, have been the subject of long-term allegations of collusion between various sections of the state security forces (the police, army and intelligence services) and loyalist paramilitary organisations. Most of those killed were active republicans, members of the Irish Republican Army (IRA), members or elected officials of the Irish republican political party Sinn Fein or (as in the case of Roseann) simply relatives, friends or workmates of republicans. Many of these deaths are currently being investigated by the Police Ombudsman for Northern Ireland as part of a series of linked inquiries looking at police collusion with the Mid-Ulster UVF in East Tyrone, and loyalists in South Derry.[2] These killings provide the focus of this book.

By the 1980s Mid-Ulster was a major site of the conflict. The IRA was highly active there, and a crucial element in republican military and political strategy. They engaged in a series of attacks on outlying police and military installations. Their campaign included killing many British soldiers, policemen of the Royal Ulster Constabulary (RUC) and members of the locally recruited Ulster Defence Regiment (UDR). There were also many civilian victims. They included people killed for doing work building or repairing military and police barracks. Almost invariably these victims were from the unionist/Protestant community. This was a heavily militarised area with a massive police and army presence. Very active here too were specialist counterinsurgency units of the British military, most obviously the SAS. Mid-Ulster (East Tyrone in particular) witnessed many of the most controversial state 'shoot-to-kill' incidents in this period. Chief among them was the 'set-piece' ambush at Loughgall in 1987 in which eight IRA Volunteers (and a civilian) were shot dead by the SAS – the largest single loss of life suffered by the IRA since the 1920s. Loyalists were very active here too. Mid-Ulster is deeply divided along political and sectarian lines. In the 1970s it formed part of the 'murder triangle', an area infamous for a large number of sectarian killings carried out by local loyalist groups who included many members of the RUC and UDR in their ranks. Loyalists in rural areas of the North often drew their support and activists from the self-same communities as did the security forces. From the late 1980s onward Mid-Ulster loyalists would embark on an escalating campaign of attacks and killings. That included many of the deaths examined here and in which collusion between loyalists and the security forces has long been suspected.

What is Collusion?

As a term, collusion has become part of the dispute over dealing with the past. Various official inquiries over the last decade and more have developed contrasting ways in which to understand what collusion means and how (if it all) it should be applied in law. It is a politically and ideologically potent word.[3] What then is collusion? Stated broadly, collusion might be understood as any form of (usually) organised or premeditated and generally secret collaboration or connivance aimed at an illicit, mutually beneficial end. In Northern Ireland collusion has essentially been used to describe state-sponsored violence and secret collaboration between state forces and paramilitary groups. Academically, it has been understood as a 'local term for the widespread practise of using "counter-gangs" or death squads to eliminate or terrorise those who oppose the policies and actions of the powerful'.[4] From a victims' group perspective it has been defined as an 'indirect campaign of murder which involved the manipulation of loyalist paramilitaries who were provided with security information and who then killed with the knowledge that they were free from prosecution'.[5] In official terms, it was first understood as a series of 'serious acts and omissions' by security force members resulting in people being killed or injured.[6]

The most substantive formal definition was provided by retired Canadian Judge Peter Cory. In 2002 Cory was asked by the British and Irish governments to carry out initial inquiries into a number of high-profile cases where allegations of collusion had been made. Cory approached the problem of definition by using various synonyms for the verb 'collude' ('to conspire, to collaborate, to plot, to scheme') to form the basis of his deliberately broad view. He placed particular emphasis on collusion being synonymous with 'connivance'; variously understood as: to 'deliberately overlook', 'to ignore', 'to turn a blind eye', 'to pretend ignorance or unawareness of something one ought morally, or officially or legally to oppose', 'to fail to take action against a known wrongdoing or misbehaviour – usually used with connive at the violation of a law', 'to be indulgent, tolerant or secretly in favour or sympathy' or 'to cooperate secretly: to have a secret understanding'.[7] Defining collusion as a 'secret understanding', and as broadly as possible, was intentional on Cory's part – justified by the need to instil and re-establish public confidence in the rule of law.

There has been much dispute over the breadth of Cory's definition, part of the 'politics of victimhood' and a wider rollback of human rights in the post-conflict era.[8] A much criticised 'variable definitional approach' adopted in several official inquiries has sometimes meant collusion could not be found because it was seen to have no legal standing.[9] Others, both north and south of the border, have endorsed Cory's approach.[10] This study will follow the latter's lead. Here, state collusion will be understood as the involvement of state agents (members of the police, army, prison and intelligence services) or state officials (government ministers, legal officers, civil servants), directly or indirectly, through commission, omission, collaboration or connivance, with armed non-state groups or agents, in wrongful acts usually (although not exclusively) involving or related to non-state political violence and extrajudicial killing.[11]

Further, it is important that collusion should not simply be attributed to, or examined in terms of, individual actions or attitudes. Collusion has been ideologically and historically framed and shaped by the structures of a prevailing social order and a specific complex of power relations. It occurs within particular institutional settings. At times, collusion is the outcome of the instrumental logic of those institutions, evidenced in broad patterns of institutional policies and practices. What we might therefore understand as institutional collusion can be defined in similar terms to institutional racism, where patterns of such wrongful acts or omissions 'overtly or covertly reside in the policies, procedures or operations and culture of public or private institutions' and form a set of practices 'inhered in the apparatus of the state and the structures of society'.[12]

Loyalism, Counterinsurgency and Collusion

This book is concerned with state collusion with loyalist organisations. State connivance and use of agents was not limited to loyalist groups, as was shown by the death of Denis Donaldson in 2005. A long-time senior republican, close to the leadership of Sinn Fein, he was killed after he was revealed to have been an informer, working for the police and MI5 for over 20 years.[13] Likewise, there have been disclosures over the role of 'Stakeknife', the British Army's 'best agent', a senior IRA man – reputed to be a leading figure within its internal security unit or 'nutting squad' – claimed to have been involved in dozens of killings.[14] Many were of members of the IRA itself, identified by this British agent and informer as agents and informers. Stakeknife's primary counterinsurgency role was to undermine the capacity of the IRA to continue its armed campaign. The vital story of agent and informer infiltration of republican organisations is one not yet fully told. Such matters lie beyond the remit and purpose of this work and deserve a full-blown study of their own.

The victims considered here were from the nationalist/Catholic community. They were killed by loyalists. No victims are more important than any other. The loss felt by other families, often at the hands of republicans, were as grievously felt as those examined here. Throughout the conflict over 3,500 people lost their lives. Of those, some 2,100 were killed by republicans. Around 50 per cent of all victims were killed by the Provisional IRA (PIRA). Loyalists killed just over 1,000 people, the security forces some 367. Catholic civilians were roughly twice as likely to be killed as their Protestant counterparts. Just over 1,200 Catholic civilians died, nearly 700 Protestant. Members of the security forces made up almost a third of all victims. Just over 500 members of the regular British Army were killed, 303 members of the RUC and RUC Reserve, and 206 members of the UDR and its replacement the Royal Irish Regiment.[15] Many security force and Protestant civilian victims were in Mid-Ulster, most at the hands of republicans.

The story of collusion, exemplified by what happened in Mid-Ulster, involves a range of factors, many with a resonance and relevance that goes far beyond the borders of the North. The patterns of individual cases of collusion need to be seen against this broader backdrop. It includes the role of British military counterinsurgency and continuities with its thought and practice back through the 'small wars' of empire. The myths of British counterinsurgency, not least its supposed adherence to the rule of law, resonate in debates about the nature of collusion. It was not so much a doctrine of 'minimum force', but of 'necessity' that had a pivotal part to play. The longer-term history of British state practice in Ireland matters too, as does the development of the legal and policing institutions of the Northern Ireland state from partition onwards. In some ways collusion was nothing new. It was also a feature throughout the long years of the conflict from 1969 to 1998, and much of what happened in Mid-Ulster later was foreshadowed by what had gone before. There were, though, changes too. A growing focus on 'intelligence' became an abiding feature of Northern Ireland's 'long war'. This placed an ever greater emphasis on the role of agents and informers and creating spaces of deniability over what it is those agents and informers might be permitted, or asked to do.

Overarching all was the British state's primary counterinsurgency concern, defeating the IRA, in whatever form that might take. A driving force behind British state collusion in the latter years of the conflict was to sap the capacity of republicans to continue armed resistance. Set-piece shoot-to-kill ambushes were a feature of an ever more active counterinsurgency campaign from the 1980s onwards and nowhere more so than in Mid-Ulster. Cases of collusion where IRA Volunteers were the victims should be seen in this light. Counterinsurgency is primarily concerned with recasting the political terrain and in the North that would involve shaping the politics of the 'endgame'. The killing of Sinn Fein activists, members and elected officials forms an important part of that story and was a prominent feature of conflict in Mid-Ulster, particularly in South Derry. The story of collusion is also bound up in the long-term segregation of a sectarian social and political order. Grassroots divisions, interwoven with the institutions of the state, meant that localised internecine conflicts could combine with a broader strategic desire to instil fear and demoralise opposition through the killing of relatives, friends and loved ones. Taken together this is what would shape the state of collusion.

1
British Counterinsurgency and the Roots of Collusion

Collusion and British Counterinsurgency

Despite considerable failings, a 2012 report by Sir Desmond de Silva into the loyalist killing of human rights lawyer Pat Finucane in 1989 confirmed collusion between British military intelligence and RUC Special Branch with loyalist paramilitaries during the conflict in Northern Ireland was widespread, institutionalised and strategic in nature. Long suspected, the true scale still came as a shock – not least that 85 per cent of all intelligence held by loyalists in the late 1980s, which was used to plan their escalating campaign, originated from state intelligence sources.[1] At the centre of these activities, pivotal in disseminating this tsunami of state-sourced information, was Brian Nelson. At that time Nelson was the chief intelligence officer of the Ulster Defence Association (UDA). He was also a British Army agent working for the key British Army intelligence unit operating in the North, the Force Research Unit (FRU). Nelson, said de Silva, passed on intelligence to better target 'republican personalities' at the instigation and behest of his FRU handlers.[2] The FRU, MI5 and Nelson were also intimately involved in the importation of a large cache of weapons into Northern Ireland in late 1987 that greatly facilitated the upsurge in loyalist killing and assassination that was to follow. So much so that by 1993 (for the first time in decades), loyalists were responsible for more killings in the North than anyone else, including the IRA. Discussions within the highest government, military, police and intelligence circles over the rules governing the handling of agents and informers changed nothing until the conflict was over. Such things will be examined more later. Suffice to say at this point a picture emerges of loyalist paramilitary groups, under the guidance of state agencies such as the FRU, and via the work of agents like Nelson, becoming a more deadly, sometimes more targeted force. In large part, this was the result of what has been termed a growing British state 'interest in the increased military professionalisation' of loyalists.[3]

There was not, of course, a single cause of such institutional collusion. Rather it was the outcome of a confluence of forces. Much focus falls on the divided nature of Northern Irish society and the links between sectarian social relations, power structures and state institutions. The long-term sectarianised character of state and society in Northern Ireland undoubtedly played an important role. So also an intelligence-led attritional strategy that generated a grey zone of official deniability around the criminal actions of state agents and informers designed to defeat an intractable, armed enemy.[4] Crucial too, however, was a longer-term history of British state counterinsurgency thought and practice, driven less by a doctrine of 'minimum force' than of 'necessity'.[5] It is that context – of British thinking and conduct of 'small wars', of counterinsurgency campaigns rooted in colonial and imperial rule – with which the story of collusion might therefore begin.

At the core of our concerns lie two questions: what was the extent, form and rationale of collusion, and what made collusion as a form of state practice possible? There are no simple answers, but the practice and thought that form the tradition of British Counterinsurgency (COIN) are a necessary if insufficient condition. A critical analysis of the roots of collusion in British COIN challenges two of its longstanding myths. First, that it is characterised by a commitment to a minimum force doctrine combined with a non-coercive 'hearts and minds' approach. Second, that it has been invariably constrained by adherence to the rule of law. Rather, it will be argued, the realities of the British COIN tradition form a critical backdrop to the ways of thinking and acting evidenced in the collusive practices of state actors in Northern Ireland. Illuminating key dimensions of British counterinsurgency therefore casts a light on how collusion, as an example of covert, coercive state violence, could come to be.

This is not to suggest that there is a direct or simple cause-and-effect relationship between this body of counterinsurgency theory and collusion – or that other factors, which need to be explored, are not important too. Rather, the threads identified within this lineage of British COIN illustrate a series of linkages, paradigms of theory and practice, that weave the fabric of a longer-term cultural and institutional context within which collusion becomes possible. This is analogous, in many ways, to the corporate memory and institutional culture that facilitated the use of torture by 'cruel Britannia'.[6] In this perspective, collusion can be understood as an expedient coercive state practice, premised on a 'doctrine of necessity', designed to remove 'enemies' and induce fear in a target population via a strategy of proxy assassination in which the appearance of adherence to the rule of law is a political end shaping the specific forms of state violence involved. Far from being an aberration in the tradition of British counterinsurgency violence, collusion emerges instead as exemplary.

What is Counterinsurgency?

What then is counterinsurgency? The current British Army field manual on counterinsurgency defines it as 'those military, law enforcement, political, economic, psychological and civic actions taken to defeat an insurgency, while addressing the root causes'.[7] Published in the wake of the chaos and destruction wreaked in Kandahar and Basra, it stresses that while this includes 'low-intensity operations' such as those 'on the streets of Northern Ireland ... counterinsurgency is warfare'. Force and other means are therefore integrated and interwoven into a coherent strategy designed to overcome insurgency, understood as any 'organised, violent subversion used to effect or prevent political control, as a challenge to established authority'. As the US Army's counterinsurgency manual argues, separating the insurgent from the population therefore emerges as the key means of defeating opposition.[8] Counterinsurgency is a 'population-centric' subset of warfare, a 'military activity centred on civilians' in which people's attitudes, actions, outlook, expectations and (by no means least) fears become the primary contested ground.[9]

According to General David Petraeus, who co-authored the manual, 'the biggest of the big ideas' underpinning the US 'surge' strategy he led in Iraq in 2007 was the 'recognition that the decisive terrain (in a counterinsurgency campaign) is the human terrain'.[10] Local 'cultures', understood as 'protocols for system behaviour' are scrutinised to predict and impact upon the actions and perceptions of those identified as part of an 'insurgent eco-system'.[11] The aim is to effect 'behavioural change' through, for example, 'psychological operations' as a planned means 'to convey selected information and indicators' to an audience in order to 'influence their emotions, motives [and] objective reasoning'.[12] The 'principal defining characteristic' of counterinsurgency is its core concern with 'moulding the population's perceptions'.[13] The management of the subject people is therefore directed towards the counterinsurgent imposing or 'maximising his own interests'.[14] Success is defined by winning a 'competition to mobilize' support not only within the local population but at 'home, internationally and among allied and neutral countries'. Victory may be less concerned with the total military defeat of insurgents than with their long-term neutralisation through 'stability operations' and the creation of 'popular support for permanent, institutionalized anti-terrorist measures'.

Of course this does not mean that force and 'hard power' do not continue to have a central role – far from it. The 'wider political purpose' of counterinsurgency always lies at its core, writes Brigadier Gavin Bulloch, author of the British counterinsurgency manual, who himself served in the North. It is the 'political potential' rather than 'military power' of insurgents that represents 'the true nature of the threat'.[15] Finding means to undermine the support base for insurgent groups is therefore the 'strategic centre of gravity', with the end being to 'shatter the enemy's moral and physical cohesion rather than seek his wholesale destruction'. In that process, however, the 'physical destruction of the enemy still has an important part to play'. Military involvement in 'deep operations' may also be through 'covert and clandestine action by special units'.[16] While formal adherence to the rule of law is advocated, physical destruction is also calculated on the 'degree of attrition necessary'. The normative culture of legal compliance and military professionalism co-exist with 'necessity' in the calibration of the extent and nature of state force and killing required to reshape the political terrain in a way conducive to the ends and interests of the state. The aim of counterinsurgency is also then to employ state violence and other means to define the balance of post-conflict political forces. Thus if post-conflict 'reconciliation' is a 'two-way process' it is one 'best undertaken from a position of strength'.[17]

'The British Army', one former solider has argued, 'is a counterinsurgency army'.[18] Historically its principal mission has been to 'acquire police imperial possessions' ensuring no one has 'amassed as much experience in counterinsurgency as Great Britain'. No one, it is claimed, does it 'better than the British'.[19] Likewise General Sir Mike Jackson, once head of the British Army and commander of British forces during the occupation of Iraq, extolled the virtues of this 'peculiarly British way' of going about 'military business' whose origins go back into Britain's imperial past 'at least a couple of centuries to Ireland, to India a century and a half ago, to Africa about the same time and, indeed, to Iraq almost a century ago'.[20] The campaign in Northern Ireland is for Jackson an exemplar of British counterinsurgency, characterising the army's role as to 'prevent the unlawful use of violence' while creating the conditions for a political resolution to the problem of having 'two peoples on one piece of territory'.[21] As he sees it, the 'trick' in counterinsurgency is 'applying force that has profound political connotations', balancing a concern not to be seen as either 'too harsh' or 'too faint-hearted' in a battle for 'hearts and minds'.[22]

There is considerable debate about whether this much-vaunted, British approach to counterinsurgency has been as distinct as often argued.[23] Some have seen it as a tradition largely invented following the invasion of Iraq as an essentially spurious means to contrast British strategy with that of their supposedly more gung-ho and violent American counterparts. This possibility is ironic given that US commentators were often pivotal in valorising a mythic British prowess for counterinsurgency in the first place. As the appalling, costly failures in Iraq and Afghanistan became all too apparent, the Ministry of Defence also sought to formally celebrate a distinct British approach to counterinsurgency, not least by citing the example of Northern Ireland, despite it actually being 'a bruising encounter characterized by a vicious undercover intelligence war'.[24] So the British military and state has increasingly come to see itself as 'peculiarly' well versed in the conduct of counterinsurgency campaigns, a conceit that continues into the present despite the fact that recent years have seen a revisionist assault on the idea that British counterinsurgency was more benign in practice (or even in theory) than its imperial counterparts.[25]

Small Wars and Imperial Policing

To consider some of the roots of collusion as state practice it is worth placing things in the context of the longer lineage of British counterinsurgency thought and praxis. The writings of three former British Army officers are important here. Their work not only spans a century of theorising 'irregular warfare' but each is also linked with Ireland. They are Charles E. Callwell, Charles Gwynn and Frank Kitson. All are regarded by the British Army as central to the tradition of British COIN.[26] If the theory as well as the practice of British counterinsurgency has deep imperial roots, until relatively recently this tradition of 'warrior-scholarship' rarely mentioned Ireland. From the outset, however, counterinsurgency thinking, colonialism and Ireland were intimately interlinked. The British Army *Counterinsurgency* field manual charts the foundation of British COIN from the publication of Major General Sir Charles E. Callwell's *Small Wars: Their Principles and Practice* in 1896.[27] Appearing at the height of late Victorian imperial hubris, *Small Wars* became the standard text on counterinsurgency for the British Army up until the Second World War and 'firmly established [Callwell's] reputation as the army's foremost expert on colonial warfare'.[28] Indeed the post-9/11 US and British invasion and occupation of Afghanistan and Iraq saw a resurgence of interest in *Small Wars* and cemented Callwell's 'credentials as the founding father of modern counter-insurgency'.

Small Wars makes no mention of Ireland but there is a considerable Irish connection through its author. Callwell was of solidly Ulster capital and Anglo-Irish landed stock, one of a generation of Anglo-Irish military men who rose to influential high office within the upper echelons of the British Army in the period prior to the First World War.[29] He was particularly close to the most powerful and highly political of this coterie of unionist senior military figures – one-time chief of the Imperial General Staff, Field Marshall Sir Henry Wilson, 'whom he [Callwell] had known since boyhood'.[30] Wilson played a leading behind-the-scenes role encouraging the Curragh Mutiny and unionist opposition to Home Rule in March 1914.[31] Following the introduction of partition, Wilson was elected unionist MP for North Down in 1922 and appointed senior military adviser to the newly installed Northern Ireland government, to act as the 'strong man of Ulster'.[32] A few months later he was assassinated by the IRA and it was his 'fellow Irish Unionist and war veteran' Callwell who 'devoutly compiled' and published Wilson's controversial *Life and Letters*.[33] His own experiences as a 'soldier of empire', fighting in Afghanistan and South Africa and later in the intelligence branch of the War Office, informed Callwell's views on the conduct of 'small wars'. His book was also a compendium of various works on 'irregular warfare' and a study of not only British but also French, German and Russian colonial campaigns (as well as the genocidal efforts of the US against 'Red Indians'). For Callwell, 'small wars' meant imperial and colonial wars and his lessons were primarily aimed at a British Army operating as an 'imperial police force'.[34] In this light, the absence of Ireland from the pages of *Small Wars* is perhaps all the more conspicuous.

Callwell saw the decisive factor in achieving victory in conflicts that 'dog the footsteps of the pioneers of civilisation', fought against 'lesser races' and 'savage enemies', as what he termed the 'moral force of civilisation'.[35] This idea of 'moral force' was central to his thinking, and more important as a foundation for the development of British COIN theory than any conception of 'minimum force'. More so than in conventional warfare, Callwell argued, force was to be used less for outright military victory than for its impact on insurgents and their base of popular support; what he termed the 'moral effect' of organised violence. 'Moral force' (essentially a synonym for instilling a sense of awestruck fear) was more 'potent' than 'physical force' in defeating colonial insurgents. As Callwell put it, in campaigns against 'savages and guerrillas' the important thing was to develop a 'system of overawing and terrifying [because that was] the great object always to be kept in view'.[36] 'Impressionable lower races' lacked the moral character and fibre that civilisation bestowed on imperial powers so 'must be made to feel a moral inferiority throughout' and come to 'recognise that the forces of civilisation are dominant and not to be denied'.[37] This was in essence a 'shock and awe' strategy, designed to ensure that the uncivilised or 'semi-civilised' enemy 'maintain his respect for the forces of civilisation'.[38] In brief, social Darwinian racism shaped the origins of modern counterinsurgency thought.[39]

Counterinsurgency force was therefore understood from the outset as a form of 'exemplary violence' or a 'performative of power'.[40] Nor was this a 'minimum force' doctrine. Callwell was a stout advocate of a strategy of 'butcher and bolt'; raids undertaken to destroy crops, livestock and buildings, to raze whole villages to the ground and lay waste to conquered areas that 'fanatics and savages [could be] thoroughly brought to book and cowed ... [so they would not] rise up again'.[41] On the other hand, while not 'minimal', this was not wanton, but purposeful and strategic violence. For Callwell, the 'end view' always to be kept in mind was the need to employ violence sufficient to punish and 'overawe' the enemy, but not so much as to lead them to 'exasperation [or] driven to desperation'.[42] The state should use whatever exemplary violence was needed to have the 'moral effect' of instilling the fear necessary to achieve the desired political outcome. As the foundation of a British COIN tradition, we might think of it as a coercive 'hearts and minds' strategy devoid of a 'minimum force' doctrine.

Major General Sir Charles Gwynn's *Imperial Policing*, first published in 1934, became a standard text for training British Army imperial officers for decades thereafter.[43] Like Callwell, Gwynn was an Irish Protestant (born in Donegal) though his family had somewhat greater political complexity.[44] Gwynn served in the British Army during the First World War and later became commandant of the British Army's Staff College.[45] In *Imperial Policing* Gwynn examined Britain's various post-1918 colonial campaigns to establish 'lessons to be learnt' on the application of military power in imperial 'small wars', now recast as 'policing duties'. Family connections and the record of the Black and Tans may, again, have ensured Ireland's absence, leading Gwynn to consider it 'inadvisable to draw on experience in Ireland, instructive from a military point of view as many of them were'.[46] In any case, the humiliation of defeat made revisiting counterinsurgency in Ireland uncomfortable within British military circles.[47]

Gwynn established four general principles for the conduct of counterinsurgency based on two core concepts: the military should act as an 'aid to the civil power' and the force employed should be 'the minimum the situation demands'.[48] These would have a powerful, long-term mystifying political and ideological effect promulgating the idea that British counterinsurgency was governed by law. Much later, acting as an 'aid to the civil power' would (at least in theory) form the legal and constitutional basis of the British Army's campaign in Northern Ireland. Yet Gwynn's thinking was ultimately driven by a utilitarian logic. The 'minimum force' commitment was based on a calculation of the degree of force needed to meet desired ends. Here was a 'necessity principle', not objectively founded, but subjectively formed, in the political decision to preserve the existing order. It would prove poor ground on which to forge a long-term commitment to legally binding limitations on state violence; as *Imperial Policing* itself showed.

In his analysis of the Arab Revolt (1936–9) in Palestine, for example, Gwynn's aim of demonstrating Britain's 'rule of law' commitment was framed by what he saw as the 'restrictions' placed on British troops by an 'extreme conciliatory policy', identified as the root cause of conflict.[49] He denounced 'propagandist' charges of British misconduct that then prevented bombing Arab villages from the air and continuing punitive house demolitions, in one case likening the latter to a form of progressive urban redevelopment.[50] This actually involved deliberate mass destruction, part of an escalated official reprisals policy of houses being demolished, properties looted, food stores systematically destroyed, forced labour, 'punitive village occupations' and the imposition of crushing collective fines. From 1920 British coercive policing in Palestine was modelled on the Royal Irish Constabulary and the Black and Tans, led by the head of the former and founder of the latter. An auxiliary force was overwhelmingly manned by former 'Tan' members who went on to play their part in the Palestine police and a regime built on routinised street violence and systematic brutality in prisons and interrogation rooms (including the use of waterboarding and 'suspensions').[51]

Repression gathered pace after the outbreak of the Revolt. Police violence was rampant, with beatings, summary executions and extra-judicial killings. Torture centres were set up and Arab suspects were shot 'while trying to escape'.[52] 'Bad' villages were razed to the ground. 'Policing' of the Arab revolt was built around 'premeditated, systematic, officially sanctioned brutality in the form of collective punishments and reprisals'.[53] Arabs were tied to the bonnets of military vehicles to 'deter' mine attacks, wounded fighters were left to die and others were shot while surrendering.[54] Members of the Royal Ulster Rifles were involved in one of the most notorious atrocities when 50 Arab men were rounded up and driven over a landmine in a bus, which was completely destroyed in the explosion.[55] 'Special night squads' were set up: composed of British and Jewish settler policemen moving at night (sometimes disguising themselves as Arabs) they terrorised Arab villages, humiliating and killing Arab civilians. This foreshadowed not only the 'counter-gangs' developed later by Frank Kitson in Kenya, then Northern Ireland (an antecedent of collusion itself), but also 'something of a model for subsequent Israeli Special Forces'.[56]

Yet throughout, 'moral restraint' was not absent and a 'veneer of legal respectability' was maintained.[57] Most things done were legal; sanctioned by military command, control structures and 'proper authority'. In essence, the law was modified as 'necessary', so punitive, violent state actions remained within its bounds. Here again we see a key thread in the character of British counterinsurgency, reflected in the logic of *Imperial Policing*. As Gwynn recommended, at the outbreak of the Arab Revolt the British Army formally operated as an 'aid to the civil power'. However, *de facto* a state of 'statutory martial law' existed and military law could 'justify the use of any degree of force necessary to meet and cope with the insurrection'.[58] Military courts dispensed an approximation of summary justice, Arab civilians and combatants were denied the protection of the emerging body of international law, and while formally legally accountable the prosecution of British soldiers was all but non-existent.[59] Nothing here was inconsistent with Gwynn's own support for a 'vigorous repressive policy'. He approved of military courts' imposition of the death penalty, the arrest of Arab leaders, banning organisations, that there had been 'round-ups of villages' and that rebel groups met in battle had been 'roughly handled'.[60] His only reservation (perhaps again with Ireland in mind) was that a policy of reprisals 'was always dangerous', although not because of any squeamishness on his part.[61] It was not reprisals, as such, that worried Gwynn. Rather he was opposed to a lack of 'command and control' and concerned that violent retaliation, if undertaken by 'ruthless' irregular forces, could lead to a backlash felt mainly by 'defenceless loyalists'. Instead, reprisals should be codified by rules, 'publicly stated and … duly authorised'. The message was clear: counterinsurgency violence, while it might be wholesale and overwhelming, should not be out of control or unrestrained, and preferably 'legitimised' through the authority of command structures and shaping the law to the task in hand.

The Rule of Law and 'Counter-Gangs'

Despite arguments to the contrary, of all British military theorists none is more immediately relevant to the conduct of counterinsurgency during the conflict in Northern Ireland than General Sir Frank Kitson.[62] Between 1970 and 1972 Kitson commanded 39 Brigade with overall responsibility for British troops in Belfast and, while John Newsinger rightly insists that the so-called 'Kitson experiment' was neither as original nor as comprehensively enacted as sometimes suggested, Kitson was certainly heavily involved and influential in the subsequent development of British counterinsurgency strategy in the North.[63] Before taking up this role he had earlier served in Kenya, Malaya, Muscat, Oman and Cyprus, writing of the counterinsurgency lessons he garnered from these experiences.[64] In his work Kitson provides a heavily sanitised account of his career, reducing the Kenyan campaign for example, among the 'bloodiest of post-war British military operations … to the level of a *Boys' Own* adventure story'.[65] In actuality a cumulative and concerted attempt to theorise a British national security state, his writings present a starkly militarist manifesto at the heart of which once more was a counter-insurgency doctrine of necessity.[66] Along with Maurice Tugwell and General Richard Clutterbuck, Kitson is also identified in the British Army *Counterinsurgency* manual as someone who 'developed and offered more up to date principles and guidelines' on how to 'defeat the two scourges of the late Twentieth century ... insurgency and terrorism'.[67]

Several themes course through Kitson's work. There is a considerable focus on the importance of intelligence and propaganda, the use of covert operations and (of most direct relevance to the issue of collusion) on the role of police Special Branch and the recruitment of local covert militia forces; or what were termed 'pseudo-' or 'counter-gangs'.[68] Given a post-1945 imperative to at least appear committed to international law and human rights standards, Kitson and his contemporaries were also more vexed by the need to order the rule of law to counterinsurgency ends. This had been far less of a worry for the likes of Callwell, and only partly so for Gwynn, writing when there was little call for imperial powers to recognise the legal status of colonial subjects who continued to be excluded, implicitly or explicitly, from constraints on the use of force used against civilians.[69] It was a time, Kitson noted wistfully, when 'soldiers were able to carry out their tasks without excessive wear and tear on their consciences'.[70]

His 'rule of law' commitment might best be seen in this light: as necessary in theory, if not in practice, to ward off potential criticism of a failure to meet new international legal standards. In this he was not alone. British counterinsurgency has tended to shy away from formally suspending legal norms (i.e. through declaring martial law), seen as politically difficult and counterproductive. Thus Kitson's near contemporary Robert Thompson, widely credited with making political aims central to counterinsurgency practice, identified adherence to the rule of law as one of his core principles.[71] Thompson's experience of the Malayan 'Emergency' (1948–60) and acting as an adviser to the US during the Vietnam War informed his work, which is still regarded as pivotal for British counterinsurgency thinking (despite the appalling record of brutality evident in both). Illegality and widespread repressive and coercive state violence have been revealed recently to have characterised British policy in Malaya.[72] The 'British tradition' of counterinsurgency is one that has generally sought to give the *appearance* of maintaining legal norms and normalcy, whatever the *reality*.

Kitson (who served in Malaya at the same time as Thompson) echoed his contemporary in a twin focus on the political dimensions of counterinsurgency and the issue of the rule of law.[73] For a soldier there were two 'yardsticks' to measure right and wrong: the law and 'expediency'. At first sight his view on the law appears absolutist. Whatever course of action is available to a soldier, he insisted, if it is 'illegal it must be avoided'.[74] Because insurgency and subversion are defined by being 'unlawful' and 'unconstitutional', counterinsurgency should never be undertaken 'in any other than a lawful and constitutional way'.[75] Indeed, alongside acting as an 'aid to the civil power', winning the 'war for the minds of the people' and establishing an effective intelligence organisation, a commitment that 'everything done by a government and its agents in combatting insurgency must be legal' formed the four core principles of Kitson's counterinsurgency thesis.[76]

How does such an absolute commitment to abiding by the rule of law sit alongside 'expediency'? Any apparent contradiction is not as great as it first appears. What constitutes legality (and how it is shaped and adapted according to circumstances, ends and interests) is what matters. 'It is a function of government to make new laws', insisted Kitson, and 'if necessary' to adapt the way the law is administered creating 'a legal system adequate to the needs of the moment'.[77] In other words, expediency governs the legal order. As recently argued, Kitson's 'theorising was not interested in the ethics of counter-insurgency – just in getting the job done'.[78] In that vein he was entirely in step with the utilitarian strain at the core of the British counterinsurgency tradition in which the 'ethics' governing the deployment of coercive state violence were premised on calculating the state's own self-identified need.

Kitson suggested two ways in which the law could work during an insurgency. One was for it to remain 'impartial', ensuring (even when new 'tough' laws were introduced) that equality before the law was a governing principle and 'the officers of the law will recognise no difference between the forces of government, the enemy, or the uncommitted part of the population'.[79] Yet, while this might be 'morally right', Kitson argued it was often 'unworkable'. Necessity might require an alternative path, which is captured in his (with good reason) oft-quoted maxim that 'law should be used as just another weapon in the government's arsenal, and in this case it becomes little more than a propaganda cover for the disposal of unwanted members of the public'. Entirely in keeping with the COIN tradition, the key problem was to ensure that the civil authorities generated a juridical order allowing state agents to do 'what was necessary' to preserve its interests. The quandary for the political system was to find ways to ensure the protection of state agents in conducting counterinsurgency operations by making, if required, what might otherwise be illegal, legal.

For Kitson, intelligence work, covert operations and the use of special forces were central to counterinsurgency. In Kenya, creating an effective intelligence system was his first priority and framed much of his later thinking.[80] The need for an 'effective' intelligence system was also his key reason for advocating a 'necessary adaption' of the administration of the law and the entire process of arrest, interrogation and imprisonment.[81] This was a strategy aimed at maximising the potential for recruiting informers and agents, and dissuading others from following the insurgent path.[82] The rapid expansion of intelligence organisation, Kitson also noted (with considerable understatement), might lead to 'the possibility of the odd indiscretion'. These should be accepted by the government, he argued, as 'essential risks [so that] the necessary action is taken'.

A former RUC Special Branch officer has recently argued that 'nothing that transpired' in Northern Ireland 'resembled Kitson's tactics'.[83] Rather, there was a 'rule of law approach ... broadly in keeping with classic British counterinsurgency' such as that 'successfully' conducted in Malaya. However, a focus on arrest and imprisonment is entirely consistent with Kitson's stringent counterinsurgency doctrine, while the 'success' in Malaya rested on 'violently extracted collaboration' by British forces able 'to inflict the greatest harm of the civilian population'.[84] For Kitson, streamlining the law to pursue an aggressive arrest strategy was an important weapon in a broader arsenal that included deploying special forces, counter-gangs and the primacy of intelligence.

Likewise, echoing Kitson (perhaps unsurprisingly), the same former long-time RUC man argues that counter-gangs were never used in the North.[85] The 'briefest study of the counter-gang concept' shows it relies on 'co-ethnicity', and 'teams of proselytised Provos partnering the Army' never happened. Kitson was certainly an unequivocal advocate of the effectiveness of 'counter-gangs', and their creation and deployment was clearly central to his conception of counterinsurgency. He did not, however, invent the idea. As Raymond Murray noted long ago, Kitson was 'no innovator'; his 'model' was the product of a longstanding tradition of British colonial policy and principles of counterinsurgency.[86] A wider reliance on 'locally recruited allies' in a variety of guises (as a source of intelligence or the necessary manpower on the ground) was characteristic of virtually all of Britain's counterinsurgency campaigns before and since, up to and including the wars in Iraq and Afghanistan.[87]

In Kenya 'counter-gangs' were also but one strand of what amounted to a campaign of state terror. Alongside it a force of some 25,000 'local loyalists', operating in 'loosely controlled small units', was the 'most efficient and most covert method of delivering a policy of state-sponsored terror' and ensuring the compliance of the population.[88] Given that he could write in the late 1970s of having had to waste too much time 'investigating fictitious atrocities allegedly committed by loyalists', it seems reasonable to assume this campaign of state terror in the countryside troubled Kitson's conscience little, regarded as a permissible means to meet the government's 'first duty' during an emergency: to 'regain the allegiance of the population'.[89] The recent official recognition provided by the 2011 British High Court judgement of the regime of systematic torture deployed against thousands of those held in British-run detention camps, similarly casts a mournfully belated light on the realities of a counterinsurgency campaign that is much at odds with Kitson's self-congratulatory narrative.[90]

There is evidence too of Kitson having a direct role in introducing the pseudo-gang tactic into the North: exemplified in his establishing the Military Reaction Force (MRF) in the early 1970s, the forerunner and template of later covert units such as the Special Reconnaissance Unit (SRU), 14th Intelligence Company and the FRU. Certainly 'guerrilla defectors' have often been a feature of 'pseudo-operations' but they are not necessarily synonymous with each other. You do not need to uncover hordes of 'proselytised Provos' to find evidence of 'false flag' activity. The defining feature involves deploying covert forces, often made up of agents or intelligence personnel (such as with the MRF) that mimic the forms and actions of the enemy, with a focus again on gathering intelligence and carrying out 'black ops'. In that sense such units can be more akin to 'death squads', understood as 'clandestine, irregular organisations, often paramilitary in nature, which carry out extra-judicial executions … against clearly defined individuals or groups of people [that] operate with the support, complicity or acquiescence of government'.[91]

2

Northern Ireland and the Roots of Collusion

McGurk's Bar and the MRF

On 4 December 1971, members of the UVF planted a bomb at an entranceway of McGurk's Bar in North Belfast.[1] The explosion obliterated the bar killing 15 people; until the 1998 Omagh bombing this was the largest loss of life from a single incident during the conflict. Although this mass atrocity was claimed by the 'Empire Loyalists' (a UVF *nom-de-guerre*), political, police and military officials quickly and deliberately attributed blame to the IRA, saying the massacre was an 'own goal' resulting from a premature explosion. This became the official narrative for years to come, further undermining lingering faith in the rule of law for many who knew different. Despite considerable forensic evidence to the contrary, an RUC 'pre-disposition' prevented any meaningful investigation of loyalist culpability.[2] Eyewitness accounts contradicting 'investigative bias' were interpreted as an 'orchestrated plot'.[3] Nationalist statements blaming loyalists were denounced as 'propaganda'. The unionist government used the bombing to justify the recent (utterly disastrous) introduction of internment, in which no loyalists had been arrested. For Whitehall, attributing blame to loyalists would have 'raised serious questions ... over why loyalist paramilitaries had not been interned'.[4] They didn't. Indeed, British military intelligence would propagate the 'own goal' story as part of a wider 'psy-ops' strategy to discredit republicans. Army public relations had recently been overhauled in light of past experience of late colonial campaigns. It would soon be nicknamed the 'Lisburn Lie Machine', the 'most unreliable of the many agencies involved in the conflict'.[5] Such 'psychological warfare' was then led by 'hard-line paratroop officer Maurice Tugwell', later lauded as a key British counterinsurgency thinker.[6]

Disseminating the 'own goal' story may also have been to deny the British Army's own role. While more dubious, and shrouded in mystery, there have long been allegations of British intelligence involvement in the McGurk's Bar bombing.[7] These swirl around the activities of the shadowy MRF, the unit formed by Frank Kitson shortly after he took over command in Belfast.[8] What is certain is the MRF was a British Army 'surveillance unit', involved in a range of covert operations, which also took control of agent handling for the military in the 1970s. Its very existence was long denied, 'hidden beneath an extraordinary web of cover names and secrecy'.[9] In an attempt to 'professionalise' the use of covert military units, as early as 1973 the MRF had morphed into the SRU.[10] Despite official denials to the contrary, the SRU included members of the SAS. This was done secretly, given government fears of the 'political implications if news leaked out' – public knowledge of SAS deployment would draw unwanted comparisons with earlier colonial campaigns.[11] Secrecy was maintained by the fiction of the return of SAS men to their original regimental designations, before they were then deployed to form a core of the covert members of the SRU. The MRF (and SRU) also proved to be the 'precursor and inspiration, a decade later, of the Force Research Unit'.[12]

As well as infiltration and intelligence gathering, members of the MRF were involved in direct attacks and assassinations, some of an avowedly sectarian nature.[13] They included the May 1972 shooting dead of Patrick McVeigh, a 44-year-old father of six and member of the Catholic Ex-Servicemen's Association. McVeigh was shot in Andersonstown in Belfast from a car that made its escape via a nearby military checkpoint.[14] A month earlier two brothers, John and Gerard Conway, were shot and badly injured (again in West Belfast) as they made their way to work. The members of the MRF responsible apparently mistook them for two local IRA men. The following September, 19-year-old Daniel Rooney was killed and a friend wounded as they stood chatting on a street corner near the Falls Road. They were shot by a covert unit of six British soldiers who claimed they were armed. They were not. According to then chief of staff of the British Army, the MRF involved 'soldiers in plain clothes ... exploiting ex-members or supporters of the IRA'.[15] One former member recently revealed that 'we were not there to act like an army unit. We were there to act like a terror group.'[16] It was a 'shoot-first, take-no-prisoners, man-hunting squad'.[17] In other words, the MRF was a pseudo-gang.

Revolution, 'Reprisal' and Partition

The McGurk's Bar bombing and the secret state assassination campaign of the MRF took place during some of the darkest days of the conflict.

Yet the story of covert state activity and collusion precedes the outbreak of the 'Troubles' in 1969 and should be seen in that longer-term context. The partition of Ireland in 1920 created a northern state born amid the divisions of the Home Rule Crisis and Irish Revolution, as well as the cataclysmic, epoch-shaping, mass slaughter of the First World War. While Charles Gwynn chose not to dwell on the lessons for 'imperial policing' events in Ireland provided, British strategy demonstrated that coercive counterinsurgency approaches were much to the fore.[18]

In the summer of 1920, for example, British Prime Minister Lloyd George gave 'tacit approval' for the creation of what was called a 'counter-murder society'.[19] The chief of police in Ireland (and later in Palestine), Major General Sir Henry Tudor, then created two paramilitary auxiliary divisions. Demobbed ex-British soldiers were drafted en masse into the 'auxiliaries' (made up of ex-officers, which acted as a specialist, proactive counterinsurgency force) and the notorious 'Black and Tans'.[20] The record of 'reprisals' carried out by both, including extrajudicial killings, destruction of homes and workplaces and the targeting of known or 'suspected' republicans, ensured 'Black and Tan' became a byword for state terror, coercion and oppression. This 'counter-murder' campaign was not conducted by an ill-disciplined, out-of-control mob. It was a counter-revolutionary war that fought 'terror, as they saw it, with terror'.[21] Reprisals were far from indiscriminate. Those carrying them out, as a British military intelligence officer of the day argued, whether 'under orders of the authorities' or not 'almost invariably knew the victims they selected, knew that they were guilty although their knowledge would not convict in a court of law'.[22] A localised, reciprocal, tit-for-tat dynamic developed in particular areas between revolutionary IRA violence and Royal Irish Constabulary and British Army counter-revolutionary terror.[23] If 'reprisals' could be condemned as an 'impossible policy', that had 'none of the forms of law', they could also be seen as a 'safety valve' for vengeance.[24]

Allegations of official sanction and complicity in a reprisals policy were vigorously denied.[25] However, there was considerable high-level state ambivalence at the very least, if not outright support, for grassroots state violence. From early 1920 as an 'unofficial … reprisal movement' grew within the RIC, sometimes giving itself cover names such as the 'Anti-Sinn Fein Society', this was 'officially tolerated and encouraged'.[26] Ostensible, public British government opposition to reprisals was paralleled by advocating an unofficial practice of 'counter-murder'.[27]

Charles Callwell's close friend and 'strong man of Ulster' Sir Henry Wilson noted that Lloyd George thought the head of the RIC 'or someone was murdering two S.F.'s [Sinn Feiners] to every loyalist the S.F.'s murdered' and that such 'counter-murder was the best answer to IRA killings'.[28] War Secretary Winston Churchill argued that the way to defeat Sinn Fein was 'gunning rather that burning … [and to] let the police get at the gunmen whom they knew but could not legally convict'.[29] According to Wilson, Churchill saw 'very little harm' that the RIC had 'marked down certain SFs, in their opinion the actual murderers and instigators, and then coolly went and shot them without question or trial'.[30]

Foreshadowing Charles Gwynn's view, Wilson himself was 'horrified', but only because (like the military authorities) he wanted an authorised and regularised 'reprisal' policy.[31] Then chief of the Imperial General Staff, Wilson also echoed Callwell in advocating the 'moral effect' of counterinsurgency killing. He wanted lists established with the names of known 'Sinn Feiners' posted on church doors, and 'whenever a policeman is murdered, pick five by lot and shoot them'.[32] A policy of 'shooting by roster', as Charles Callwell noted.[33] 'If these men ought to be murdered', wrote Wilson, 'then the Government ought to murder them'.[34] In seeking clear, command-and-control structures for such actions, Wilson was entirely in tune with the wider army leadership which pressed for a 'system of official reprisals'.[35] Ever the canny politician, Lloyd George, with an eye on international public opinion, argued that no government could take such responsibility and 'preferred to let the police have their heads and to observe the effect of "unauthorised" reprisals'.[36]

Policing the State

The creation of partition also saw previously pro-state paramilitary forces drafted into the policing and coercive structures of the newly founded northern state. The original UVF had been formed in 1912, providing armed opposition to potential British government introduction of Home Rule for Ireland, with considerable elite political and military support. During the First World War it was incorporated, structures largely intact, into the British Army as the 36th (Ulster) Division. Mass casualties suffered by the Ulster Division at the Battle of the Somme would become a foundational, iconic and ideologically potent loyalist sacrificial symbol, through to the present.[37] By 1920 the escalation of the IRA's campaign not only saw both British government and unionism fix on partition as its preferred political solution, but the re-formation of the UVF in the North as a paramilitary force.[38] By year's end unionism had a private army, still an 'illegal organisation', of 20,000 to 30,000 men.[39] Thereafter the UVF was incorporated into the Belfast regime's emerging state security apparatus.

Simultaneously British Army chief of staff and unofficial military adviser to the new Northern Ireland government, it was Henry Wilson who recommended the formation of the RUC and an auxiliary 'Ulster Special Constabulary' (USC), or B Specials. Churchill had already suggested 'arming 20,000 Orangemen', but for Wilson establishing control was key.[40] The constitution of Northern Ireland's security forces came to exemplify the new state's 'sectarian-populist flavour'.[41] The creation of an armed police force, and a mass, paramilitary auxiliary in the B Specials, circumvented a supposed prohibition on the Belfast government raising a military force. As a 'sectarian Protestant force' the B Specials also came to occupy a crucial position in cementing the cross-class alliance that underpinned unionist rule. Professionalism in policing was cast aside in favour of 'retaining the force's essentially populist character'.[42]

Extrajudicial killings and reprisals were also a feature of the emerging policing order. In the wake of the signing of the 1921 treaty that confirmed partition, amid pogroms and a state of virtual civil war, the IRA went on a violent offensive. It was met with a campaign of assassinations by the Specials. The most notorious case occurred in North Belfast months later. After the IRA shot dead two Specials, others (in uniform) broke into the home of a well-known pub owner, Owen MacMahon.[43] They lined MacMahon, his five sons and a barman against a wall and shot them. Only two sons survived. The killers were likely a gang, made up of RUC men and Specials, that carried out a wave of 'reprisals' across Belfast over several years, 'apparently able to operate with impunity during curfew hours'.[44] Victims included both Sinn Fein members and ordinary Catholics. The 'reprisal squad' was believed to have been set up by the head of the RUC detective division in the city and led by a well-known district inspector. Both were pivotal in shaping the Specials in the city and recruiting its members, mostly from the loyalist Shankill Road.

For the unionist regime, in place for decades to follow, localised communal social networks were often interwoven and embedded in the structures of unionist hegemony and the apparatus of surveillance, control and coercion it put into place. This was most obviously so in terms of policing. From the foundation of the state, the RUC was always overwhelmingly drawn from the unionist community.[45] The B Specials, in turn, acted as a substantial reserve force and state militia, its membership virtually all Protestant.[46] Mobilised in times of political crisis, the 'B men', working in their own localities and utilising intimate, local knowledge, were 'extremely effective in suppressing resistance to Unionist rule'.[47] The police were also able to call upon the arsenal of regularly employed draconian powers conferred on the state by the Special Powers Act (SPA), 'emergency' legislation that became permanent. The SPA became 'part of the fabric of daily control' and, as violence declined, government justification shifted. 'Exceptional' measures, initially said to be required to establish order, became, instead, 'necessary to maintain peace'.[48] Through 50 years of unionist control the SPA provided a readily available means to adapt the rule of law to counterinsurgency ends. Together, extraordinary law, armed police and paramilitary auxiliary, formed the powerful, primary means to enforce rule.[49] Police partisanship saw Catholic dissent as 'subversion' while 'Protestant sectarianism' was 'construed as an expression of ultra-loyalty to the state and treated leniently'.[50] RUC Special Branch maintained close surveillance of suspected republicans, but would at first deny the very existence of the UVF in the 1960s and even claimed to have 'no records on loyalists'.[51] If they had such records they did not use them.

Essentially crafted as a counterinsurgency force, and seeing their role as 'protecting the state and the unionist community against nationalist subversion', the B Specials would be deployed across the decades to 'keep the Catholic community under close scrutiny'.[52] Nationalist antagonism towards the B Specials was borne out of 'harassment and humiliation' experienced at their hands, accentuated by 'the fact [they] often knew their tormentors by name … as neighbours [who were] armed, uniformed, paid and entrusted with special powers'.[53] In contrast to a nostalgia-infused and ideologically powerful vision of the pre-conflict Northern Irish countryside as a place of peace and tranquillity, this was, rather, a long-term condition of 'imposed normality'.[54] This was a situation more akin to that of other colonial police forces, many of whom modelled themselves on the RUC and USC – something often celebrated by the RUC themselves. Even today the 'global brand' of the RUC is often presented as a template for postcolonial and counterinsurgent policing, not least in post-invasion Iraq.[55]

Discredited and disbanded after the outbreak of the conflict in 1970, the 'B men' were immediately replaced by the UDR, some of whose members soon developed their own litany of abuse, illegality and collusion.[56] Indeed, initially many of its recruits (in some areas all its local commanders) were former B Specials.[57] Like its predecessor, the UDR operated much like a militia in its own locality, its role far greater in the countryside than major towns and cities. Deploying local knowledge in a divided society was central to its function. This 'local knowledge', and a continuous presence amid the regular turnover of British Army units deployed in the North, would make the UDR a vital resource for the military. However, local recruitment also made UDR soldiers highly vulnerable to republican attack, particularly off-duty. A total of 206 UDR/Royal Irish Regiment soldiers were killed during the conflict, the majority (162) while off-duty.[58] A further 60 retired UDR members were killed. Neighbour knowledge was not a one-way street and this could make for a vicious, internecine dynamic of violence, pitching communities and families, as well as organisations, against one another. An initial boost of Catholic recruitment soon fell away so the UDR was, again, essentially a Protestant-only force, viewed by the military as playing an important political role in 'reassuring the Protestant population'.[59] According to the British Army, this provided an avenue for those who might otherwise be tempted to join loyalist groups and (in their view at least) helped ensure 'extreme loyalist violence was relatively rare'.[60] Local recruitment ran the risk of 'partisan' attitudes and security breaches by the UDR but, they concluded, these too were 'rare'.

After its formation extensive, chronic collusion between the UDR and loyalist paramilitaries was, in fact, both soon evident and long known. A report by the Social Democratic and Labour Party (SDLP) in the early 1980s noted not only that the UDR had 'by far the worst record for serious sectarian crimes' of any British military force, but was 'known to have been seriously infiltrated' by loyalist groups.[61] As a result, far from being upholders of 'law and order', it was seen 'more as a menace' by nationalists. Many former and serving UDR members certainly found their way into the ranks of the loyalist paramilitary groups. Nor was the extensive involvement of UDR members in loyalist paramilitary organisations any secret to the authorities from the earliest years of the conflict onwards. Both 'senior officers in the British army and successive secretaries of state', it has been argued, were 'fully aware of the sectarian nature of the UDR' and that it was 'riddled' with members of loyalists groups.[62] Indeed, the UDR has been likened to both a pseudo-gang and an eighteenth-century yeomanry, part of whose function was to control 'the worst excesses of loyalist sectarianism by placing loyalists in uniform under the command of English officers and contain unrest by tactics of intimidation and harassment'.[63] In this sense the UDR provided an official, locally based conduit for grassroots loyalism and, through two decades, 'operated a system of low-level state terror that was tolerated by the authorities because it fitted the overall goals of the security apparatus'. The 'important task' of 'instilling fear into nationalist population' bore comparison with the function of 'colonial militia elsewhere' – an analogy that was ironically evident in the army's canteen culture, where UDR members would refer to regular troops as 'redcoats', and found themselves called 'native levies' in return.[64] As well as direct involvement in bombings and killings, by the late 1980s members of the UDR were central in the wholesale leaking of intelligence files and photos of suspected republicans to loyalist groups.[65] 'Lost' or 'stolen' UDR weapons had a similar tendency to turn up in loyalist hands.

Collusion, Bombings and Sectarian Killings

The most notorious case of collusion in the 1970s involved members of the UDR, along with other state force personnel.[66] The 'Glennane Gang', as it became known, was named after a Co. Armagh farm. For a period of over five years in the mid-1970s, in the heart of what became known as the 'murder triangle', this farmhouse 'served as a kind of engine room for murder and mayhem in mid-Ulster'.[67] The gang was responsible for some of the most infamous and costly loyalist killings. These included the Miami Showband massacre in 1975 and the Dublin and Monaghan bombings in 1974, in which 33 people were killed – the greatest loss of life on a single day throughout the conflict.[68] The Glennane Gang has also become a byword for collusion. It included several serving, or former, members of the RUC and UDR. To all intents and purposes the illegal UVF paramilitary unit operating in this area, at that time, was all but indistinguishable from the security forces. They were involved in a series of sectarian assassinations, including organising mass killings in bars in neighbouring nationalist towns and villages.[69] British state military and political officials were also aware of these activities. By early 1976 they knew the farmhouse had been used as a 'staging post' for the Dublin and Monaghan bombings and placed it under surveillance'.[70]

Yet this did not stop the Glennane Gang's ferocious campaign targeting and killing Catholics in their homes – the 'killers were still free to strike'. Nor did it end attacks on bars. The bombing of the Step Inn, in Keady in August 1976, is a case in point, and a chilling comparison to the pattern of events in years to come. Having received warning of a planned explosion, the Glennane farmhouse was under surveillance, but with 'gaping holes during the hours of darkness' when the surveillance was withdrawn.[71] The farm's owner had been warned that the farm was being watched, by a UDR captain who also supplied the explosives for the attack. Despite knowing the farm had been under suspicion the bombers (including several members of the security forces) carried out the attack within hours of the surveillance being lifted, apparently unconcerned they would be stopped or arrested. The massive car bomb placed outside the Step Inn killed two people and seriously injured 22 others. Although RUC Special Branch had considerable evidence, both before and after the bombing, of who planned and carried out the attack, this information was withheld from CID investigators and no search was made of the farm. A later report concluded even though state authorities in the North knew the farm had been a 'centre for illegal activities' since the start of 1976, 'and probably for some time before that ... those activities were allowed to continue for another two years'. This meant senior security forces officers permitted a 'climate to develop in which loyalist subversives could believe they could attack with impunity'.[72]

In all the Glennane Gang has been implicated in almost 90 killings of Catholics and nationalists in this period.[73] There have also long been allegations of military intelligence involvement in attacks such as the Dublin and Monaghan bombings and the Miami Showband massacre, and that the gang received help and support from higher up the chain of command, in what amounted to a campaign of total war.[74] Its activities were only brought to a halt in 1978 after one of its members, John Weir, was arrested for murder and confessed, naming others involved. At the time Weir was also a serving member of the local RUC Special Patrol Group, a counterinsurgency unit he later said 'saw itself as being at war with the IRA and regarded loyalist paramilitaries as allies'.[75] Several arrests and convictions followed, although they resulted in derisory sentences. In one judgement, Lord Chief Justice Lowry (the most senior legal figure in the North), perversely argued that, as police officers charged with the duty to maintain justice, even if guilty of serious, violent crime, any sentence 'would be imposed on a different and lower scale from that appropriate to terrorists'.[76] These 'unfortunate men', he noted, in passing the most lenient sentence possible, had 'done the State some services', and though acting wrongly, had felt 'more than ordinary police work was needed and was justified to rid the land of the pestilence which has been in existence'. Collusion, it has been suggested, was not something from which the legal process was wholly immune.

The scale of killings carried out by the Glennane Gang make them stand out, but their record of collusion was far from unique. From the start of the conflict, collusion had been both 'formal' and 'informal'. Formal collusion involves state ordered and 'sanctioned use of loyalist gangs' to eliminate dissent. Informal collusion includes security force members operating 'in tandem with paramilitary groups' or passing information 'without official sanction'.[77] In terms of the latter, for example, membership of the UDA – a mass loyalist paramilitary group set up in the early years of the conflict – was widespread within the UDR. Yet even in the worst year of the conflict in 1972 (when nearly 500 people lost their lives, over half at the hands of republicans) a senior British Army officer could view part of the UDR sympathising with the aims of the UDA as inevitable, and understood an 'important (but unspoken) function of the UDR' to be a means of channelling 'Protestant energies which might otherwise become disruptive'.[78] That year loyalists killed 121 people, the majority (71) victims of the UDA and their counterpart the Ulster Freedom Fighters (UFF). The loyalist 'theft' or 'loss' of weapons from official stores, in which collusion was suspected, was endemic. Between October 1970 and mid-March 1973, the UDR alone 'lost' 222 weapons, 141 of which were never recovered.[79] Most were taken during 'well-co-ordinated raids on armouries'.[80] 'Our boys were able to enter and take over a UDR camp', a leading UDA commander would later say, 'and clear it out of weapons'.

Official use of informers and agents had long been a feature of the political and policing landscape. This would become an increasing aspect of state counterinsurgency in the latter years of the conflict, but was far from absent earlier. As is often the case, much here is mired in controversy, and reliant on thin threads of evidence. For example, Albert 'Ginger' Baker, a British soldier who ostensibly absconded from his regiment returning to his native Belfast in 1971, became a leading member of a brutal UDA gang that carried out vicious 'romper room' torturing and killings of Catholics.[81] During an upsurge in UDA violence in February 1973, he launched a grenade attack on a minibus carrying 14

Catholic workmen in East Belfast that killed 50-year-old Paddy Heenan and severely wounded many more. Months later he handed himself in to the police in England and was convicted for four sectarian killings. Baker would claim to have been working for British military intelligence, part of an MRF campaign designed to terrorise the Catholic community and turn it against the IRA. He also alleged state collusion in loyalist bomb attacks in Dublin that foreshadowed the 1974 Dublin and Monaghan bombings. While doubt has been cast on some of Baker's claims, only in 2015 did Paddy Heenan's family serve a writ on Frank Kitson and the Ministry of Defence (MoD) for their part in fostering loyalist gangs at this time.[82]

Eliminating Enemies

On the morning of 16 January 1981 three loyalist gunmen sledgehammered the door of the isolated farmhouse home, near Coalisland in East Tyrone, of well-known political activist Bernadette McAliskey. In front of their children, she and her husband Michael were shot many times then, badly wounded, left for dead. The attackers were, however, prevented from making their escape (rather than being prevented from carrying out the attack) by four paratroopers, possibly SAS, dug in nearby to keep the McAliskey home under surveillance. The telephone wires had been cut so one soldier set off to call for help. The Paras said their radio was not working. Nor did they give medical aid as the wounded couple lay near death for some 20 minutes. The Paras left when four soldiers from another regiment arrived, giving help that probably saved the McAliskeys' lives. The three gunmen were members of the UDA. One, a former member of the UDR, had only stopped shooting when his gun could fire no more.[83]

The sort of covert operations undertaken by the MRF in the early 1970s (some targeting republicans) would find later echoes. In patterns that would become increasingly familiar, the start of the 1980s saw a series of killings and attacks, including that on the McAliskeys, in which collusion (if not direct state involvement) has long been suspected. By then, a focus on intelligence and covert action was already becoming a more prevailing feature of state strategy. The initial militarisation of conflict gave way to 'criminalisation', 'containment' and the 'long war'. Northern Ireland was a place 'closer to home', where the treatment of a 'white' European population was more exposed to the glare of international opinion and there was a political premium to deny unwanted colonial comparisons. Conducting a counterinsurgency campaign in this context meant that covertness and deniability became all the more 'necessary' as the means to preserve the appearance of 'constitutional normalcy'.[84] However, even if partly contained, the IRA's violent campaign also showed no sign of abating. Even as the Thatcher government came to power in 1979, republicans carried out a number of high-profile and devastating attacks. In late August they killed Lord Mountbatten and three others (including two boys aged 15 and 14, the latter his grandson) in a bomb attack off the coast of his estate in Sligo. On the same day the IRA also blew up 18 British soldiers at Narrow Water, Warrenpoint, near the Irish border; the largest single loss of life suffered by the British Army throughout the conflict.[85] A few months earlier the Irish National Liberation Army (INLA) had killed the shadow Northern Ireland Secretary Airey Neave, on the eve of the Conservatives entering office. Neave was a close aide and confidant to Margaret Thatcher, primed to take charge in the North and a keen advocate of intensifying the counterinsurgency campaign.[86] As with the killing a decade later of Ian Gow (who had vehemently opposed talks with republicans), Thatcher experienced 'deep personal grief' at the loss of this 'very dear friend'.[87]

Campaigns against the 1976 removal of special category status for prisoners convicted of conflict offences were also coming to dominate the political sphere. Within the H-Blocks of Long Kesh/the Maze, republican prisoners, refusing to put on prison uniforms (some for several years), were 'on the blanket' and 'no-wash' protests.[88] The work of the National H-Blocks Committee outside, in which Bernadette McAliskey was the most well-known and pivotal figure, was drawing increasing national and international attention to the issue.[89] The erupting crisis would result in the hunger strikes of 1980 and 1981; the first major confrontations of the Thatcherite era. These were epoch-shaping political moments. Against this background, attacks were launched against several senior figures within the H-Blocks Committee, the Irish Republican Socialist Party (IRSP – the political voice of the INLA), or both, culminating in the attempted killing of Bernadette McAliskey.

The first victim of this assassination campaign was John Turnley, a former British Army officer from a landowning unionist family who had become a republican, councillor for the Irish Independence Party and member of the National H-Blocks Committee. He was shot dead by loyalists in early June 1980.[90] While John Turnley had no connection to the IRSP or INLA, Robert McConnell, one of four UDA men convicted of his killing (among them his brother Eric), said he was told otherwise. More significantly, McConnell also testified that he and the others had been working for the SAS, who provided weapons, ammunition and intelligence, as well as discussing a number of potential targets, John Turnley included.[91] Suspicions were also raised when it became known that the UDA men had been stopped, questioned and released not long after the shooting and that Eric McConnell's RUC interview notes had been destroyed because they contained 'sensitive information'. Another of the gang, William McClelland, was a former member of both the UDR and Prison Service, facts withheld from the trial.[92] Bernadette McAliskey and Miriam Daly were among other republican targets Robert McConnell said he talked over with SAS handlers. A Queen's University lecturer, Miriam Daly had been a leading figure within the IRSP and was also very prominent on the H-Blocks Committee. A few weeks after John Turnley was killed, Miriam Daly was found dead, her legs bound, in the hallway of her West Belfast home. Gunmen had cut the telephone wires, entered the house in Andersonstown, seized Miriam, and then waited for the return of her husband, also prominent in the IRSP. When he did not appear, they shot Miriam, using a pillow to drown the sound. It was a ruthlessly efficient, well-planned attack carried out in a staunch republican area – of a kind unprecedented for loyalists.

The following October two further members of the IRSP were killed, Ronnie Bunting and Noel Lyttle. Ronnie Bunting was a long-time left republican activist who emerged from the student radicalism of the civil rights movement to join, first, the official IRA, then the INLA. Being a republican from a Protestant background would have been enough to ensure Ronnie Bunting received more than his share of attention and antagonism from loyalists and state security forces alike. This was all the more so because he was the son of Major Ronald Bunting. During the violent street confrontations of the conflict's early years, Ronald Bunting had been a high-profile ally of Ian Paisley, until the two had fallen out a short time later. Whatever their political differences, however, it was to his father that Ronnie Bunting at times turned when in greatest need. 'His father always stood by him, through thick and thin', recalls Ronnie Bunting's widow Suzanne, 'they used to throw Ronnie out onto the street when they let him out of Castlereagh [Interrogation Centre]. He would phone his father, who would come to pick him up.'[93] At the inquest into his killing, it was Ronald Bunting who insisted a series of police death threats against his son was entered into the official record. 'I always remember him saying they had different politics but Ronnie had a right to his views', says Suzanne, 'and he should never have been persecuted, let alone murdered for them'.

Like the Dalys, the Buntings lived (in their case with their three young children) in the middle of a republican area of West Belfast, considered immune from loyalist attack. Death threats during interrogation, and the belief Airey Neave's assassination would lead to a government response had, however, heightened a sense of threat. 'We'll pay for it, she'll want her pound of flesh', was Ronnie Bunting's view on Thatcher's likely reaction.[94] In the early hours of 15 October 1980, two armed, masked men broke into the Bunting's house. Noel Lyttle, a friend and fellow IRSP member, was staying the night. The Buntings had a bolt on their bedroom door, left off and the landing light on so their children could 'toddle in if need be'. On hearing the front door sledgehammered, the Buntings rushed to put the bar in place, but were too late. 'They came straight to that door before we even got it closed', remembers Suzanne, 'so they knew the layout of the house beforehand. They were at the door as we reached it jumping out of bed.'[95] The Buntings tried to push closed the door as the gunmen pushed from the other side. One gunman got his hand round the door and fired, hitting Suzanne in the hand. She fell back on the bed as the gunmen came in and started shooting Ronnie. 'I didn't want to see it', says Suzanne, 'you expect one or two shots but they just kept going, shot after shot. I looked up and this bastard was standing there, emptying his gun into him. I just blew a fuse.' Suzanne jumped onto the attacker's back. 'He was trying to get his hand round to shoot me', she recalls, 'then the other one shot me and I fell off his back. When he got a few steps down he raised his gun and shot me in the mouth.' Ronnie Bunting was killed, shot nine times. Suzanne was hit four times herself. Noel Lyttle, who had gone to bed in the next room where the couple's baby lay in his cot, was also shot. He would die before reaching hospital. As Suzanne got onto her hands and knees, struggling for life, her eldest daughter Fiona, just seven, came from behind her. Suzanne called to her to get help. Fiona had to crawl over her father's body, her mother severely injured beside him, to get down the stairs and go for help. Suzanne would survive her wounds only after ten days in intensive care.

As well as apparent prior knowledge of the house, other features of the killing of Ronnie Bunting and Noel Lyttle stand out. Before the attack reports suggest the area was 'flooded with British troops', a British Army checkpoint, said to be checking everyone in and out, was in place up to half an hour before. But when the attack happened, 'they were all gone'. Recent calls for a fresh investigation have followed claims a specialist unit of the RUC had the house under 24-hour surveillance, lifted just before the shootings.[96] The attack was also 'very professional'.[97] The gunmen were dressed in 'military-type gear. They were wearing balaclavas, khaki ribbed jumpers with shoulder and elbow patches, and khaki trousers pushed in their army boots.' 'They were cool, calm, collected', Suzanne would recall, 'they didn't speak at all, except on the way out. As they went, half-way down the stairs, the other one said to the fella who had shot me in the mouth "come on", called him Georgie or Geordie, "hurry up". They just walked in, did the job and walked out again.'[98] Unusually, particularly given such a well-known victim, no loyalist organisation claimed responsibility for the attack. Unusually too no getaway car was found. The weapons used were not recovered and no one was ever arrested or convicted.

For the Bunting family, not least the children, the legacy of a lost father has been long and lasting. 'A lot of people concentrate on the horror of the attack', says Suzanne Bunting, 'but it was the loss that was more important. The loss was massive, the attack wasn't. The younger children were only three and 15 months so don't remember him at all. It's hard for kids to get over and they would still sometimes get angry. It's one thing to lose him, another to think they got away with it.' Suzanne Bunting believes her attackers were either SAS or trained loyalists acting as British agents, and with clear political purpose. 'It couldn't have been done without help', she explains, 'and I have always felt Miriam and Ronnie's deaths were connected, to each other and to Airey Neave. This was the fallout. They were the brains, political heads. It was being directed against prominent thinkers within the Irish republican socialist movement. There were lots of other people they could have taken out but they were irreplaceable.' A few months later saw the attempt to kill Bernadette McAliskey in her East Tyrone home – a mark of what had been and sign of things to come.

3
An Intelligence War

An unfortunate attitude ... then persisted within RUC Special Branch and the Force Research Unit. Namely, that they were not bound by the law and were above and beyond its reach.[1]

[R/15, a former senior RUC officer] said there was a reluctance to give official recognition to what Special Branch was doing, the effect of which would be to authorise agents of the State to allow informants to take part in activities that could lead to the commission of terrorist offences. [R/15] said that the gist that he took from the Government's response was, in effect, 'carry on with what you are doing but don't tell us the details'.[2]

Phases of Counterinsurgency

Distinct phases have been identified in British counterinsurgency policy during the Northern Ireland conflict.[3] For some, an initial 'militarisation' phase (late 1960s to mid-1970s) gave way to 'criminalisation' from then through to the early 1990s, followed by an 'accommodation' phase with the onset of the peace process. Certainly 'militarisation', or a 'war model', in the early 1970s saw a high number of state killings, particularly of Catholic/nationalist civilians.[4] This presented the state with several problems, not least because such repression proved counterproductive, feeding a rapid and devastating escalation of violence, and generating (rather than dissipating) levels of resistance to the state. The 'war model' also involved employing counterinsurgency strategies and repressive force used in other colonial campaigns, creating a profound paradox. Such an approach underscored the view of those (not least the state's principal enemy, the IRA) who argued Northern Ireland was, indeed, Britain's 'last colony', even as government rhetoric specifically sought to deny it. The problem, therefore, became one of how to conduct a counterinsurgency campaign capable of achieving the state's military goals, while maintaining and advancing its political and ideological ends – not least in preserving the self-projected legitimacy of the state, by arguing that liberal democratic norms, values and practices were being upheld. This was critical in shaping the emerging state strategy of 'criminalisation', 'normalisation' and 'containment'.[5] The ideological battle would be fought on the terrain of 'criminalising' and depoliticising the opposition (leading directly to the prison protests and ultimately the 1981 republican hunger strike), while the use of force was increasingly calibrated by this overarching political logic.

However, typologies of state counterinsurgency campaigns are often more distinct in theory than in practice. In reality phases are far from 'watertight compartments'.[6] In the midst of 'militarisation', for example, the state (or elements within it) could still favour and pursue alternative, political approaches, as evidenced by the 1972 Conservative government talks with republicans and the failed Sunningdale power-sharing agreement of 1974.[7] Similarly, during the prolonged (if often breached) IRA ceasefire of 1975, a Labour government – giving at least some consideration to a 'withdrawal' option – held protracted secret talks with the republican leadership.[8] All such efforts ultimately failed – due, in no small part, to the simultaneous resort to violence by non-state groups, as well as the contradictory and countervailing use of coercive and lethal state force, exemplified in the Bloody Sunday massacre of January 1972.[9] Likewise, while 'proclaiming a stance of criminalisation', it has been argued that 'a government may covertly pursue policies that are consistent with suppression, such as a policy of targeted assassinations or a "shoot-to-kill" policy'.[10]

We might go further and say that, far from being in any way mutually exclusive, 'criminalisation' and covert 'targeted assassinations' can be intrinsically tied to one another. Thus a close interrelationship has been identified between shifting legal and political strategies and the state's use of lethal force.[11] In this view, the ending of 'militarisation' in 1974, though followed by a 'normalisation' phase, was superseded from 1981 to 1994 by another distinct strategic moment – 'the alliance of active counterinsurgency and extraordinary law'.[12] Central here were important developments in counterinsurgency practice emerging more fully at the start of the 1980s. The wake of the 1981 hunger strike witnessed a 're-established [and] more systematic ... active counterinsurgency'.[13] This would be exemplified in the strategic deployment of specialist units of the British military (the SAS) and the emergence of a shoot-to-kill policy, not least via set-piece ambushes of republican combatants, concentrated in certain areas.[14] The use of 'massive and deadly firepower' combined with the further adaptation of emergency laws, the subverting of legal due process and the militarisation of the RUC. This was the backdrop to an intensified intelligence war and ever greater focus on the state use of informers and agents that, in large part, came to define collusion in the same period.

Counterinsurgency, Informers and Policing

The importance of intelligence as a feature of irregular warfare developed, if intermittently, throughout the tradition of British counter-insurgency.[15] So, over a century ago, Charles Callwell argued that a 'well organised and well served intelligence department' was more essential in a war against 'guerrillas' than any other.[16] Likewise, while still much focused on 'firepower and mobility', Charles Gwynn wrote that without a 'reliable force of native police as a source of intelligence', insurgency was 'obviously difficult to suppress'.[17] He also called for a 'unified intelligence effort' and an early version of 'police primacy', where military intelligence supported the police.[18] Intelligence came more to the fore in Britain's post-1945 British colonial campaigns. For example, counterinsurgency in Kenya saw attempts to integrate military and police Special Branch efforts to collect information, primarily through a 'network of informers and agents'. Here, too, the pseudo-gang was 'refined to an art form'. Information was first used to 'turn' insurgents, then counter-gangs became the intelligence-gathering means to identify, locate, capture and kill 'real gangs'.[19] No one viewed intelligence work as more vital to counterinsurgency than Frank Kitson.

Some argue that the counterinsurgency strategy in the North in the early years of conflict was marked by inefficiency, an 'intelligence vacuum' and tense competition between the independent networks, and vying interests, of various intelligence organisations.[20] With RUC Special Branch, military intelligence groups like the SRU and 14th Intelligence Company, the SAS and MI5 operating simultaneously, the counterinsurgency and state intelligence-gathering field was certainly crowded. Efforts to bring these various agencies closer together and develop 'more sophisticated' intelligence techniques were well underway long before the decade's end. The creation of regional Tasking and Co-ordinating Groups (TCGs) from 1978 onward, for example, were designed to do just that.[21] Geographically mirroring the organisation of the British

Army, the three TCGs acted as 'integrated intelligence centres'. They were based in Derry, Castlereagh and Gough Barracks in Armagh, mirroring too the organisation of the state's recently created main interrogation centres – around which soon swirled well-founded allegations of abuse, ill-treatment and torture.[22] The TCGs included representatives of the British Army, MI5 and RUC CID, but were headed by a senior RUC Special Branch officer – reflecting the belief that 'the police had to play a controlling part in the decision-making process, in the planning and execution of operations right to the end'.[23] The TCGs became pivotal in the counterinsurgency campaign. One central task was to facilitate 'what security chiefs called "executive action" – locking together intelligence from informers with the surveillance and ambushing activities of undercover units'.[24] They were also able to declare areas 'out of bounds', to uniformed patrols, where covert operations were taking place.

By the start of the 1980s state counterinsurgency had become increasingly 'intelligence-driven'. By then, too, the primary source of intelligence for all branches of the state forces was agents and informers. Often (contentiously) celebrated in mainstream academic analysis as what 'fundamentally defeated the IRA', the use of informers and agents is widely recognised as an ever more important cornerstone of state counterinsurgency in the North from the early 1980s onwards.[25] Such counterinsurgency 'success' is also generally acknowledged to have come at the price of employing 'highly dubious methods' that might also be seen to raise (seldom explored) 'major ethical questions'.[26] Yet, despite being understood to have involved 'overt collaboration' in killing, these analyses also tend to argue that such practices fell far short of 'a concerted state policy to use informants to commit murder'.[27] That remains to be seen. Certainly, it is generally agreed, informer- and agent-derived intelligence became central to the emerging strategy of 'active' counterinsurgency.

This combined with the increased militarisation of policing. As the structure of the TCGs demonstrates, a focus on 'police primacy' was introduced from the late 1970s onwards. The political and ideological logic of police primacy was to represent the conflict as less a war than a struggle against 'terrorism' and criminality. It was always something of a chimera. While full-time RUC numbers increased significantly (and a shift from part time to full time was also evident within the UDR), regular British Army troop numbers, though somewhat reduced, remained high throughout the conflict.[28] The British Army also took the lead in the most militarised areas, while the use of counterinsurgency military units, if anything, intensified. 'Ulsterisation' was never as complete as often suggested. Above all 'police primacy' meant the primacy of police-centred counterinsurgency. In practical and strategic terms it saw the expansion and development of the police's capacity to carry out a counterinsurgency campaign, not least through the creation of specialist, militarised units within the RUC, such as E4A. Along with counterinsurgent military units like the SAS, these would soon be at the centre of allegations of a shoot-to-kill policy. RUC Special Branch was also placed at the heart of the counterinsurgency endeavour. It became a 'force within a force'. The apparent shift from army to police primacy was paralleled by a move from investigative to intelligence-led policing.[29] Counterinsurgency was prioritised over all other aspects of policing. Streamlining the ways agents and informers were recruited, employed and protected undermined the core legal basis of policing – concerned with 'the prevention and detection of crime ... with far-reaching consequences' – not least on the character of collusion.[30]

Handling Informers, Changing the Rules

The central place of 'human assets' in the state's counterinsurgency campaign was signalled by the introduction of substantial structural and procedural changes to the way the RUC handled agents, informers and intelligence. These changes, mooted before, were brought in fully from March 1981. They were based on an internal report, drawn up by Sir Patrick Walker and commissioned by the newly installed head of the RUC, Sir John Hermon. Again, Walker provides some continuity with the imperial roots of counterinsurgency. Later head of MI5, he was 'the last Director General with a colonial background'.[31] Born in Malaya, Walker grew up in Kenya, and then served as a colonial administrator in Uganda 'at the end of empire'.[32] He joined MI5 when independence was declared. Walker seems to never have lost a mandarin cast of mind or his yearning for halcyon colonial days. While there had been 'great hostility' to Britain's imperial role 'as something to make apologies for', he later nostalgically reflected, people 'are coming to recognise that the stability of British colonial rule, and the gradual improvements achieved under it, did benefit the majority of people, and were in many ways something of value'.[33] Walker's 1980 report on the RUC introduced radical changes and established a centralised intelligence and agent-handling system that built the primacy of intelligence-gathering and counterinsurgency operations into the DNA of policing practices.

At that time Walker was second in command of MI5 in the North, highlighting the fundamental part played by the secret service in both reshaping policing and forging the new phase of this intelligence-led war. MI5 was instrumental in designing these crucial changes to policing, which were implemented in secret rather than being the result of legislation or any public policy process.[34] The Walker report may have 'given the lead role' in policing to RUC Special Branch but 'MI5, having devised the strategy, played a significant role behind the scenes. They pulled the strings.' They also ensured that the primacy of counterinsurgency was enshrined as the dominant paradigm of policing – a process that not only reconstituted the very nature of policing, but helped entrench a culture of systemic collusion. Intelligence gathering and informer recruitment would now take precedence in all aspects of policing crime.

There were three key changes. First, as the report noted, many police officers had developed 'in the course of their duties a wide range of trusted contacts', of whom other police officers might not be aware. CID members, in particular, often had their own networks of informers.[35] This was no longer allowed. All RUC officers (again notably in CID) were required to hand over details of any contacts, sources or networks of informers to Special Branch, who were now solely in charge of handling any 'agent or source reporting on subversive organisations'.[36] Second, new guidelines were issued for the conduct of interviews that prioritised, over all else, gathering intelligence on insurgent organisations and Special Branch informer recruitment. All police interviews were to be viewed as 'an important source of intelligence', whether or not it directly involved 'subversive crimes'.[37] CID officers should 'seize every opportunity to acquire intelligence on subversive organisations', even once confessions for 'ordinary crimes' had been obtained. Anyone being questioned with potential 'intelligence of value' was to be interrogated by Special Branch and any charges delayed until that could take place. Not stated, this could also allow for charges to be dropped as a part of a deal to recruit informers. Indeed, CID officers were always to be 'alert [to] the opportunity to recruit' informants during the course of an interrogation. If such an opportunity arose, 'Special Branch must be involved at an early stage both in de-briefing and handling an agent'. Finally, all arrests planned by CID required prior clearance from Special Branch so the latter could 'ensure that no agents of either RUC or the

Army are involved'. Any decision to charge an informer or agent had to be the result of 'a conscious decision by both Special Branch and CID in which *the balance of advantage has been carefully weighed* [my italics]'.

One-time Special Branch head (and later head of the RUC), Sir Ronnie Flanagan, described the Walker report as simply concerned with the 'proper management' of information to defeat 'subversive criminality'.[38] It was much more than that. This was a system that institutionalised intelligence gathering and informer recruitment in exchange for deferring arrest and imprisonment, and the prevention of the arrest of agents, once recruited, even if they had been involved in criminal acts and extensive wrongdoing. It was a calculated, bureaucratised conduit to systematic collusion as a means of conducting a counterinsurgency campaign.

Intelligence 'Leaks'

The build-up of state intelligence also had direct bearing on the nature of collusion. By the late 1980s the security forces were far and away the most important source of intelligence for loyalists. Indeed, the scope and scale of the 'leaking' of intelligence from the security forces to loyalist paramilitaries, revealed in the de Silva report into the killing of Patrick Finucane, is astounding. For example, after dismissing any 'questionable' reports of 'leaks', de Silva still found 270 separate instances of information being handed over to the UDA alone in less than a two-year period between 1987 and 1989.[39] This included 'accurate and sensitive targeting information on republicans; information about the identity of informers; advance notice of arrests and operations; and, on occasion, weapons'.[40] Nearly half of the leaks involved information for targeting republicans.[41]

This was known at the time by state authorities – though there is little evidence they then acted on that knowledge. Several MI5 reports throughout the mid to late 1980s found that the vast majority of leaked information came from members of the RUC and the UDR.[42] RUC men were more likely to hand over 'general information and warnings to paramilitaries of impending security forces operations', while their UDR counterparts tended more towards 'the passing of montages or photographs and collusion in supplying weapons'.[43] Both were as likely to leak as each other but UDR members, it was blithely noted, were more susceptible to involvement in 'murder, manslaughter [and] firearms offences'. Certainly intelligence on 'republican targets' had 'greatly increased', particularly after the signing of the Anglo-Irish Agreement in 1985. Such 'leaks' were not restricted to 'low-level' intelligence or solely carried out by junior officers.[44] There was ample evidence that the UDA received highly sensitive RUC and military files, including intelligence reports. Members of RUC counterinsurgency units, like E4A, were notably linked to loyalists. Much also suggests that senior UDR and RUC officers 'may have been providing assistance to loyalist paramilitaries', particularly in terms of procuring weapons. The weight of evidence that a 'small number of comparatively senior figures' was involved in giving 'assistance' to loyalists was 'sufficiently compelling and consistent' to lead de Silva to conclude it was likely true.

Indeed, incredibly the claim that 85 per cent of loyalist intelligence had originated from state files is likely to be an underestimate.[45] It involved literally thousands of documents handed over to loyalists. This was a widespread and endemic practice that was pivotal in developing the capacity for violence shown by loyalist organisations in this period, particularly where directed against republicans. 'I have no doubt', noted de Silva, 'that most UDA targeting and attacks during the late 1980s could be traced back to initial security force leaks', ensuring the UDA was 'in a position to mount an effective campaign'.[46] State-sourced intelligence made possible the UDA's developing strategy of accelerated violence, something known by intelligence agencies at the time. Figures given by de Silva for this tidal wave of leaked intelligence did not even include details of what was handed over to the UVF. Nor did it include state-sourced information systematically given to Brian Nelson, who (during the late 1980s) was simultaneously head of intelligence for the UDA and a British military intelligence agent.[47]

The FRU and Brian Nelson

Alongside RUC Special Branch, at the heart of much collusive activity was the main intelligence unit of the British military operating in the North – the FRU. The FRU had been set up around 1980 at the behest of General Sir James Glover, the 'mandarin of British intelligence', to consolidate the army's running of agents.[48] It was the latest reincarnation of British military intelligence, following on from what had gone before (such as the MRF) and setting a pattern for what would come after. Ostensibly in place to support RUC Special Branch, it ran an independent, parallel intelligence system while (it is claimed) sometimes providing 'the RUC with a token of its product to cover political niceties'.[49] Designed to operate alongside 14th Intelligence Company and the SAS, the FRU's existence was, for many years, completely unknown beyond intelligence circles. Its commander reported directly to the highest echelons of the British Army.[50] By the late 1980s the FRU was run by Colonel Gordon Kerr. Brian Nelson was recruited by the FRU in the mid-1980s. A native of Belfast and former British soldier, Nelson soon became chief intelligence officer of the UDA, responsible for the collation, upkeep and dissemination of intelligence used in launching loyalist attacks. This allowed Nelson to act as a conduit for state intelligence and targeting information (including the names, addresses, photographs, layout of homes, transport and movement details of 'suspected' republicans) used in the rising number of loyalist assassinations in the late 1980s, including that of Pat Finucane.[51]

Gordon Kerr would claim that Nelson only provided sufficient intelligence and resources to maintain his cover within the organisation and that he then passed on details of information provided to his FRU handlers. This is contradicted by the substantial evidence that many loyalists strongly suspected (if not simply being aware) that Nelson was a state agent – not least given his evident open access to military and police files. It is a defence of Nelson's activities demolished by de Silva, who suspected that Nelson's dissemination of material targeting 'republican personalities' was instigated by, and done at the behest of, the FRU.[52] Nelson's handlers were aware that state intelligence was distributed to UDA commanders, allowing them to act 'independently', which 'greatly enhanced the UDA's potential for murder' while escaping arrest.[53] The FRU's aim in engineering Nelson's advance to head of intelligence, declared Gordon Kerr, was to 'persuade the UDA to centralise their targeting activity through Nelson and to concentrate their targeting on known PIRA activists'.[54] That Nelson also provided intelligence for targeting republicans to the 'more aggressive' UVF (who previously lacked such material) showed, however, this was anything but a strategy to 'save lives', and that was 'clearly understood' by Nelson's handlers.[55]

This was the exact reverse of Kerr's later justification for Nelson's activities. Rather, the FRU and other branches of the security state had (as noted) a growing interest in the 'military professionalisation' of loyalists.[56] Having agents and informers in crucial roles within armed non-state groups (loyalist and republican) allowed them to substantially influence, if not direct, their violent actions, making them pivotal to the thrust of state counterinsurgency policy. Nelson was the primary means for the FRU to get sensitive intelligence material into loyalist hands, and only his (inadvertent) arrest in 1990 ended his activities.[57] His subsequent conviction, two years later, came only after a guilty plea deal was agreed. That helped ensure his trial lasted less than a day, marked only by a vigorous defence of Nelson's actions mounted by Kerr. Nelson served half a ten-year sentence and lived under a false identity when released.[58] How unusual Nelson's case was remains an open question. One dominant narrative argues that his removal, and along with him a loyalist 'old guard', allowed a new generation to mount the escalation in attacks and killings witnessed in the early 1990s.[59] Yet much suggests that loyalist groups were still riddled with informers and agents long after Nelson was gone. Their involvement in widespread serious crime, including murder, would continue into the new millennium.[60]

What can be said is that under FRU guidance, and through the work of agents like Nelson, loyalist paramilitary groups became a more lethally effective force. Their killing capacity was increased, the ability to prevent attacks on 'republican personalities' reduced, and republican deaths made more likely – as was the likelihood that the perpetrators would escape capture. Even as the number of blatantly sectarian victims grew, this looks like nothing so much as a systematic attempt to kill, demoralise and defeat the 'enemy' (the IRA and its supporters) at arm's length and beyond the bounds of the law. It takes considerable effort not to see this as a strategy of targeted assassination by proxy – or that this is very much in keeping with the 'calibration of lethal force' in the tradition of British counterinsurgency.[61]

Agents, Informers and a Void of Law

The rules (or their lack) governing the handling of agents and informers is central to any discussion about collusion; not least in terms of what it was they were not only permitted, but directed, to do. This was a major focus for de Silva's examination of collusion. He spends a considerable amount of time and energy looking at discussions among Cabinet members and with Northern Ireland Office (NIO) officials, senior legal figures and high-ranking members of the RUC, army and intelligence services, as to whether or not there should be guidelines for, essentially, what crimes agents and informers might 'necessarily' be allowed to commit and what crimes should be beyond the bounds of what was permitted. Certainly, de Silva's report shows that this issue regularly exercised the minds of senior members of the police and military, who consistently raised the matter at the highest political level. It is a big issue for de Silva because he wants to argue that the absence of such clear guidelines or a legal framework helped make possible collusion, and the involvement of state agents in serious wrongdoing, up to and including murder. However, de Silva also wants to explain all this in a very particular way. That is because, despite being so regularly discussed within the highest echelons of the state, no meaningful or enforceable rules, or limits, on the actions of agents and informers were brought in throughout this period. Nothing, in that sense, was done. This raises the question why?

During Nelson's trial, Gordon Kerr complained about the 'armchair rules' for the handling of informers which supposedly prevented them from being involved in criminal activity.[62] In reality, there was virtually no regulation (and little guidance) on what both handlers and agents could, or could not, do. No statutory framework existed at all, only 'non-statutory guidance and direction', characterised by a 'looseness of terminology … and judicial uncertainty'[63] – a situation rendered even more opaque when 'the "accessory" is a police informer or agent'. RUC guidelines pre-dated the conflict and the RUC themselves admitted they could not be 'strictly adhered to' without undermining an 'effective intelligence network'.[64] For Army Intelligence, the guiding principles in place in the late 1980s and early 1990s were those issued in July 1986, by the recently appointed Commander of Land Forces for Northern Ireland, Major General Tony Jeapes.[65] Jeapes (uniquely for someone in his new role) had previously been commanding officer of the SAS and been responsible for the development of its strategy in the North in the early 1970s. He had earlier served in the SAS in Malaya and Dhofar in the late 1950s and 1960s. Jeapes took up his senior role in the North at the same time as a new General Officer Commanding was appointed, Lieutenant General Robert Pascoe. Both were 'open to the idea of using Special Forces for ambushes'.[66]

An absolute prohibition on undertaking, or sanctioning, illegal acts seemed, on the face of it, to be central to army guidance. The official military 'instructions for source control and handling' stated it was 'unlawful for any person to authorise an illegal act'.[67] At least, that was the theory. Yet, as Gordon Kerr's comments illustrate, the practice was somewhat different – and seems to have been widely understood as such within intelligence and political circles. This is crucial and points towards a vital, violently productive, space between an ostensible public and official norm of adherence to the law and the everyday practice of intelligence and counterinsurgency operatives, working in the context of a non-public institutional norm, where the law was rendered indeterminate. Kerr's perspective suggests that the theoretical condition of legal compliance could never be met, even while it had to be publicly stated. In addition, while those legal standards were only ever 'guidance', they lacked the potentially prohibitive force of a statutory basis.

Certainly there was no lack of awareness of the issue of agent handling at the highest levels of the state – far from it.[68] De Silva shows that substantive discussion of the matter was taking place between various state political, military, policing and civil administrative agencies (and at the highest level) from at least March 1987 and continued, without legislative resolution, throughout the early 1990s. Indeed, he argues, this was not a question that suddenly emerged in the late 1980s, concluding that the absence of clear legal guidance for handling informers was likely an issue to have arisen throughout the conflict. Nor was it something that had been hidden from government. 'It was manifestly not the case', argues de Silva, 'that agent-handlers were seeking to conceal the general nature of their activities from those in authority; on the contrary, they wanted the political leadership to provide a clear framework and direction'. It was, then, an issue 'considered extensively at Cabinet level and Government Ministers were clearly aware that agents were being handled in Northern Ireland without reference to adequate guidelines because no such framework existed. Ministers nonetheless continued to place a high priority on pursuing an intelligence-led approach to the terrorist threat. The result of this was that agent handlers and their supervisors were being asked to perform a task ... *that, in some cases, could not be carried out in a way that was both effective and lawful* [my italics].'[69]

In other words, from the outset there was a distinct 'lack of political will' to introduce formal changes or resolve 'grey areas' involving 'the demands placed on the intelligence sector and its legal capacity to achieve its objectives'; a perspective shared by the NIO and senior legal advisers.[70] While ministers were 'fully seized of the problem', the NIO were not enthusiastic about formally resolving matters and attempts to ensure 'fairly slow progress' appear to have been realised.[71] A 'hot potato' for the NIO, 'key legal people' were apparently 'reticent, to say the least', to change the existing system, 'despite the fact that *what actually goes on is known or assumed by many* [my italics]'.[72] One consequence was that neither FRU nor RUC Special Branch handlers apparently received any formal 'training or briefing on the legal implications of agent-running'. This was not the result of a lack of awareness of the problem but because such training was impossible 'given the absence of a statutory framework on which to base any such training or guidance'.[73] Even when new agent handler guidelines were eventually drawn up in 1990 by the NIO, and later adopted by military intelligence and MI5, they were viewed by the Solicitor General as 'unpromising territory for Ministerial approval' because they amounted to little more than a call not to get caught.[74]

Brian Nelson's conviction precipitated another review, this time chaired by Sir John Blelloch (believed to have been an MI5 officer in the North during the 1981 hunger strike).[75] Despite having been adopted by the intelligence agencies, Blelloch found that these guidelines could not be formally approved by ministers 'for fear that that may involve them in allegations of conspiratorial criminality'.[76] A further internal review chaired by the NIO Permanent Secretary of State Sir John Chilcot (later chair of the Iraq War Inquiry) did little but extend unresolved senior-level discussions beyond the IRA and loyalist ceasefires of 1994. Conservative government political sensitivities were by then particularly acute given parliamentary reliance on the support of unionists who, paradoxically, viewed the IRA ceasefire as 'another source of menace'.[77] Throughout, state fears that legal uncertainty would prevent the recruitment and use of agents and informers, at the forefront of counterinsurgency activities, proved unfounded.[78]

Informers, Collusion and Deniability

In his report Desmond de Silva has a very specific interpretation to explain the absence of a regulatory framework for handling agents and the 'wilful and abject failure' to put legislation in place. In essence de Silva characterises these discussions as a concerted, but ultimately doomed, attempt to arrive at some consensus on implementing rules governing the criminal acts of agents. It is a reading of events that now extends into the government's later, post-de Silva 'lessons learnt' document. It is now, in other words, the official narrative of what took place.[79] This line of argument rests on a built-in *a priori* assumption adopted by de Silva. It is 'self-evident', he asserts, 'that the implementation of such an inherently difficult task as penetrating terrorist groups with agents would require the development of a detailed legal and policy framework'.[80] In other words, establishing clear and binding rules for the handling of agents would have been a 'good' thing, not only for moral, legal or rights-based reasons, but also in operational terms – in order to better achieve the strategic counterinsurgency ends for which agents and informers were being used. Throughout, de Silva then assumes, this shaped the viewpoint and thinking that informed government decision making. It is similarly taken to explain why the issue was raised by high-ranking members of the police and the army – that they were pressing for government-sanctioned rules on agent handling as, among other things, the best means of achieving their strategic ends. The absence of any agreement on putting any such rules in place until after the conflict was over therefore emerges, in this perspective, as an apparent matter of regret for all concerned; in other words as a failure of policy making.

Yet there is another, more critical, way of viewing this evidence, which is to understand the absence of such guidelines not as a failure of policy but, rather, its purpose – to open up a space of legal obscurity and plausible deniability that facilitated, rather than hampered, counterinsurgency practice. Not having clear laws and guidelines in place as to how informers and agents should be handled, and how they in turn should act, might instead be seen as the means to allow them to be handled and act in ways that were, to all intents and purposes, contrary to the rule of law, but consistent with the end goal of counterinsurgency: the defeat of the IRA and the preservation of the state's order. An alternative assessment of what was taking place might rather understand the 'wilful failure' to put a regulatory framework in place to be (while certainly 'wilful') only a 'failure' in the immediate sense of not creating a legal basis for actions that were intended to facilitate the 'successful' achievement of this wider objective. Apart from anything else, if collusion is understood to include deliberately 'turning a blind eye' to wrongdoing, this, in itself, would constitute institutionalised collusion at the highest political level. De Silva might then have lent more weight to his own conclusion, that the 'system [for agent handling] appears to have facilitated political deniability ... rather than creating mechanisms for an appropriate level of political oversight'.[81] This was not a policy failure – it was the point.

Indeed, de Silva's report contains much evidence to support this alternative reading, including one telling comment, from a former senior RUC officer, recalling a remarkable meeting, held with Margaret Thatcher and members of her Cabinet, in the late 1980s. When Thatcher asked what was needed to 'combat terrorism effectively', she was told by the RUC officer that 'he regarded as essential a sound legislative basis on which intelligence operations could be conducted lawfully', and that the management of agents and informers was made 'infinitely more difficult because they were operating in a grey area, and in the absence of a sound legal framework'.[82] The recalled government response is highly significant – 'essentially that the issue was too difficult to handle, and that SB [Special Branch] should continue as before. [R/15] said there was a reluctance to give official recognition to what SB was doing, the effect of which would be to authorise agents of the State to allow informants to take part in activities that could lead to the commission of terrorist offences. [R/15] said that the *gist that he took from the government's response was, in effect, "carry on with what you are doing but don't tell us the details"* [my italics].'[83]

In other words, the lack of a statutory framework for the handling of informers was not understood by senior political figures as a difficulty so much as a means by which counterinsurgency actions and practices could take place that could, otherwise, not be defended legally or politically. There was an instrumental and strategic advantage in recognising, but not formally acknowledging, the *modus operandi* of Special Branch at the time. Nor was this an isolated incident. Rather, according to de Silva, it is 'strikingly consistent with the picture revealed by UK Government files'. Indeed, legislation would not be put into place until after the signing of the Good Friday Agreement (when the conflict essentially ended) in the form of the Regulation of Investigatory Powers Act 2000 (RIPA). In other words, until after the conflict was, to all intents and purposes, over. Despite protestations to the contrary, the 'grey spaces' did not inhibit the counterinsurgency use of informers and agents but rather facilitated the political deniability of 'exceptional' practice.

Senior military and police figures undoubtedly expressed concerns about the lack of a clear legal basis for their actions, although there is little evidence to suggest this was from a desire to prevent collusive practices, as de Silva assumes. Rather, much points to a fear (shared by senior members of the military, police and intelligence agencies) that operating in a 'grey area' of 'twilight legality' might leave them criminally accountable for their actions at some future point, while their political masters sheltered behind official denial. For example, amid (ultimately failed) attempts to charge members of the RUC for conducting a shoot-to-kill policy in the wake of the Stalker Affair, senior RUC officers argued that informer handler guidelines were regularly breached and left

RUC officers open to possible prosecution.[84] Indeed it is striking that the key issue raised throughout was not that such actions and practices should be stopped, but that guidelines and the law needed to be changed in order to protect the position (and prevent the prosecution) of agents and their handlers. In other words, to give legal sanction and prevent potential legal culpability for what was being done, rather than stopping the activities themselves.

It was a position shared by other senior state officials. The problem, according to John Chilcot, was that 'existing law appears to leave agents, handlers and others involved in the intelligence process – including Ministers – unduly exposed'.[85] Fears of later exposure to culpability echo what has, more recently, been referred to as the 'Ulsterisation of blame'.[86] Something of this view is, again, captured in the (seemingly embittered) words of Gordon Kerr to the Stevens III inquiry in 2002: 'I believe the wilful neglect in this matter lies with successive governments who despite calling for counter terrorist intelligence measures ... have *deliberately failed to address* [my italics] the need for a more complete legal framework and more detailed guidelines'.[87] Putting a 'clear framework' in place would have involved a declared, legally binding, official sanction of such practices. The 'lack of a political will' to introduce legislation is what helped generate a space of deniability, which limited the chain of potential responsibility and absolved the government of direct culpability. What, then, we can more broadly ask, might the consequences be for the cultures existing within state institutions, when such lines are knowingly blurred – and those working within them at a high level know, but do not formally acknowledge, that wrongdoing and serious law-breaking is taking place?

Covering Up Collusion

The search for truth about collusion has often been presented as a narrative of unbroken and dogged official investigation. However, public disclosure of the role of agents and informers has had to wait some considerable time, and is very far from complete. How it was portrayed when the conflict was still ongoing was also, significantly, very different – notably in the first Stevens collusion inquiry, published in 1990, which is viewed as a key stepping stone on this journey towards official accountability.[88] Indeed, the first Stevens Inquiry had only been set up after loyalists sought to justify the 1989 killing of Loughlin

Maginn by plastering walls with some of the mass of intelligence files and photos in their possession.[89] At that time, Stevens concluded that the problem of collusion was limited to a 'small number of individuals', no 'documents of any higher security classification' had been handed over and collusion was 'neither widespread nor institutionalised'.[90] He even suggested that the British Army and RUC had, in essence, rectified matters. In response, the then secretary of state, Sir Peter Brooke, noted that no RUC officers had been charged, and 'misbehaviour' by a 'few individual members' of the UDR did not 'lessen his conviction' that it, too, was 'fundamentally sound'.[91] A second inquiry in 1994 added little else.[92] Collusion as a 'rotten apple', low-level problem of the past, became the official line, echoed by the RUC and military hierarchy, government and much of the media.[93] It would be the dominant narrative for many years to come. Suggestions that collusion was endemic, state-sanctioned or systematic were long dismissed as republican propaganda. A quarter of a century later, Stevens acknowledged that collusion was clearly 'far more widespread and extensive' than he initially found.[94]

Brooke also said that both the army and the RUC had given their 'full co-operation at every level' to the first Stevens Inquiry. This was not true. Stevens had, in fact, faced RUC and military 'obstruction' that was 'cultural in its nature and widespread'.[95] Both the RUC and British Army went to extraordinary lengths to prevent the full picture of collusion emerging. Far from cooperating, the primary aim of those leading the state's continuing counterinsurgency efforts was to deceive, deflect and obstruct. Consequently, files and intelligence were withheld and loyalists facing impending arrests were tipped off.[96] On the eve of arresting Nelson himself, Stevens' team offices (and many of their records) were destroyed in a fire. The fire alarms were not working and telephone lines were dead, and yet the RUC concluded that it was not started deliberately.[97] Years later, Sir John Stevens said it was a 'deliberate act of arson' – a conclusion Desmond de Silva had 'no reason to doubt'.[98] Yet, this starkest example of 'obstruction' of an official inquiry, likely carried out by members of the security forces, 'remains unexplained'.[99]

Only a decade later, long after the Good Friday Agreement had brought an end to the conflict, was Stevens able to access official British Army and RUC documents he had been told did not exist. Senior military and police officers had been pivotal in blocking access. They included Sir John Waters, the most senior British officer in the North, who sanctioned withholding army intelligence files from Stevens.[100] He may have done so after discussion with the head of the RUC. For de Silva, that 'senior Army officers' went so far as to deny that the military ran agents at all, was a 'deplorable' attempt by 'public servants' to conceal 'the fact that a figure at the heart of this matter was an Army agent'.[101] Judge Peter Cory was even more damning. The apparent willingness of RUC Special Branch and military intelligence to collude together 'to protect their perceived interest', said Cory, evidenced 'the unfortunate attitude that then persisted within RUC SB [Special Branch] and FRU. Namely, that they were not bound by the law and were above and beyond its reach.'[102] Nothing suggests that Stevens' early inquiries caused those conducting counterinsurgency to change what they were doing. The response of both loyalists and 'their allies within the Security forces' was merely to 'sharpen up their act'.[103] This took the form, says Tony Geraghty, of striking 'more precisely at genuine IRA targets or, and this suited them just as well, close proxies in the form of parents, children and siblings' of republicans.

The Liberal Ideology of Collusion

States might reasonably cite a principle of self-defence as justification for utilising a range of means at their disposal (political, diplomatic and military), including intelligence-led operations and the use of agents and informers, when faced with violent political opposition or armed insurgency. Most (if not all) states have employed 'human intelligence' for such ends.[104] That said, within liberal democracies, any such practices are normally defended as continuing to conform to the norms and practices of the rule of law, even when the juridical order has been substantially reshaped, or subverted, by 'emergency' measures. Of course, it is precisely the place and role of the rule of law in the use of agents and informers in Northern Ireland that is under scrutiny. The darkest, starkest problems in the relationship between the covert practices of the state and the juridical order emerge if such collusive intelligence work is seen to have been pivotal in conducting a state campaign of targeted assassination and extrajudicial killing (including the killing of 'non-combatants') by proxy.

How then might all this be understood and what does it tell us about the relationship between the practices of state violence, the exercise of power and the rule of law? A recent critique of the rise of a 'torture culture' in post-9/11 America has argued that the founding tenets of liberal democracies contain both the conditions for abhorrence towards the use of torture and the philosophical underpinnings for its justification.[105] The theoretical antagonism of liberalism (broadly understood) towards torture is even more fulsome than against state killing because it ranks the cruelty inherent in torture as 'the first among vices', exemplifying the 'terrorizing' effect of the 'tyrannical political relationships liberalism hates most'. Despite this, the self-same 'liberal' ideas that make torture so 'morally unacceptable … at a deeper level … can justify interrogational torture in the face of danger', at least for the purpose of intelligence gathering; the flawed logic of the so-called 'ticking bomb' scenario.[106] That such liberalism insists upon limited governments that 'exercise their power only for instrumental and pragmatic purposes' makes possible viewing torture as 'civilised', when aimed at 'preventing future harms'.[107] Here, torture becomes divorced from cruelty, 'authorised and administered by decent human beings, who might abhor what circumstances force them to do'. Justified on the pragmatic basis of preventing a supposed future 'greater evil' is what has been called the 'liberal ideology of torture'.[108] This is the triumph of a doctrine of necessity – and one directly analogous to that which underpinned institutionalised collusion.

In the context of an 'emergency', or belief of an impending 'catastrophe', a doctrine of apparent pragmatic necessity determines what becomes 'allowable' for liberal democracies, even to the extent of using forms of violence (such as torture) that apparently stand in absolute contradiction to the 'values' ostensibly being defended (such as the absolute prohibition of torture). Given the bureaucratic orders and institutional settings of state agencies, there is, in addition, a tendency towards the corrosive normalisation of forms of (otherwise impermissible) violence. This is particularly so where the resort to secrecy, to offset the rise of a public culture of ostensibly prohibited forms of state violence, does not so much avoid the normalisation of such violence as merely 'layer on top of it the normalisation of state secrecy'.[109] Secrecy within state institutional orders, and the cumulative experience of rules-breaching violence carried out by state agents, similarly shifts the normative ground upon which they operate. In the absence of 'bright-light rules', as 'necessity' trumps all else, the limits of the permissible are seen to be porous, expansive and highly contingent on circumstance, while rights-based criticisms are dismissed as absolutist – not least, perhaps, because adherence to 'values' may be of considerably less significance than the defence and promotion of interests.

Just such a doctrine of 'necessity', rather than a singular commitment to the principle of minimum force, or a non-coercive battle for hearts and minds, has also been evident throughout the history of British military counterinsurgency thinking.[110] Proclamations of adherence to the rule of law, as a cornerstone of British counterinsurgency, act as a form of 'magical realism' where expediency subverts norms and standards behind a mask of legality.[111] This was evident in the history of counter-insurgency in the North, not least in the use of agents and informers in the conduct of the intelligence war. The key problem for the political system was to create a juridical order that could, at one and the same time, protect the state agents carrying out counterinsurgency operations that might normally be deemed illegal, but which allowed state agents to do 'what was necessary' to preserve state interests. The norms of the military professional and wider liberal values may, at times, have shaped and restrained the resort to force.[112] However, they did so tempered by the overarching logic of necessity and the blurred lines of the 'dirty war'. Yet the very idea of 'necessity' is itself a politically powerful mask and illusion – an enabling fiction, often presented in objective terms that, however, always involves subjective political judgement and decision.[113] It is always a matter of 'necessary' for what, and 'necessary' for whom'? Even where an act is deemed 'necessary' to preserve the existing order, this presumes agreement that the existing order is worth preserving.

Such subjective 'necessity' decisions were defined by the 'emergency' the state felt it was facing in Northern Ireland and, in turn, shaped the counterinsurgency campaign it then waged. From this point of view, state actors, operating within the wilfully created legal vacuum surrounding how they should handle agents and informers, had to 'break the order to save it'. The attitude of a counterinsurgency military practitioner such as FRU head Gordon Kerr was very much in tune with this line of thinking and exemplifies the 'doctrine of necessity' at the heart of the British COIN tradition. In the North, state counterinsurgency led to a broad reframing of the legal sanction of violent state practices. 'Special' and 'emergency' laws – some well-established, others new – and apparently mundane and perfunctory changes to legal and bureaucratic processes, covered much. The creation of a lacuna in the law, by not setting clear legal limits on the actions of agents, informers and their handlers, should be seen in this light. It involved (what we might see as) the bureaucratic normalisation, or 'civilising', of a culture of collusion. This is not a situation that came about through oversight or an absence of thought. Rather, it involved the public projection of a myth of legality, which could permit the conduct of counterinsurgency operations regarded as 'necessary', to meet the end goal of defeating (or at least successfully containing) the state's primary 'enemy' – the IRA.

4
Arming Loyalism

Providing Weapons

The capacity of loyalists to significantly increase their violent campaign also depended on having access to a new arsenal of weapons. These came from several (often police or military) sources, but a crucial part was played by a large cache imported from South Africa in December 1987.[1] It included over 200 Czech-made assault rifles, some 90 Browning pistols, anti-personnel grenades, several RPG-7 rocket launchers and thousands of rounds of ammunition.[2] The history of these weapons casts some light on the sordid, complex world of international arms deals. Most were originally captured by the Israelis from the Palestine Liberation Organization in 1982, who gave them to their Lebanese, Christian, phalange allies. The shipment in 1987 was arranged by Douglas Bernhardt, an American-born, Geneva-based arms dealer, who sourced them from a Lebanese counterpart.[3] Bernhardt was working in collaboration with Armscor, the apartheid-era South African state weapons company. Some of the imported arms were seized not long after being landed in the North. However, many were not, and were used in at least 70 loyalist killings, likely more.[4] This 're-arming of loyalists' fed directly into the 'major upsurge in sectarian killings in the first half of the 1990s'.[5] In the previous six years loyalists killed 71 people, in the six years after they killed 229, many using the imported guns. Many of these victims were shot dead in Mid-Ulster.

There have long been allegations that Brian Nelson and his FRU handlers were closely involved in arranging and facilitating this arms shipment.[6] In 1985, with the full knowledge and support of his army handlers, Nelson had travelled to South Africa, at the behest of the head of the UDA, to arrange an arms shipment via a contact (originally from Northern Ireland) who worked for Armscor.[7] While this failed to transpire because of a lack of loyalist funds, the links developed by Nelson would be the same as those that facilitated the 1987 shipment. Desmond de

Silva followed others in refuting such accusations.[8] The 1987 shipment, he said, was a 'separate operation' with which 'Nelson and the FRU had no involvement'.[9] Indeed, despite his key intelligence role within the UDA, de Silva accepted Nelson's contention that he (and by implication his handlers) did not know the origin of the imported arms until several months later – even though the 'bulk of the UDA's share of the weapons had already been captured by the RUC'.[10] Conversely, de Silva reserves special praise for security force efforts in seizing loyalist weapons, including a portion of the 1987 shipment captured in January and February 1988. For de Silva, this was ultimate proof refuting 'untenable' arguments that loyalists were 'simply State-sponsored forces'. Not only had British intelligence, the police and the army not been aware of, or involved in, this massive arms shipment beforehand, he concluded, they did all they could to stop the weapons being used by loyalists afterward.

Much here rests on less than solid ground. Whether or not the FRU and MI5 records to which de Silva had access were wholly accurate and complete is at least questionable.[11] Certainly the findings of a more recent Police Ombudsman's report into the 1994 Loughinisland massacre (which looked at the 1987 arms smuggling) stand in stark contrast to such conclusions, painting a very different portrait of the foreknowledge of state agencies and the role of state agents and informers. Rather, it is said, the 'origins' of the 1987 arms shipment categorically lay in Nelson's 1985 visit to South Africa, organised 'with security force oversight' by a 'senior member of the UDA who provided information for the RUC's Special Branch'.[12] Likewise, throughout the next two years, the RUC had a wealth of intelligence of a 'conspiracy' of various loyalist paramilitary groups, including the UDA, organising to acquire weapons from South Africa.[13] Alongside the UDA, this involved leading figures in the UVF and the recently formed, mass-based paramilitary group Ulster Resistance. Contrary to de Silva's conclusions, state agencies were therefore 'aware of the plans of the UVF, UDA and Ulster Resistance to import a significant consignment of weaponry'.[14] Among those centrally involved was a senior loyalist RUC informant.[15]

Leading UDA figures, many who worked closely with Brian Nelson, directed plans throughout. A bank robbery, which funded the arms deal, was 'carried out by and on behalf of the UDA' in the months after Nelson became chief of intelligence for the organisation.[16] Alongside their 'command and control' of loyalist paramilitary groups and their part in 'murder [and] conspiracy to murder', the report concluded that 'informants [were] involved in the procurement and distribution of the weapons, including individuals at the most senior levels of the organisation(s) responsible for the importation'.[17] RUC Special Branch was aware months prior to the arms smuggling that proceeds from the robbery were to be used 'to finance a large arms deal exploiting a South African connection' and were 'monitoring' the situation alongside 'the Security Service'. 'Everybody seemed to know about' the arms shipment, one UVF figure later said, 'the whole thing was so transparent that I started to worry if it had been infiltrated from the beginning'.[18] In private, many (both loyalists and security force members) admitted that 'the weapons were allowed to reach the province'.[19] Indeed, even if the official line was taken at face value, it surely beggars belief that, at no point, did any of the intelligence agencies at least ask Nelson, head of UDA intelligence, to try and find out what was going on.

Arms, Ulster Resistance and the Mid-Ulster UVF

De Silva argued that neither Nelson 'nor any other person in the UDA' was involved in the arms shipment because it was the work of Ulster Resistance.[20] This was patently wrong. Ulster Resistance was, though, deeply involved, its members playing 'the most critical part in the operation'. Founded in 1986, by the leadership of the Democratic Unionist Party (DUP), Ulster Resistance was conceived as a mass-based 'sort of clean-living paramilitary group', through which 'loyalist politicians and business elements sought to harness the political potential of paramilitary muscle' in opposition to the Anglo-Irish Agreement.[21] It was 'in effect the fusion of Paisley's Third Force and [the] Ulster Clubs'; two earlier attempts to create a mass loyalist militia. Presented as a 'citizen's army', complete with warlike rhetoric and military paraphernalia, it appeared to be 'Paisley's attempt to prepare for armed conflict with the state'.[22]

Ulster Resistance also illustrates well the (often politically contingent) fluidity and permeability of boundaries between unionist parties, loyalist paramilitaries and locally recruited police and military. Senior DUP figures occupied leadership positions. This provided 'a degree of legitimacy and respectability essential for the support of God-fearing residents of rural Ulster' from which most of its members came.[23] Former and serving security force members were included in its ranks.[24] So too were leading loyalists, including UDA men in key roles. They included

John McMichael, head of the UDA and close associate of Nelson, whose rise as UDA intelligence coordinator McMichael fostered. Along with a Mid-Ulster UVF commander, McMichael was also a leading figure in the Ulster Clubs, a network of loyalist gun clubs with some 20,000 members, originally founded in Mid-Ulster. In 1985 Nelson's contact in South Africa was the uncle of the Ulster Club's chairman, who worked for Armscor.[25] McMichael had been central in developing arms links in South Africa. It has also been suggested that 'for many years' he had been a 'useful conduit for acting on British intelligence targeting information and may have been one among many informers and agents operating at senior levels in the UDA/UFF'.[26]

After the 1987 arms shipment Ulster Resistance was involved in another attempt to obtain weapons from South Africa, using the same links.[27] In 1989 three of its members were arrested in Paris, along with arms dealer Douglas Bernhardt and a South African diplomat. They were looking to exchange weapons for sensitive military technology information, stolen from an army base in Newtownards and much sought by Armscor and the embargoed South African Defence Force. One of the 'Paris Three' was a serving UDR sergeant.[28] Another was Noel Little. From Markethill, Armagh, Little was a former UDR soldier, chair of the Armagh Ulster Clubs and head of Ulster Resistance, long close to Ian Paisley. Little's daughter is now a DUP MP. The DUP and Paisley would, however, begin to publicly distance themselves from Ulster Resistance as its links to arms shipments emerged. In fact, Little had also been briefly held soon after part of the 1987 arms shipment had been seized, and his telephone number was found on the wrist of an arrested UDA commander – given to the latter by John McMichael 'in case he got into any trouble in Armagh'. Little later said he always suspected that British intelligence 'turned a blind eye' to the 1987 shipment because Nelson could not have known about it and 'not told his handler'. His own eventual arrest, and (albeit brief) imprisonment, he attributed to straying into 'secrets and commerce, a step too far for the British authorities'. Little had been Ulster Resistance's contact with Armscor. However, a 'former senior' Armscor employee said arrangements always 'needed to be agreed by McMichael and by his intelligence officer – Brian Nelson'.[29] 'Everything', he said, 'had to be run by the head of intelligence'.

The 1987 arms shipment was jointly undertaken by Ulster Resistance, the UDA and the UVF in Mid-Ulster. The Mid-Ulster UVF, based in Portadown and led by Robin Jackson and Billy Wright, would be to the fore in the subsequent devastating rise of loyalist attacks.[30] The media focus on the 'bogeyman' Wright may have exaggerated his role. Likewise the make-up of the UVF in rural areas often relied less on recruiting from working-class estates than among 'farmers and businessmen, many of whom would be seen as "pillars of the community"' – the self-same social milieu from which came many RUC and UDR members.[31] Yet, both Jackson and Wright were central figures in the new loyalist offensive. Between 1988 and August 1994 86 people were killed in East Tyrone, and the UVF was responsible for half that number – many with guns imported as part of the 1987 arms shipment.[32]

As mentioned, some have argued that this upsurge in loyalist violence in the late 1980s and early 1990s was due to the rise of a younger, more militant leadership replacing an older, corrupt and heavily infiltrated old guard.[33] In this view, losing control of agents and informers, following the Stevens investigations, is seen as part of the cause. Security force 'high-level penetration' of the UDA, it is suggested, was lost, and resulted in the resurgence of loyalist violence.[34] So, paradoxically, attempts to re-enforce the rule of law, exemplified in Nelson's arrest and removal, are taken as a 'watershed' that 'tipped the balance in favour of a violent regeneration of the UDA'.[35] Security force 'double agents' within loyalism, from this perspective, 'worked primarily to the detriment of loyalist paramilitaries', while only a 'very, very small number of junior and marginal members of the security forces' helped loyalists.[36] Indeed, a supposed inability of the police and military to penetrate 'parts of the UVF in Mid-Ulster' is what is said led to 'high levels of violence' in the area.[37] There is an echo here of the tortured logic evidenced in Gordon Kerr's defence of Nelson at his trial. It is an argument that also rests on a timeline of the escalation of loyalist violence which diminishes, ignores or denies this earlier arming of loyalism, when FRU agent Nelson was very much still in play. Similarly, it requires a belief (with little evidence) that state infiltration of loyalist groups largely ended, or was absent in places like Mid-Ulster. Much suggests otherwise, though whether agents were in place in the Mid-Ulster UVF has been 'among the great unknowns from the Troubles'.[38]

Seizures, Police 'Failures' and Loyalism Rearmed

Within weeks of the 1987 arms shipment around a third had been captured by the RUC. However, 'most of Ulster Resistance's share' of the weapons (and a 'good part' of the UVF's) remained intact'.[39] Ulster Resistance also soon 'reached an agreement' with the UDA and UVF to share 'a portion of its haul with them'.[40] As noted, for de Silva, RUC weapons seizures were taken as proof positive that loyalists were not simply acting as 'state-sponsored forces'. Again, the picture that emerges from the later Loughinisland report reveals a darker story. Certainly, on 8 January 1988, a specialist unit of the RUC stopped three cars at a road checkpoint near the large RUC/army base just outside Portadown, Co. Armagh. Two were found to be heavily laden with weapons and all three drivers, led by the UDA commander in North Belfast, were arrested and subsequently jailed.[41] This was an intelligence-led operation run by the TCG for the area. As elsewhere, the TCG (South) brought together senior members of RUC Special Branch and British intelligence and specialist units (including the SAS) to conduct covert operations. At that time it was led by Ian Phoenix, a senior figure in RUC Special Branch, long experienced in organising and running its counterinsurgency efforts.[42] A former member of the British Parachute Regiment, his military background made Phoenix peculiarly well placed to coordinate police and military counterinsurgency operations.[43] He also became a keen advocate of a 'more aggressive' counterinsurgency campaign and the deployment of the SAS in actions against the IRA.[44] When the SAS killed eight IRA Volunteers in the Loughgall ambush in 1987, Phoenix led the RUC support operations. Shortly after, in late 1987, he took up his TCG role coordinating covert operations throughout Armagh and Tyrone.[45] For Phoenix this was also home ground, as he had been born and raised in a small village in East Tyrone, a few miles away from both Loughgall and where the weapons haul was captured.[46] The precise actions of the TCG in the search for weapons are shrouded in some mystery, as the relevant records are lost, likely destroyed.[47]

What we do know is that a substantial surveillance operation had been in place for some time. Both the RUC counterinsurgency unit E4A and the British Army were involved in tracking leading loyalists as they met to organise the distribution of the arms shipment. The RUC had those involved in moving the weapons under close surveillance and seem to have had a good idea that the cache of imported weapons were being stored in and around the small Co. Armagh village of Tandragee.[48] Indeed, on the morning of their arrest, the three drivers were followed to Tandragee, where they were met and escorted to the weapons hide. At that point, however, the RUC surveillance appears to have been 'temporarily unsighted'. Only afterwards did the E4A unit pick up again the (now weapons-laden) cars. The exact location of the weapons dump apparently therefore remained unknown. However, it was in any case clear the weapons had been stored close by. Special Branch intelligence also indicated the arms seized were only a portion of the total. Despite this, not until four days later did the CID detectives investigating find out the weapons had been kept at a farm between Tandragee and the nearby village of Markethill – home to another of the loyalists under surveillance. Even then, although CID carried out searches in the area one notable location was left untouched. It was a farm with a particularly dark and violent place in the story of collusion, home in the 1970s to the 'Glennane Gang'. It was here the Dublin and Monaghan bombings had been planned and the bomb used stored, and from which several of the bombers left to carry out the atrocity.[49] Here, too, 'this group of loyalists, UDR men and RUC officers met, drilled and conspired in the 1970s on a regular basis'.[50]

The Glennane farm belonged to local man James Mitchell. CID detectives said they would have 'torn apart' Mitchell's farm after the 1987 arms shipment had they been aware of its past. Yet that history could not have been entirely unknown to those involved in the world of intelligence and counterinsurgency.[51] Indeed, Mitchell had been convicted for 'keeping a major UVF arms dump' on his farm before, one of those charged after John Weir's confession.[52] Mitchell was also a former RUC Reserve Officer. Even after his arrest on arms charges in 1978, he continued to serve in that role for almost a year, before being allowed to resign. Strikingly, he then only received a one-year suspended sentence, a derisory decision mirrored by those for others in the gang who were also members of the security forces.[53]

Despite this violent history, when the RUC knew a large cache of weapons had been hidden in the Tandragee-Markethill area in 1988, it seems no one thought to search James Mitchell's farm. This, despite the fact that one of the senior RUC officers 'on the ground' during the 'loss of surveillance at a crucial time' and the search for the weapons had been involved in questioning Mitchell in the 1970s. Yet, at no point did he propose searching Mitchell's farm – something for which, says the Police Ombudsman for Northern Ireland, Michael Maguire, there is 'no logical explanation'.[54] Indeed, despite Mitchell's record of involvement with the Glennane Gang, earlier conviction and alleged involvement in storing UVF weapons in the early 1980s, and that 'within a week' of the

Mahon Road arrests the RUC knew he attended a meeting with several other leading loyalists 'to discuss the arms seizure', the police never even questioned Mitchell about the 1987 imported arms.[55] Everything suggests that Mitchell's farm was where the arms were kept.[56] Later intelligence indicated as much. It also suggested that, within hours of the 8 January arrests, Mitchell had been tipped off by a member of the RUC that his farm might be searched. The remaining stock of weapons was moved soon after.[57] Contrary to other accounts, a further police seizure of some imported weapons in Belfast a month later was not the result of ongoing searches or intelligence passed on by Special Branch.[58] In sum, Special Branch's withholding of intelligence, and the failure to consider searching Mitchell's farm, 'permitted the prompt undetected removal of the remaining weapons', and so allowed their later use in dozens of killings, including those at Loughinisland.[59] Given the 'gravity of the conspiracy', concludes Michael Maguire, the decision not to investigate leading loyalists implicated in the importation of the weapons, several of them informants, was 'indefensible'.

Throughout, Mid-Ulster loyalism was at the centre of this massive rearming effort. A cache of weapons was found around Tandragee and Markethill in February 1987.[60] In November 1988 more South African weapons were found in the same area, some alongside Ulster Resistance red berets and parts of a surface-to-air missile stolen from an arms factory in Castlereagh, presumably bound for Armscor.[61] A few months later an Ulster Resistance member and former UDR man from Richhill, Co. Armagh was convicted for possessing explosives.[62] Intelligence sources also indicated that a significant portion of the weapons from Mitchell's farm, including the type of automatic weapon used in the Loughinisland massacre, found its way into the hands of Robin Jackson. Among those named by Weir in the late 1970s, Robin Jackson was said to have had a leading role in the Miami Showband massacre and been one of the bombers believed to have set off from Mitchell's farm to carry out the attacks in Dublin and Monaghan.[63] A former member of the UDR, Jackson is believed to have been responsible for many other loyalist killings and atrocities committed in the Mid-Ulster area over decades. Indeed, he is alleged to be responsible for more deaths than virtually anyone else involved in the conflict. Former senior British Army intelligence officer and 'dirty tricks' whistle-blower Colin Wallace described Jackson as 'a professional assassin'.[64] Despite this, Jackson spent remarkably little time in jail. 'The state', said Wallace, 'not only knew

[Jackson] was doing it, its servants encouraged him to kill their political opponents and protected him'. Justice Barron concluded that Jackson was 'reliably said to have relationships with British intelligence and/or RUC Special Branch'.[65] In other words, Jackson was either a police informer or British Army agent, perhaps both. It has been claimed he had very close links to British military intelligence, as allegedly did several other members of the Glennane Gang.[66] In 1988, at the time the UVF collaborated with Ulster Resistance and the UDA to import weapons into the North and store them in the Armagh countryside, Robin Jackson was the UVF's Mid-Ulster commander.

5
Shooting to Kill: Targeting Republican Combatants

The British Government's main military objective in the 1980s was the destruction of PIRA, rather than resolving the conflict.[1]

I never did find evidence of a shoot-to-kill policy as such. There was no written instruction, nothing pinned up on a noticeboard. But there was a clear understanding on the part of the men whose job it was to pull the trigger that that was what was expected of them.[2]

The way that the standard units and the specialist units should work together to get success can be compared with an old-fashioned tiger hunt.[3]

War and Mid-Ulster

On the evening of 8 May 1987, the SAS shot dead eight members of the IRA as they attacked a part-time police station in the small village of Loughgall, Co. Armagh. A Catholic civilian was also killed and his brother badly wounded.[4] As well as being the greatest single loss of life the IRA suffered throughout the conflict, the Loughgall ambush virtually wiped out the leadership of what was, until then, the militarily potent, and strategically important, East Tyrone Brigade. Considerable controversy continues to surround the Loughgall ambush. Not least, whether several of those killed might rather have been arrested, or were shot dead after being captured or having surrendered. If exceptional in scale, Loughgall is also emblematic of how Mid-Ulster had become a critical site of the battle between insurgency and counterinsurgency during the 1980s, the pattern of 'set-piece killings' that formed a key element of that struggle, and of the violent contours shaping the context within which collusion took place.

By the mid-1980s, Tyrone and nearby border areas had become a key focus of a newly invigorated republican military strategy. A post-hunger strike rise in Sinn Fein support paralleled an upsurge in IRA recruitment and a vastly expanded arsenal of sophisticated weapons from Libya.[5] In part inspired by classic guerrilla theories, the East Tyrone IRA undertook an 'intensification campaign', aimed at creating a 'liberated zone' ungoverned by the state. This became a crucial front in the IRA's overall strategy and took the form of a series of coordinated attacks on isolated, rural military and police installations.[6] So, for example, Ballygawley RUC station was attacked in December 1985, leaving two police officers dead.[7] Mortar attacks on UDR bases in Castlederg and Carrickmore followed, as did one on Birches RUC station near Portadown, on 11 August 1986, when – in a tactic later employed at Loughgall – a mechanical digger containing a bomb was driven into (and demolished) the building.[8] In total the IRA attacked over 100 bases, demolishing 33 military installations, in the five years after 1985.[9]

Crucially, too, this campaign involved targeting contractors involved in building and maintaining military installations, as well as members of the British Army, UDR and RUC.[10] This was part of a deadly 'ratcheting up' of attacks launched by various sides in the conflict. For example, the IRA first employed a 'human' or 'proxy bomb' in an attack on a border checkpoint, near Derry, in October 1990, which left dead five British soldiers and local man Patsy Gillespie (who worked at an army base in the city).[11] While unconnected, this came just two days after the loyalist killing of Frank Hughes in Dungannon, and two days before that of East Tyrone Sinn Fein worker Tommy Casey. IRA attacks on builders involved in work on military installations culminated in the January 1992 killing of eight civilian workers, all of whom were Protestants. A roadside bomb was exploded under the workers' van at Teebane crossroads as they returned from doing repairs on a British Army base, near Omagh.[12] This occurred just three weeks before an RUC officer killed three people (including two party workers) in the main Sinn Fein offices in West Belfast.[13] The day after the Teebane massacre, five Catholics were shot dead in a betting shop on the Ormeau Road by the UFF, who claimed this was carried out in retaliation for what happened at Teebane. The Ormeau Road massacre, in turn, has itself been the subject of long-term allegations of state collusion with loyalist paramilitaries.[14]

'Set-Piece' Operations and Shooting to Kill

The state was no passive or neutral observer in this period of heightened conflict, not least (as in East Tyrone) where its own strategic concerns were to the fore. In this sense collusion should not be seen in isolation, but rather viewed in relation to broader state counterinsurgency – particularly evidence of a shoot-to-kill policy, conducted primarily by specialist units of the RUC and British Army, directed against republicans. Allegations of a state shoot-to-kill policy remain highly controversial. Many continue to flatly deny such an approach existed, that incidents such as Loughgall were 'very rare' and that arrests were 'always the explicit aim' in covert operations.[15] However, much suggests that shoot-to-kill formed part of a counterinsurgency strategy, particularly in the form of 'set-piece' killings, as at Loughgall.

Such killings were marked by 'the deployment of specialist police or military units, evidence of foreplanning in the confrontation (usually informer information), little apparent attempt to arrest rather than kill, and massive use of firepower against the deceased'.[16] Thus, at Loughgall, the carefully planned, intelligence-led deployment of several dozen SAS and specialist RUC personnel lying in wait resulted in the SAS firing over 1,000 times.[17] As a vital site of confrontation between insurgents and counterinsurgents, from the state's perspective, there was a clear military and political logic to employing the set-piece tactic in East Tyrone, and on a scale unmatched elsewhere. Stated coldly, in East Tyrone it became increasingly 'convenient' for the state to pursue the permanent removal of key IRA combatants, via 'set-piece' killings, 'in contrived circumstances where the use of lethal force was legally permissible (or at least would be accepted as such in a domestic court)'.[18]

In the British Army's own assessment, its strategy during the 1980s was directed, not towards 'resolving the conflict', but to advancing a campaign of 'attrition' aimed at the 'destruction' of the IRA.[19] Alongside arrests this included covert operations, such as Loughgall, in which 'several of their [IRA] most experienced operators' were killed.[20] This was regarded as a tactic for which the IRA 'never found a solution' and so were 'brought to believe that there was no answer to Army covert operations … probably a key factor' in convincing republicans 'they would not win through violence'.[21] Others have identified set-piece killings as emblematic of a distinct phase of intelligence-led counterinsurgency, characterised by state use of lethal force that went to the bounds of the rule of law and beyond. This included RUC use of 'maximum force – a synonym for shooting dead – against suspects in situations where a lesser degree of force is an option'.[22] Such a 'discernible shift', in the pattern of 'state confrontation' with 'paramilitary actors', marked the new phase of the 'alliance of counter-insurgency and extraordinary law'.[23] Overwhelmingly that involved attacks on republicans. Throughout the conflict loyalists accounted for only 5 per cent of state victims.[24] When it came to killing members of armed non-state organisations, there is little doubt at whom the state's guns were pointed.

A rise in republican fatalities echoes this 'discernible shift'. As with the general pattern of conflict deaths, the tumultuous years of the early 1970s witnessed the largest number of republicans killed (77 in 1972 alone and some 213 from 1971 to 1976).[25] However, there is a notable rise in the killing of active republicans in the late 1980s when compared with the previous decade.[26] Much also suggests that this involved a state strategy of 'selective assassination'.[27] While some republican deaths were the result of other factors (such as the 1987 feud between the INLA and Irish People's Liberation Organisation, and premature explosions) most republican combatants killed in this period were victims of the British Army or the RUC. Almost all were in the IRA. This is not as obvious as it might seem, but rather suggests a strategic shift in the use of lethal force by state forces in the late 1980s and early 1990s. For the British Army the intent was to 'wear down' the IRA and deliver a crucial counterinsurgency blow, by undermining their will, and capacity, to continue.[28]

'Set-piece' killings of IRA members were central to this marked rise of fatalities. From 1981 to 1994, 40 per cent of all direct state killings occurred in set-piece settings. These involved ambushes and instigated confrontations directed against targets (whose identities were known) often in the process of launching or preparing attacks of their own, usually on military targets or installations.[29] Again, the overwhelming majority of set-piece killings were of IRA combatants; virtually none targeted loyalists.[30] This reflects the British Army's strategic (and British government's political) focus. Despite the upsurge of loyalist killings in the late 1980s and early 1990s, the British Army's own analysis of Operation Banner tellingly limits discussion of loyalist activity at this time to the single observation that they 'continued to operate against the Catholic community but on a fairly limited scale'.[31] Between the official deployment of the SAS in 1976 and 1987, no loyalists were killed by British Army undercover units. Indeed, of the 58 shoot-to-kill victims shot by the British Army from 1982 to 1992 only one was a loyalist.[32] Likewise, the RUC killed 26 people in the same period. Of these only one was a loyalist paramilitary. Aside from one other, all their remaining victims were either members of the IRA or Sinn Fein, or simply

Catholics.[33] As Mark Urban noted, the absence of loyalist victims of state covert set-piece killings discredited 'the idea, so frequently voiced in the authorities' dealings with the court and the media – of chance meetings between undercover forces and armed republican terrorists, since the odds of stumbling on and shooting a loyalist would appear to be almost as high'.[34]

At the time, that was the routine argument offered to deny that set-piece killings were the result of careful state planning. This has, of course, since been revised and replaced by an insistence on the operational primacy of arrest as a defence for the unavoidable and 'necessary' use of lethal force.[35] It is a perspective long advanced by former members of the SAS. Any increase in the number of operations ending in the deaths of IRA combatants from the mid-1980s onward, this argument continues, was 'less a function of a determination by the Government to take the gloves off after the Brighton bombing ... than of the increased scope and scale of IRA operations'.[36] In this view, the 'rising kill rate' from SAS planned operations after December 1983 was due to an increase in the volume and visibility of IRA activity. Again, that remains to be seen, but what is beyond dispute is that the SAS were very much to the fore in this new phase of violence. An earlier campaign, primarily targeting republicans in Armagh in late 1977–8, was eclipsed by the greater use of specialist units in covert operations in the 1980s.[37] Of the 58 shoot-to-kill victims of the British Army from 1982 to 1992, 45 were shot by undercover British soldiers, including 37 by the SAS. Seven others were killed by the (closely linked) 14th Intelligence Company.

While supposedly falling 'a long way short of orders to kill', this dramatic increase in lethality 'coincided with a change in [the] terminology' governing SAS operations.[38] The SAS were no longer on 'hard arrests or surveillance' operations but now manned 'Aggressive Observation posts' or were involved in 'Observation Post/Reactives'.[39] This apparently innocuous, euphemistic and sterilising language paralleled an authorised escalation of set-piece killings. Senior approval by way of 'commendations and decorations that followed clean kills of IRA players showed that arrests were only one of the acceptable results of such operations'.[40] One general reportedly told officers there was 'a crate of champagne to the first man who puts a body in my in-tray'.[41]

In June 1989 the most senior British Army officer in the North, Lieutenant General Sir John Waters, issued instructions outlining how 'standard' and 'specialist' units should work together, and likened 'set-piece' operations to an 'old-fashioned tiger hunt'.[42] 'The most experienced hunters', insisted Waters, 'are placed in what is judged to be the very best position from which to get a shot. The beaters surround the area of the jungle where the tigers are expected to be and drive them on to the guns. Beating requires great skill and coordination to prevent the tigers breaking out of the cordon, or killing some of the beaters. Frequently the tigers break back, make a mistake, and expose themselves to the beaters. This is the opportunity for the beaters, who also carry guns, to get a tiger.' Waters (who went on to become Commander-in-Chief of UK Land Forces) was also instrumental in denying the first Stevens Inquiry access to army files and intelligence casting considerable light on the nature of collusion.[43] Criticism of Waters' 'tiger hunt' comments made by a senior military colleague at the time was not concerned with his substantive view. Rather, the 'main worry' was that such 'quotable phrases [were] almost bound to reach unauthorised ears', and 'bitter experience' suggested this would cause 'embarrassment to the Army department and Ministers'.[44]

Here was, what we might call, a 'code red' impunity culture. A formal, seemingly minor, change in operational language suggested an ongoing public commitment and continuity in policy, practice and adherence to legal norms. But this language embodied significant operational changes. They then combined with the more informal, yet powerful, norms and relations within the institutional setting of the military to auger the onset of a more forceful and lethally focused shoot-to-kill strategy. This echoes the culture that John Stalker (then deputy chief constable of Manchester) found within counterinsurgency units of the RUC, before he was removed from investigating allegations of a police shoot-to-kill policy in the mid-1980s.[45] There was at least, Stalker argued, a 'police inclination … to shoot suspects dead without warning', such that the 'suspicion of deliberate assassination was not unreasonable'. If not a 'policy' or 'written instruction', with 'nothing pinned up on a noticeboard … *there was a clear understanding on the part of the men whose job it was to pull the trigger that that was what was expected of them* [my italics]'.[46] Such permissive institutional cultures are particularly significant when taking shape within hierarchical social orders, such as those to be found within the police and army. Simultaneously, the absence of a written policy helps generate a fiction necessary for the continued denial of wrongful acts. As the SAS was provided with the 'best possible intelligence of forthcoming attacks', so that a 'clean kill of IRA' members could be achieved, it was equally important for the state to ensure 'their actions would be deemed reasonable by the legal system'.[47]

These set-piece, shoot-to-kill operations were also specifically designed in such a way as to provide a 'cloak of domestic legality [to make] "legal" killings that were effectively extra-judicial'.[48] The test of 'reasonable force' was central here, and illustrative of Kitson's maxim of adapting the law to provide legal justification for counterinsurgency violence. In theory, British soldiers and the RUC were just as subject to the domestic law governing the use of lethal force as anyone else. This formed part of the wider, politically and ideologically potent, insistence that the conflict was not a 'war' and that 'constitutional normalcy' was being maintained.[49] The reality was considerably different, due largely to the combination of 'emergency' powers and the systematic bending of due process. Instead, from the earliest years of the conflict onwards authorised impunity for state forces was the order of the day.[50] In addition, by the early 1980s the 'supergrass strategy' (using uncorroborated informer evidence to obtain mass convictions), itself a subversion of the legal system, had largely failed.[51] This forced alternatives to an arrest-based strategy further up the state's coercive agenda. Likewise, an increase in available intelligence combined to place a greater focus on specialist counterinsurgency units that operated in a '"grey", legal, moral and political environment'.[52] In turn, the ever greater reliance on 'special operations' created an ever more regular recourse to – and potential legal conundrum with – the defence of 'reasonable force'.

Again, an extremely expansive interpretation by non-jury Diplock courts of 'reasonable force' for state killings was evident from the early years of the conflict – notably, for example, in the case of Patrick McElhone, a farmer shot dead by the British Army on his East Tyrone farm in 1974.[53] Unarmed, entirely innocent and posing no threat, the court found that Patrick McElhone's shooting was 'reasonable' because of the 'wartime situation' and the nature of (what was an entirely typical) local nationalist area.[54] One (minority) appeal judge declared that this gave 'an unlimited licence to the security forces'.[55] Lord Diplock would himself expand 'reasonable force' even further, to include a British soldier's 'belief' (whether true or not) that his victim 'was a member of the Provisional IRA who, if he got away, was likely sooner or later to participate in acts of violence'.[56] A deliberately vague, muddied and highly permissive understanding of 'reasonable force' therefore emerged, particularly in shoot-to-kill cases. Lord Chief Justice Gibson (later killed by the IRA) likened British soldiers involved in the killing of an unarmed man to a Wild West posse who, 'if they don't bring them back peaceably they shoot them', and broadened 'reasonable force' still further by arguing that 'shooting may be justified as a method of arrest'.[57] Acquitting the RUC men responsible for the shoot-to-kill deaths of Gervais McKerr, Eugene Toman and Sean Burns in Lurgan in November 1982, Gibson declared they were 'absolutely blameless in the matter' and commended them for 'their courage and determination in bringing the three deceased men to justice, in this case the final court of justice'.[58]

Broad interpretations of 'reasonable force' were also the ground on which British Army specialist units based the legal defence of their actions. A phalanx of army lawyers, expert in the law of minimum force, also 'acquired an understanding of the kind of statements that would make the soldiers' actions appear reasonable in the eyes of the court'.[59] So, for example the language used by the SAS men who killed three members of the IRA in Gibraltar in 1988, 'owed as much to the well-proven approach of their Army Legal Service lawyers as it did to being a genuine account of the events'.[60] With military lawyers readily available to help soldiers prepare their accounts, the result was a stream of state killing cases where victims seemed to have developed a habit of making sudden, suspicious movements, even when unarmed; apparently demonstrating a somewhat strange 'urge to reach for weapons which they were not carrying'.[61]

The court system itself was also substantially remoulded and subverted, not least the inquest system.[62] Major changes introduced in 1981 curbed the powers of inquests in several key ways, preventing meaningful investigations in state killing cases.[63] RUC and British Army witnesses had never been compelled to attend inquests, but were now able to provide unsworn 'witness statements', which became the vehicle for 'imminent threat' narratives that were uncontestable by cross-examination. Inquests could now also be adjourned for many years, and, when held, saw evidence withheld by Public Interest Immunity Certificates, issued on the grounds of 'national security'. Finally, inquests could no longer issue verdicts but were, instead, restricted to issuing 'findings' confined to the basic facts of the death. On the eve of the counterinsurgency phase of the conflict, inquests were, in essence, rendered ineffectual as accountability mechanisms in state killing cases. No British solider or member of the RUC would be found guilty for a set-piece killing.

Set-Piece Shoot-to-Kill and Mid-Ulster

Certainly East Tyrone was a major focus of set-piece ambushes and the evidence suggests a deliberate, theatre-based, sustained British military covert campaign. Of the 58 shoot-to-kill victims of undercover British soldiers between 1982 and 1992, 40 per cent were killed in and around East Tyrone, with the vast majority (20) killed between 1987 and 1992.[64] There were more set-piece killings here than anywhere else. All were victims of the SAS and most were killed in large-scale set-piece ambushes. In total, 26 IRA combatants were assassinated in East Tyrone in the nine years between 1983 and 1992. Loughgall was therefore by no means the end of the story. Other killings included those of Gerard and Martin Harte and Brian Mullin in an ambush in Drumnakilly in August 1990, and of Martin McGaughey and Dessie Grew, again near Loughgall, the following October. Three IRA men were shot dead by a waiting SAS unit in the village of Coagh in June 1991, and four more in an SAS ambush in Clonoe, near Dungannon, in February 1992.[65] Many of these killings are the subject of continuing court cases. In at least one, at Clonoe, the SAS actions were belatedly adjudged to be 'unjustified'.[66]

A distinct, attritional pattern of deaths therefore emerges, and not only in terms of East Tyrone's proportion of set-piece casualties. Of the 53 Tyrone IRA victims listed from 1972 to 1992, 19 died during the first decade. But only six of these were killed by the security forces and only two (a mere 4 per cent of the overall total) by undercover British units. They included the death of Paul Duffy, the first Tyrone IRA victim of the SAS, killed in 1978.[67] On the other hand, from 1983 to 1992, 34 members of the IRA were killed (65 per cent of the total) and, of these, 75 per cent were shot dead by the SAS. Something similar (though notably far less intense) emerges in the pattern of IRA fatalities evident in other parts of Mid-Ulster. In North Antrim, for example, the IRA lost six members. The first killed here by the British Army (Henry Hogan and Declan Martin) were shot dead by undercover British soldiers in Dunloy as late as 1984.[68] Likewise in South Derry, the same year witnessed the first IRA Volunteer killed by the British Army – again by the SAS, and in highly disputed circumstances.[69] Another, Francis Bradley, was killed by the SAS in South Derry just over a year later.

If 'used sparingly' in other areas in the 1980s and early 1990s, the set-piece tactic was 'rampant in East Tyrone', making the eight set-piece ambushes in the area appear to have been the result of a 'deliberate policy choice', and part of a larger 'East Tyrone-specific campaign'.[70] Many targeted highly experienced IRA activists, and while Loughgall was met with retaliation (13 security force members were killed in the area in 1988) there was then an overall decline in local IRA activity.[71] Equally striking are parallels with IRA deaths in Mid-Ulster at the hands of loyalists. After two decades of conflict, Liam Ryan was the first East Tyrone IRA Volunteer killed by loyalists. A year later three more were shot dead, at Cappagh. Similarly, in North Antrim and South Derry respectively, Gerard Casey and Jimmy Kelly (one of the four men killed at Castlerock) were, at one and the same time, the last IRA victims of the conflict in these areas, and the first to have been shot dead by loyalists.[72] Here again, in time and space, an overlap between the pattern of set-piece killings and those of IRA activists shot dead by loyalists in Mid-Ulster seems to emerge. While far more difficult to substantiate, the prevalence of shoot-to-kill operations in Mid-Ulster may also provide an insight into the prevailing ethos, culture and habitus holding sway over the attitudes and actions of security forces in the area at this time, and the generation of a permissive context within which collusion, directed against republicans, becomes all the more thinkable and doable.

'Sudden movement', reasonable force arguments to defend set-piece killings were similarly to the fore in Mid-Ulster cases. When Colm McGirr and Brian Campbell were shot dead when returning to an arms dump in Clonoe, in December 1983, the SAS men who killed them claimed they had already retrieved the weapons when called upon to halt.[73] Both, it was claimed, then 'spun round very fast', with Brian Campbell supposedly pointing at the British soldiers.[74] As Raymond Murray noted, the SAS testimonies were not only remarkably similar to each other but repeated 'the same pattern of sentences' emphasising imminent threat to life used in Army statements in other cases.[75] Shot while wounded on the ground, Brian Campbell (one soldier said) moved his leg so he 'thought he was about to fire on us'. A third man, who was wounded but escaped in a car, claimed both of those killed were unarmed and that no arrest was attempted.[76] When the unarmed William Price was shot by the SAS in July 1984, first in the legs then (injured and sitting) in the head, the British soldier who killed him acknowledged he 'did not see a gun', but that Price had 'moved his hands into a position that suggested to me he was holding a gun'.[77] The SAS soldiers were said to have 'whooped hysterically like Indians in an American wild west film' after the shooting.[78] Likewise, in South Derry, Francis Bradley was shot dead while retrieving weapons near an isolated farmhouse in February 1986. After shouting halt, the SAS statements read, Francis had a 'rifle in both hands, traversing in an aggressive manner in our direction'.[79] SAS testimonies read into the inquest record bore the now 'familiar phraseology of threats to their lives and movements'.[80]

Then there was Loughgall itself.[81] As well as the SAS, this involved 'scores of officers' from the 'RUC's elite paramilitary wing', the Headquarters Mobile Support Unit, in support.[82] Anything up to 14 IRA members planned to destroy the barracks in Loughgall, by planting a huge bomb in the bucket of a digger to be driven through the perimeter gates.[83] All eight of the IRA combatants killed had multiple gunshots, including wounds to the head. They included Patrick Kelly, officer commanding (OC) of the IRA in East Tyrone, and Jim Lynagh, one of the IRA's 'most wanted activists in Northern Ireland' and widely credited as the architect of the 'intensification' strategy.[84] Here in microcosm was counterinsurgency practice in East Tyrone. The briefing beforehand made it clear this was to be an 'OP/React … a coded term for an ambush'. The operation itself had 'more in common with what the [SAS] practises in the jungles of Brunei' than was 'considered normal' in Northern Ireland.[85] If sowing the seeds of doubt about informers was part of the strategy, those repercussions still resonate within the broad ranks of republicanism in the area to the present day.[86] Some reports suggest the SAS unit 'celebrated with champagne' on their return to Mahon Road Barracks.[87] None were to appear at the subsequent inquest.

Legal battles surrounding many Mid-Ulster set-piece killings continue decades later. Inquests into the killings at Loughgall were only reopened in 2016 and the cases remain ongoing. Likewise an inquest into the 1992 Clonoe ambush has yet to be heard. However, in 2011 the High Court examined some of the circumstances of the Clonoe attack in a civil case brought by Aidan McKeever; the unarmed, severely wounded driver of the getaway car and only republican survivor of the ambush.[88] This set-piece operation, carried out by both the SAS and 14th Intelligence Company, left four IRA combatants dead in a hail of gunfire. In court, the 'imminent threat to life' defence unravelled and fell apart under cross-examination of the only soldier to give evidence. His testimony was described as 'utterly implausible'.[89] In particular, 'the idea that, as he claimed, a man who was unarmed and whose car had just been shot at and who may well have been – and probably was, already shot – should have got on his knees at the bonnet of the car and presented his head and shoulders above the bonnet and adopted a firing stance is simply not credible'.[90] Such actions would have been contrary to 'reason and the instinct for self-preservation' and 'insane' if taken by someone who knew they were not armed.[91] Other soldier witnesses then declined to appear, and the judge 'inferred that their evidence is likely to be unhelpful' to the Ministry of Defence.[92]

One reason the set-piece strategy was confined to relatively narrow (and isolated) geographical areas may have been to offset the potential for substantial political fallout.[93] It may also have met other counterinsurgency ends. Local 'republican' communities were acutely aware of what was happening, while people more widely were far less so. The demonstration of state 'omnipotence' through localised displays of impunity, while rendering actions 'invisible' to the wider world, generated demoralisation within communities and simultaneously isolated them further.[94] Information about such killings circulated at the same time it was denied. Shoot-to-kill and collusion allegations were voiced and reported, but non-prosecutions helped preserve evidence and impunity. Fear, dependent on both 'knowledge and uncertainty', went hand in hand with 'state legitimacy dependent on permanent official denial'.[95] A campaign of attrition against republicans and republican communities was paralleled by the formal preservation of liberal democratic legal normalcy. Shoot-to-kill was designed to serve these twin needs in a continuum of state activity (alongside collusion and the use of informers) that sought to wear down resistance and fundamentally alter people's actions and outlook.

Likewise, the neutering of accountability mechanisms and the legal fictions of 'reasonable force' narratives helped bridge the gap between what were acts of war (though killing the wounded transgressed war's laws too) where, for political reasons, a war could not be said to exist. This has a corrosive, normative effect and raises deeper questions. Can the state's claim to a monopoly of legitimate force be upheld where it uses force 'in arbitrary and extra-legal ways, killing members of the population in dubious circumstances, and then refusing to adequately investigate those circumstances?'[96] Can it then maintain a 'crisp' distinction between 'legal force and illegal paramilitarism' where such attitudes predominate? If the law becomes 'just another tool to be used by those in power to achieve partisan security and political objectives', then nothing debases the rule of law so much as when state agents employ 'lethal force … to eliminate opponents of their political masters'.[97] Where a culture is generated in which the law becomes understood as part of the state's arsenal and legal norms are trumped by necessity, this, too, is a context in which collusion can flourish.

Collusion and the Case of Gerard Casey

It is difficult to view loyalist killings of republicans in Mid-Ulster in isolation from these allegations of a shoot-to-kill policy, in operation in the same place and at the same time. Or that, just as 'clean kills' of republicans in set-piece killings were being celebrated, loyalists proved able to successfully target republicans here as never before. Likewise, the forceful prosecution of a counterinsurgency war waged in Mid-Ulster, designed to destroy one of the IRA's key battlefronts, coincided with evidence that may point towards the more widespread use of loyalists in a proxy targeted assassination campaign. The case of Gerard Casey is illustrative of many of the issues at stake.

In the early hours of 4 April 1989, 30-year-old Gerard Casey was shot dead as he lay in bed with his wife Una at their home near Rasharkin, on the South Derry–North Antrim county border. The couple's youngest child, three-month-old Geraldine, was lying in a cot beside them.[98] Just after midnight a 'rattle at the front door' was followed by two gunmen bursting into the room, dressed in green army-type jackets and black balaclavas, and armed with a shotgun and handgun.[99] One fired the shotgun at Gerard Casey, half sitting up in the bed, while the other stood over Una. As Gerard, wounded, tumbled to the floor, he was shot with the shotgun again, followed by 'an aimed shot into his chest ... while the other man also fired a (pistol) shot' as he lay dead or dying on the ground. In a deep state of shock, Una Casey ran to a neighbour's house to get help. After the RUC arrived and questioned her, Una recalls, she could not stop being repeatedly sick from the shock, and thinking, 'am I dreaming? Is this really happening? How could anyone do that? You could not do that to an animal. The house, everything, just seemed like a really bad nightmare. Afterwards I don't remember very much; I was a bit "loopy" for a couple of days.'[100]

A joiner by trade and father of four (who 'loved and always provided for his kids'), Gerard Casey had been a long-time worker for Sinn Fein. Unknown to most, he had also been a member of the North Antrim IRA for four years at the time of his death. This, along with the 'efficient, professional manner' in which his killing was carried out, raised many questions.[101] 'One man stayed outside', Una Casey remembered, 'and the other two came right up the stairs and into our bedroom. The whole time they never spoke a word'.[102] Appearing to know 'exactly where to go' suggested they 'must have known the layout of the house'. For Fr Denis Faul, it was a killing with a 'degree of military precision and discipline … not normal in loyalist assassins', leading to the 'suspicion in the Catholic community [that] the shooting of Mr Casey may have been an SAS type military covert operation'.[103] It also fitted with a pattern, then just emerging, of similar attacks on republicans and their families 'on both sides of Lough Neagh'. The getaway car was later found burnt out four miles away.[104] It had been taken earlier that evening from a home in nearby Ballymoney. Anything up to eight armed men were involved, including 'five of six men in boiler suits', who forced their way into the house. Only one ever spoke, in a 'broken Belfast accent'.[105] No one was ever caught for the killing.

That Gerard Casey was not widely known as an active republican was reflected in initial reaction to the attack. DUP leader and local MP Ian Paisley at first denounced this 'diabolical crime', condemning the 'devilish viciousness of the killers'.[106] Whatever their religious or political convictions, he added, only 'lawful authorities' should take someone's life, and so urged the government to use the 'power of the sword to prevent such attacks in the future'.[107] When, hours later, the IRA revealed Gerard Casey as a member, a contrary statement swiftly followed. This was now a death demonstrating 'the law of God has once more been proved true. Those who take the sword unlawfully will perish by the sword'.[108] For Sir John Hermon, it was a killing explained as an 'irresponsible' and 'murderous' reaction by loyalists, but that no one should be in any doubt that 'PIRA is the main threat to the whole of the island of Ireland'.[109] Unusually, a question mark emerged over whether or not any loyalist group actually claimed the killing.[110] Initially no group came forward, and when the RUC received a call from someone purporting to be from the UFF, they were unable to provide a recognised code word.[111] Gerard Casey's funeral days later witnessed a massive security force presence. 'The police were everywhere', recalls Una Casey, 'spitting at us coming out of the chapel. They had killed Gerard, then disrespected a family with kids coming out and burying their father, their husband, their son. That made me so angry.'[112]

Although Gerard Casey had been taken into Castlereagh interrogation centre several times from 1985 onwards, for much of this time he 'wasn't a known Volunteer', says Una, 'our house was never wrecked in searches and in Castlereagh he was never asked to turn informer'.[113] However, much suggests that in the period up to his death the intelligence agencies or police knew, or strongly suspected, that Gerard Casey was in the IRA. In October 1988, a 'whole crowd of police and jeeps' of the specialist Divisional Mobile Support Unit (DMSU) raided the family home. 'They searched everywhere', Una recalls, 'the kids were in bed and the police came in and tossed the wains out. They were petrified and started being sick they were so scared.'[114] Gerard was taken and held in Castlereagh for six days. This time 'they gave him a beating and threatened him', says Una, 'they told him he would be shot and they would blame loyalists for it' and he would 'never have to be put in Castlereagh again'.[115] For the first time, too, after his release, Gerard Casey contacted a solicitor and made a formal complaint. Speaking at Gerard Casey's funeral, Sinn Fein's Alex Maskey argued that there was 'no doubt that his murder originated' in Castlereagh.[116]

It is worth remembering that Maskey (as well as several other leading Sinn Fein figures) had himself only recently survived two assassination attempts, in which FRU agent Brian Nelson was deeply involved.[117] Nelson provided an 'intelligence pack' and targeting information on Sinn Fein members, including Maskey, going to great lengths (says Desmond de Silva) 'in pursuit of a conspiracy to kill'.[118] Despite finding 20 Military Intelligence Source Reports indicating Maskey was being targeted, there were 'no entries in the threat book' and no evidence Maskey was officially warned, at any time, based on Nelson's intelligence.[119] The FRU knew the UFF was trying to kill Maskey, but took no steps to stop it. Indeed their own agent would plead guilty to conspiring to kill him, having shown not only a 'willingness' but a 'determination' to do so.[120] There are also claims that FRU involvement in attempts to kill Alex Maskey had been discussed by senior military, police and intelligence officers for some time, but 'FRU handlers were not even ... asked to explain what happened [receiving instead] the charade of a pep-talk ... with a wink and a nod and no questions asked'.[121] Speaking at Gerard Casey's funeral, Maskey described those who killed him as 'just another weapon in the armoury of the British state', and that 'dirty deeds by men in uniform had helped his killers'.[122]

The October house raid on the Casey home also resulted in a legally held shotgun being removed and the RUC drawing up a map of the layout of the house.[123] While the RUC claimed this was 'common practice' to offset complaints of theft, Una Casey did not recall this ever happening before.[124] When asked where the map would be taken, a police officer told her, 'it was a DMSU patrol, it could be anywhere'.[125] This has been linked to the ease with which the gunmen found their way to the right bedroom. When it was revealed at the inquest that the map had gone missing, a senior RUC witness was asked, 'did you not wonder where the map went?'[126] Certainly, it was later revealed, Gerard Casey's personal details had been in loyalist hands prior to his death, although 'the police never came to tell him that his photo and details had been "lost"'.[127] There are parallels here, too, with other contemporaneous loyalist killings. Two months later, Liam McKee was killed with a shotgun in the bedroom of his house in Lisburn. Unconnected to the republican movement, Brian Nelson's files, used to target McKee, named him as an 'IRA member'.[128] Afterward, it is claimed, Nelson was reprimanded by his handlers for trying to 'ethnically cleanse' a Protestant area and told to 'contain his ambitions', and obey instructions, by targeting more clearly 'republican targets'.[129]

A UDR soldier (formerly in the British Army) was among those initialling convicted for killing Liam McKee, and providing intelligence – along with another UDR member – used in 14 other attacks.[130] Among those other victims was Loughlin Maginn. Like Gerard Casey a young father of four, Maginn had been subject to long-term harassment by security forces, particularly the UDR. Regularly photographed by the RUC, a layout map of his house was also made during a police raid in October 1988, after which he was taken to Gough Barracks.[131] Four months after Gerard Casey was killed, UFF gunmen (including two members of the UDR) shot dead Loughlin Maginn in his Co. Down home. To support their claim Maginn was in the IRA, the UDA 'leaked' a mass of state intelligence files, setting in motion the events leading to the slow unravelling of the role of Nelson and the FRU.[132] Linked to this shooting, material later found to have been in Nelson's possession included video of a UDR briefing on 'IRA suspects'.[133] Both the FRU and RUC Special Branch were long aware that Maginn was being targeted and that state intelligence was in loyalist hands.[134] Yet none of this was revealed to the first Stevens Inquiry, part of the 'conscious obstruction' undertaken on the instruction of senior British Army officers.[135] Nor was evidence provided implicating an RUC officer in giving loyalists intelligence on Loughlin Maginn.[136] Instead, the FRU focused on preparing Nelson to resist any interrogation about all these matters.[137]

There were patterns here, already becoming evident to families. The killing (just months before) of local Sinn Fein councillor John Davey had ramped up a growing sense of threat and insecurity. 'You knew something was going on', says Una, 'but it was like a nightmare and you just sort of got on with your life'. Patterns of security force activity in the area also raised suspicion and concern. Two months before his death, one of Gerard's brothers claimed to have been forced to stop as he drove away from the Casey home, in the early hours of the morning, by 'four policemen … dressed in boiler suits, with balaclavas pulled up [who jumped out and] trained their guns' on the car.[138] One, it is said, then pulled the others back, saying 'no, that's not him', before driving away. There are also allegations that the period leading up to the attack itself first witnessed an intense security force presence in the area, followed by virtually none at the time of the killing. 'I think it is hard for people now to believe what things were like in wee rural places', says Una Casey. 'You would have had a Chinook helicopter landing in a field behind your house. You had them constantly on the road with checkpoints. They were always stopping people. The RUC and UDR would sail up and down the road by the house [and] sit outside pointing their guns up at the window terrifying our young boys. There was a group of UDR always about the place.'[139] Then, says Una, in the time prior to the killing, 'there was nothing; no Chinooks in the field, no cop cars, no jeeps, nothing. We noticed it at the time, not being stopped, and thinking, "God, this is weird, that they are not about"'.[140]

After the shooting, the RUC failed to establish vehicle checkpoints on the roads around the isolated row of houses where the Caseys lived.[141] Along the road up to eight men 'must have escaped', original orders to establish a checkpoint were reversed.[142] When pressed at the inquest to explain why, 'security reasons' were cited and accepted by the coroner, preventing further questions. There were other substantial police failures. No fingerprints or footprint casts were taken either at the Casey home or around the burnt-out getaway car. An RUC officer said he saw the car bursting into flames a full 45 minutes after the shooting. The examination of the car consisted of an RUC constable 'leaning in the window and poking around with a tyre iron', before deciding there was 'nothing of an evidential nature'.[143] Una Casey 'never heard anything more' from the RUC after she had provided a witness statement.[144] The RUC men accused of mistreatment at Castlereagh were not questioned as part of the RUC investigation, because it was not deemed relevant.[145]

The remit of the inquest was, as in other cases, severely restricted in what it could examine. Attempts to raise various issues (such as death threats and the missing map) were prevented.[146] Cross-examination of police witnesses was prohibited. The RUC chief constable was represented by a QC, who intervened to direct the coroner away from wider questions. A later attempt to overturn the coroner's open verdict was rejected, and despite an 'avalanche of photographs and information' in other cases, the judge decided there were no facts supporting suspicions of collusion.[147] A couple of years later, in large part to get them away from ongoing police and UDR harassment, Una Casey moved her young family across the border to Donegal.[148] She remains convinced that collusion was at the heart of her husband's death.[149]

Shootings at the Battery Bar

Liam Ryan was a senior republican who, some have claimed, was the IRA intelligence officer in East Tyrone at the time of the Loughgall massacre.[150] He had himself been present at Loughgall and escaped the ambush. Ryan had earlier spent ten years living in New York, deeply involved in US-based republican fundraising and support organisations, and may have been head of the IRA in America. He returned to Ireland in 1985 and bought the Battery Bar, in Ardboe, near where he grew up, on the banks of Lough Neagh. Shortly after, he was given a large fine and ten-year probationary sentence in the US for using false documents to buy firearms; part of a cache 'found by customs officials bound for Northern Ireland'.[151]

Just before midnight on 29 November 1989, gunmen burst into the bar and shot Liam Ryan dead. They also killed 33-year-old Michael Ryan, a local farmer and married man with two young sons, the youngest only seven months old. Newly married, Liam Ryan had also only recently become a father for the first time. A third man, Pat Campbell, was seriously wounded. He had no links to the republican movement – nor did Michael Ryan. The latter was not even a regular at the bar, but had only gone to watch a local darts match. He did, though, bear more than a passing resemblance to Liam Ryan, the likely target of the attack (that would be claimed by the UVF) for whom he may have been mistaken. In any case, both men were shot again as they lay wounded on the ground.

The Battery Bar is located in a scenic, quiet, secluded spot at the end of a narrow lane, overlooking a small harbour on the western shore of the lough. Yet, in the late 1980s, this was also a heavy militarised area, not least because it was seen as a stronghold of republicanism. The very remoteness and relative inaccessibility of the area was also regarded as a defence against possible attacks by loyalists who had seldom, if ever, ventured into such a place. As with the later attack on Boyle's Bar in Cappagh, similarly sited in a remote, rural, overwhelmingly republican village, the Battery Bar shooting therefore had symbolic as well as more immediate, lethal consequences. Among other things, both incidents seem designed to undermine the idea that there were areas invulnerable to those looking to attack republicans and republican-supporting communities.

There are also echoes of the 'military precision' evident in the killing of Gerard Casey. Around 50 people were still in the main public bar as the darts match was drawing to a close. Liam Ryan was heading towards the main door of the bar to let some customers out, including Michael Devlin and Pat Campbell. A knock at the door was followed by a burst of gunfire, wounding all three men. Two armed men then forced their way in.[152] One fired towards the lounge bar while the other stood over Liam Ryan and Michael Devlin and shot them from close range with a handgun, as they lay on the ground wounded. They both died instantly. Pat Campbell, his leg badly wounded, crawled into a storeroom, only surviving because his attacker's gun jammed. Both gunmen then ran out of the bar. While he survived, like so many others injured in the conflict, the experience cast a long shadow of mental, as well as physical, scars over Pat Campbell's life.[153] Helen Ryan, who arrived at the bar just minutes before the attack, remembers being unclear where the firing was coming from, as the 'bang, bang' of the guns echoed in the narrow hall.[154] As everyone dropped to the floor, Helen hid behind the bar. After the gunmen left, those in the bar attended to the dead and wounded. Helen and her sister tied a tourniquet on Pat Campbell's leg. In the process of being renovated, the bar had no phone or outside CCTV and people feared going outside to raise the alarm. The sense of panic and fear was palpable. 'People were coming and going', says Helen, 'running around and nobody really knew what to do. Then somebody started to say the rosary.'[155]

Initial reports suggested this was a random sectarian attack, with loyalists firing 'indiscriminately' into the bar. With good reason, given such loyalist pub massacres had happened before, and would again at Greysteel and Loughinisland.[156] 'As a Catholic bar' in an 'almost entirely Catholic area', noted a local SDLP councillor, when the gunman 'sprayed the inside of the bar he probably assumed that whoever he hit would be a Catholic'.[157] More than 20 bullet holes were found in the doors, floor and furniture of the lounge bar and many more may have been killed if not for the fact (unknown to the gunman) that almost everyone was in the other, public, bar.[158] Ominously prescient of the Greysteel attack, for one eyewitness the 'bang, bang' of the rapid shots 'was like Halloween'.[159]

But the Battery Bar attack was different too. Some reported the gunmen never tried to enter the main bar. Helen Ryan was standing right behind the public bar door – 'we heard the noise of the bullets but it never opened. They could have come in and sprayed the place and there would have been a lot more than two people killed'.[160] Firing towards the lounge bar may have been to cover their escape. Rather than wholesale slaughter, as one eyewitness stated, the gunmen focused on killing the wounded and 'fired more shots from the handgun into the bodies of their dying victims and then fled': hallmarks perhaps of the targeted assassination of Liam Ryan.[161] In carrying out their task, however, the gunmen showed no compunction at shooting dead Michael Devlin, attempting to kill Pat Campbell and firing towards a bar full of people. If, as seems likely, this was a targeted attack it would have required greater planning, organisation and use of intelligence. Throughout the gunmen were also said to have acted in a 'very cool fashion'.[162]

Afterwards 'everyone was in a complete daze, crying, wailing and lamenting', and in the days that followed there was 'numbness – the whole community was just devastated'.[163] Liam Ryan's brother, Eugene, arrived at the bar shortly after, finding Michael Devlin's grief-stricken father standing outside, initially unable to get in. On seeing the bodies of the two slain men, lying side by side, Eugene was struck by their resemblance to one another. 'You wouldn't have known the difference between them', he recalls, 'they even both had glasses on. When the boys who did the shooting came to the door they couldn't have told the difference. But they had to go no further than that. They knew one of them was Liam.'[164] 'They were very alike', agrees Helen, 'you would have thought they were brothers. So you felt a sense of responsibility, because Michael had been shot and you knew that Liam was the target.'[165]

While later denied by the RUC, it was alleged Liam Ryan had been told by the police (in the weeks before his death) that his 'name and photograph were contained on a missing security force document'.[166] There were allegations, too, that an RUC man told him he would be 'shot before Christmas'.[167] The Ryan family also say a recording existed, since lost, of an RUC threat at a checkpoint that he 'had not long to go now'.[168] They recall that in the weeks preceding the shooting Liam Ryan was clearly 'jittery, living on his nerves, knowing something could happen because he had been told he was going to be killed'.[169] About a month before the attack, while Liam was staying with his brother's family, Eugene Ryan had to hand in legally held shotguns to the RUC; a demand not made before. As he left the Battery Bar on the night of the shooting, he told a local RUC sergeant 'now I know why I lost those guns. You boys knew this was going to happen.' He was asked to reapply for a gun licence three months later.[170]

Locals stated that two members of the UDR scouted the area around the bar just before the shooting.[171] One claimed that 'British Army patrols drove into the pub's car park and sat there for some time' on the two days before the attack, and that uniformed British soldiers had (unusually) come into the pub a few weeks earlier.[172] Others reported a 'heavy' security force presence on the day of the shooting, 'including patrol boats on the Lough and at the jetty' and of British Army personnel in and around Ardboe on the night of the attack itself.[173] There are competing theories regarding the gunmen's escape. A burnt-out car was found near derelict buildings four miles away, but some have suggested this was a decoy and was ablaze before the attack.[174] Some have alleged, rather, that the gunmen made their escape in one of three British Army boats that patrolled Lough Neagh.[175] This is much disputed, and sometimes explained as a result of local disbelief that loyalists could have got in and out of this isolated republican stronghold any other way.[176] While set against the scene of chaos and unreality, Helen Ryan does, though, remember there was 'no sound of a car zooming off, no screeching' after the attack.[177] Certainly, there was only 'one narrow road in and out' and a car coming from the opposite direction could easily have barred an escape. In any case, it is alleged, few checkpoints appear to have been set up, or a helicopter deployed, to secure the surrounding area.[178] Relatives also say there was little in the way of an RUC investigation. Helen Ryan, for one, was never asked to provide a statement and it was local people who 'dug many of the bullets out of the walls' after the police forensic team had gone.[179] What is known is that the weapons were the same as those used to kill Phelim McNally, and that both were part of the South African arms shipment. Indeed, it was Phelim's brother Francie, a well-known local republican in whose house Phelim was killed, who claimed the day after the Battery Bar attack that it was no 'random sectarian killing ... [but] planned deliberately with Liam Ryan the target of security force collusion'.[180]

There are vying theories, too, as to the precise motivations of those who carried out the Battery Bar shootings. Some point to local factors and the role of cross-generational tensions between near neighbours, of family 'vendettas' that, nevertheless, included (on one side at least) members of the UDR, RUC and the local unionist regime. Others focus on Liam Ryan's role in the IRA (something, it should be said, not at first acknowledged by the republican movement) and view the attack as part of the wider strategy of attrition, exemplified in the Loughgall ambush.[181] For the family of Michael Devlin, however, he was simply a Catholic man caught in the wrong place at the wrong time. After the killings his wife and brother-in-law insisted they did 'not want any retaliation ... we just want to get on and bury him in peace and live in peace, because there's so much trouble in this country'.[182]

Killings in Cappagh

In the middle of the small village of Cappagh today stands a large, stone statue of an IRA Volunteer, a monument to the many republican combatants from the local area killed during the conflict.[183] It reflects how Cappagh was long regarded – as a republican stronghold in a part of East Tyrone, set on a hillside, relatively isolated, and surrounded by fields and bog, from which the IRA recruited strongly and launched attacks. Throughout the conflict this was also an area under heavy military occupation. By the 1980s, the British Army mounted saturation surveillance here, with helicopters flying overhead and foot patrols dropped in from the air. The UDR was much in evidence and the SAS was regularly deployed in the surrounding countryside. Relations between the local population and the security forces were never good, and often far worse than that. For example, the nearby town of Coalisland found itself 'virtually under siege' in 1992, when the Parachute Regiment was stationed there.[184] A catalogue of regular low-level, fractious, hostile confrontations and cases of harassment soon ensued. After an IRA landmine near Cappagh injured one Paratrooper, others went on the rampage. The 'Coalisland riots' followed, and the Paras shot and injured three locals – one whose brother was among those recently killed in the set-piece ambush in Clonoe. The Paras involved, though declared 'not entirely innocent', walked free, and Security Minster Michael Mates said they acted in 'self-defence and as such within the law'.[185]

The few hundred people living in Cappagh and its surrounding area are overwhelming Catholic. As in many other parts of rural East Tyrone and South Derry, communal dividing lines are often as acute here as in the working-class city, if less visible to the unfamiliar eye. These social divisions, reflected in tight networks of communal and family ties, are often interwoven with stark political oppositions. If family networks coursed through the local structures of republicanism, the same is also true of unionism and loyalism. Here, however, such affiliations were also interwoven with the structures of the state; not least in terms of the ranks of the RUC and the UDR, often drawn from the self-same communities, social strata and families as the UVF in the area. Local knowledge, and networks of kith and kin, could help blur the lines between official state counterinsurgency and the actions of loyalists directed at the same 'enemy'. In other words, this was not just a question of 'dreary steeples' sectarianism and communal division – state practice counted too.

Locality matters. Cappagh's isolation and reputation made it both a difficult, but symbolically important, target. Neighbouring villages lie several miles away, likewise the nearest main town Dungannon. Getting anywhere, in and around Cappagh, involves travelling down narrow country roads, most poorly marked (if at all); something of a mystery to the uninitiated. It is easy to get lost around Cappagh. The saturation military presence also made it difficult for anyone to move around without an expectation of being stopped, questioned and potentially captured, particularly, again, if unfamiliar with local terrain. If it is easy to get lost around Cappagh, getting in and out without coming to the attention of the authorities was anything but.[186] Like the Battery Bar, launching loyalist attacks in somewhere like Cappagh was therefore a means to undermine morale and defy a myth of relative safety.

This was an area, too, where evidence of collusion between locally recruited state forces and loyalist armed groups was far from new. It formed part of that 'triangle of death' (enclosed by the towns of Portadown, Armagh and Dungannon) in which 'murder gangs', consisting of 'a combination of SAS/UDR/loyalist paramilitaries', operated in the mid-1970s.[187] In 1974 and early 1975 alone, they killed some 30 people locally – all Catholics. UDR and RUC members were among those responsible for some of the worst atrocities. For example, two members of the UDR were convicted for the 1975 Miami Showband massacre. They were part of a UVF gang that stopped the van of the popular music group at a fake checkpoint after it crossed the border. They then botched an attempt to plant a bomb on board the vehicle, intended to make it appear that the musicians were transporting explosives for the IRA. In the process, two of the gang blew themselves up, including their leader, Harris Boyle, who was said to have been an associate of British Army intelligence officer Captain Robert Nairac, as well as being involved in the 1974 Dublin and Monaghan bombings. After the bomb exploded, three members of the Miami Showband were shot dead in a particularly shocking and brutal manner.[188] Fran O'Toole, the 'good-looking' lead singer, was shot in the face 22 times. It has also been alleged that Robin Jackson was behind this attack, and several others that took place around the same time. The RUC and UVF member John Weir, who later confessed to his involvement in similar killings, argued that 'someday it will come out that there were people high up, either Special Branch or army intelligence, who were using us [but] they were not getting their hands dirty. The army, I believe, was using people to do dirty work all along the line.'[189] The Barron report into the Dublin and Monaghan bombings found Weir's testimony and sources 'authentic and credible', concluding it was 'neither fanciful nor absurd' to believe there was collusion in these lethal attacks.[190] The British government and security services continue to insist it is both. Believed to be at the centre of much of this violence throughout, Robin Jackson was still a leading figure in Mid-Ulster loyalism in the late 1980s and early 1990s.

The first killing of this earlier loyalist onslaught in which collusion played such a central part took place in Cappagh. In January 1974, loyalists fired randomly into Boyle's Bar, then situated on Cappagh's main street. Of five people inside, three were wounded. Standing in the doorway, 72-year old retired farmer Daniel Hughes was shot eleven times and killed. The description of one gunman bears comparison to Jackson.[191] A pistol employed in this attack was used in six other killings, including the brutal deaths of Francis and Bernadette Mullan, a middle-aged married couple shot multiple times in their farmhouse near the village of Moy. The gunmen also shot their two-year-old son four times in the legs.[192] A Sterling sub-machine gun, used in the 1974 Cappagh attack, was used in 13 other killings, including the Miami Showband massacre and those of three members of the O'Dowd family in their home in Ballydougan, Co. Armagh in January 1976.[193]

There is, today, another, smaller monument in Cappagh. It stands across the road from the new bar and lounge the Boyle family built in 1979, about 100 yards from the site of the 1974 attack.[194] The small cross commemorates the four local men shot dead, on 3 March 1991, in and around 'Malachy's', as the bar is known locally.[195] Three of those killed (Malcolm Nugent, Dwayne O'Donnell and John Quinn) were members of the East Tyrone IRA, the other was Thomas Armstrong. A single man, a labourer by trade and avid fan of traditional music, Thomas Armstrong lived in Cappagh with his widowed mother. He had dropped in to Malachy's for a couple of drinks around 9.00 pm that evening. He was 'the sort of fella', as his brother Michael recalls, 'who enjoyed the craic and just went out for a pint at the weekend'.[196] Thomas Armstrong was not a member of any republican organisation. Twenty-year-old Malcolm Nugent was from nearby Galbally, growing up close to the home of republican hunger striker Martin Hurson.[197] His family was steeped in republicanism and Malcolm was raised, says his sister Siobhan, with 'house raids and harassment'. His cousin Martin McGaughey was shot dead by the SAS alongside Dessie Grew in 1990. By then, around the time of the Loughgall massacre, Malcolm Nugent had already joined the IRA, aged 16, and 'took part in many IRA attacks throughout East Tyrone'. 'Things had tightened up', says Siobhan, 'tensions were high. It was a scary enough time.'[198]

Malcolm's close friend Dwayne O'Donnell, a keen Gaelic football player and cyclist, had also grown up in a republican family. His grandfather had been in the IRA in the 1920s and an uncle was 'on the blanket' in the 1970s. 'He was brought up in republicanism', says his mother Briege, 'so it was no shock to both his father and me when he became involved. I had a very good relationship with Dwayne and I knew he was involved.'[199] Aged just 14, Dwayne was arrested for collecting car numbers outside Dungannon RUC station and spent some time in a youth offenders centre. He was only 17 years old when he was shot dead. One of eight children, John Quinn also grew up near Cappagh, on a small family farm in Cranogue. He joined the IRA in his late teens. John's sister Poilin, herself a republican former prisoner, remembers the death of Martin Hurson had a big effect on him: 'Martin was only 24 when he died on hunger strike and he experienced so little of life – he was in jail, died on hunger strike and was really so young. I suppose the same goes for John.'[200] John Quinn was friends with some of those killed at Loughgall and also had long experience of regular arrests and confrontations with the security forces. Stress following a beating at the hands of the local RUC, it is believed, triggered hair loss that left him virtually bald. He is described as the head of the 'Cappagh unit' of the IRA that took part in the ambush of two SAS soldiers in the village in March 1990.[201] 'John was seen by the state as a name in the local area', says Poilin Quinn, 'and basically they had a policy of taking people out who they saw as creating hassle for them'. He was 22 years old when he was killed.

Only around 10.00 pm on the evening they were shot dead, does it seem Malcolm Nugent and John Quinn decided to go to Boyle's Bar. They were coming back from nearby Pomeroy, where they had gone to watch a Gaelic football match. They only met Dwayne O'Donnell because they stopped for food.[202] Together with another friend, Malachy Rafferty, they all then drove to Cappagh. John Quinn's older brother Damien, who was also in the car, was dropped off at his home to change. The plan was to go on to a nightclub. The car then left and 'by the time he got to the top of the stairs', says Poilin Quinn, 'Damien heard the shooting'.[203] The car was 'racing' up to the pub against another, driven by a female friend called Fiona. Around 10.30 pm, the two cars arrived at Boyle's Bar. Fiona's got there first. Driving into the car park she 'saw some figures standing there with guns, so she put her foot down on the accelerator and kept driving'.[204] At that point, the car containing the four men drove in. As they stopped, several waiting UVF gunmen opened fire with semi-automatic weapons. When he saw 'the boys in the headlights', Malcolm Nugent shouted 'there's something wrong'.[205] John Quinn began to reverse the car. Malachy Rafferty saw a balaclava and a gun and dived down as the firing started. 'If I had been any slower', he recalled, 'I wouldn't have been here to talk'. He was shot and wounded as he lay on the floor. John shouted to see if he was alright and, says Malachy, 'clasped my hand and that was it. That was him dead.' Malachy lay for some time, the car engine revving out. One gunman had opened fire through the front window of the car, hitting both John Quinn and Dwayne O'Donnell. Another emerged from near the back door of the bar, firing through the rear window. The car was riddled with bullets. Malcolm Nugent was shot as he clambered over a nearby low wall that dropped down 15 feet on the other side.[206]

While Billy Wright would later say the UVF Cappagh killings were 'probably our best', much suggests the story is not so simple. If, as it appears, the decision to go to Boyle's was unplanned, the arrival of the three IRA men was unpredictable. There is no evidence their car was followed. Despite loyalist claims to the contrary, most likely those killed were not, then, the intended targets. Rather, the intention was to attack the bar itself, where a well-known local republican was inside. Disturbed in their plans, but possibly recognising the occupants of the car, the gunmen turned their weapons there instead. Loyalists claimed they had been pre-warned of a planned IRA meeting due to take place in the bar.[207] This is hotly disputed by the families. 'There was definitely no IRA meeting in the bar that night', says Poilin Quinn, 'absolutely not. The loyalists have said there was a meeting of "top IRA people" and that is just complete nonsense, pure and simple. That is just trying to justify a policy of taking people out by saying it was a "good job". That is completely untrue. If you ask me "do you think John was the intended target that night?" No, I don't think so. I think they were going into the pub and kill everyone in there.'[208] There are, though, suggestions the security forces knew of the presence of the leading local republican, who was the real target.[209] At the same time, those in the car (particularly given John Quinn's distinctive appearance) were 'well known to the RUC' and potentially readily recognisable.[210] If the visit to the bar was not 'pre-planned', says Briege O'Donnell, 'after they [the gunmen] saw the car I don't think they fired indiscriminately either'.[211]

The gunmen then tried to force their way into the bar. At the sound of gunfire, those inside had barred the doors and dived for cover. Instead, one (presumably very tall) gunman then fired 14 times through the high window of a toilet cubicle, where Thomas Armstrong had sought shelter. Some have argued the gunmen seemed to know the layout of the bar and 'they must have been there before'.[212] The gunmen then made their getaway in two cars. One was found burnt out in the self-same quarry used by loyalists for that purpose after the 1974 attack. They left behind a scene of shock and devastation. Dwayne O'Donnell and John Quinn lay dead or dying, shot multiple times. Thomas Armstrong was found and moved to a pool table inside the bar. Only after several confused minutes was Malcolm Nugent's body found, over the wall in the field into which he had fallen.[213]

The ability of the attackers to enter and leave the area without difficulty has been the subject of considerable suspicion. As well as roads difficult to navigate at night without local knowledge, Cappagh was a 'village whose antennae are acutely attuned to strangers'.[214] The attack, journalist Peter Taylor concluded, 'was unlikely to have been carried out without some degree of assistance from the security forces'. The 'most likely' group involved was the UDR, 'the only agency in a position to pinpoint the movement of IRA Volunteers and pass on the information to the loyalist hit team'.[215] The evidence suggests that the gunmen 'knew the area', says Michael Armstrong, 'they must have known the whole way round the place and must have been there many a time. Someone from outside would not have known their way around. Whoever did it knew the roads'.[216] Families also argue that this points to the security forces. 'If you take the wrong road you can easily end up in the mountains', agrees Siobhan Nugent, 'people say Billy Wright was involved, and I suppose he could have been taken in and out very quickly. But to me, Billy Wright is part of the problem, not the main issue. Whoever did it was definitely helped by the police or the UDR. To get in and out of Cappagh you need to know your way around it, without a doubt.'[217] The alarm was quickly raised, but there appear to have been no roadblocks set up to cut off escape routes in this most heavily militarised of areas.[218]

Other suspicions attach to British troop movements. 'It is difficult now for people to understand the level of British Army presence then', says Siobhan Nugent, 'the like of the UDR and the SAS would have been around all the time'.[219] Before the shooting that presence was more intense than ever; 'everyone was remarking on it', says Briege O'Donnell.[220] Unusually, a British Army patrol had gone into Boyle's Bar a week earlier, 'taking names' and (one eyewitness said) drawing a map of the bar's layout.[221] On the day of the shooting, a notable heavy military presence was emphasised by a helicopter flying overhead. 'I remember standing talking to a fella looking up', says Michael Armstrong, 'and he said "that thing has been there since 10 o'clock this morning, it never left today"'.[222] In the hours just prior to the shooting, however, many say military patrols and checkpoints around Cappagh disappeared. 'It was more common to be stopped than not stopped in this area', says Siobhan Nugent, 'then it just so happened that they were all away'.[223] 'The army or the UDR were around just before', says Michael Armstrong, 'I heard a helicopter round the back of the house. I didn't know if they were soldiers being dropped off or picked up. Someone closer said that they had seen it was UDR and they were being lifted away. This was around 10.00 pm, so about half an hour before the shooting started and only about a mile away from Cappagh.'[224] Others say the same.[225]

The three dead IRA Volunteers were also not initially acknowledged as such, a decision likely taken to counter the demoralisation that followed so many republican deaths in the area. As with the Battery Bar attack, the Cappagh shootings were at first widely seen, and condemned, as simply sectarian – not without reason.[226] Barring the gunmen's entrance may have prevented many more deaths, akin to other loyalist bar massacres. The UVF soon claimed responsibility, lionising the attack as having 'decimated' the IRA in East Tyrone.[227] Certainly loyalist killing of IRA activists here (and elsewhere) was rare. As we have seen, if active republicans were killed in East Tyrone, it was usually the SAS who did it. Claims that Wright was himself directly involved may need to be treated with some scepticism. One, uncorroborated, loyalist statement, hastily withdrawn, was from a (since thoroughly discredited) source.[228] Killings attributed to Wright often served to bolster a ghoulish reputation. Wright and one or two other senior loyalists were questioned, but released soon after, alibis in place that were confirmed by RUC officers.[229] Whether involved or not, however, the real questions centre on allegations of security force involvement, particularly of members of the UDR. 'There was some UDR arrested and questioned at the time', says Briege O'Donnell, 'but they were released without charge. I want to know more about that.'[230]

Collusion allegations quickly gathered pace. The 'SAS-type efficiency', claimed Sinn Fein, could only happen 'in such a nationalist stronghold with the benefit of security force collusion'.[231] Suspicion was not restricted to republicans. In an area where relations with the security forces were 'strained', feelings were 'running high', with 'a general suspicion among people here that the security forces were in some way involved'.[232] Here, as in other killings, suggested Fr Denis Faul, there was a broad feeling that 'the assassins are getting help from security forces'.[233] 'It is damned suspicious', said one SDLP councillor, 'how a loyalist murder gang can operate in an area where the security forces know about everything that moves'.[234] Local people, said another, will be 'very sceptical' about the investigation to follow.[235] The RUC swiftly denied 'sweeping allegations about the incident'.[236] Little enough emerged from whatever RUC investigation took place. The RUC 'said they would leave no stone unturned', says Michael Armstrong, 'but we never heard another word, nothing after that'.[237] Dozens of statements testifying to the attack and security force movements were taken by local political and civil liberties activists, but not admitted as evidence at the inquest.[238] No one was ever charged or convicted for the Cappagh shootings. Later ballistics tests would show that the weapons used killed many other Catholics, including several collusion cases where republican family members were shot dead.[239]

The effect of the deaths on the families was deep and long lasting. 'For years in our house we wouldn't bring up John's name', remembers Poilin Quinn, 'it was just too painful for mum. My parents never got over it.' 'He was so young, they all were', Poilin continues, 'I have children the same age myself now and at that age then they would have been arrested and interrogated. Thank God that has totally changed and that is not a path they have to take.'[240] Briege O'Donnell remembers 'driving down the road and all of a sudden tears would be running down my face. Or I would be standing at the sink, peeling potatoes, and it would all just come over you. There are all these wee reminders. But we had all the other, younger children so you couldn't let them see you going to pieces. The children used to cry as well, it had a big impact on all of us. Dwayne and his brother Barry were very close, like twins really. Dwayne being killed had a big impact on him; Barry found it very difficult. Twenty years later my daughter said she heard her father mention Dwayne's name for the first time.'[241] On family occasions, says Siobhan Nugent, 'you are aware of Malcolm not being there.'[242] She also remembers taunts from security forces and one 'big tall UDR' man laughing, during a house raid, and saying 'we got him'. 'You were the target of things like that for years', says Siobhan. For Michael Armstrong, it was the devastating, silencing effect his brother's death had on his mother, and the sense of loss he would sometimes feel seeing familiar things and 'forget he was dead and think "where is he?" You always think he should be there.'[243] For all the Cappagh families the issue of collusion remains their most pressing concern. 'Collusion was a mechanism for enforcing policy', Poilin Quinn insists, 'blatant, but they got away with it. They used the loyalist paramilitaries and, when they outlived their usefulness, they got rid of them too. They were the victims of collusion as well. People might wonder "how did they get away with all that?" Because they were working within the confines of the way the law had been set up.'[244]

6
Stopping Sinn Fein: Collusion as Political Force

Targeting Sinn Fein

Just after 10.00 pm on 14 February 1989, loyalists shot dead veteran republican and local Sinn Fein councillor John Davey, as he drove into the narrow lane leading to his home in the small South Derry village of Gulladuff.[1] He was returning from a meeting of Magherafelt Council to which he was first elected four years earlier – part of the first wave of the party's emerging, post-hunger strike, entry into electoral politics. As an active republican since the border campaign of the 1950s, interned during the 1970s and a prominent figure within republicanism since, John Davey's election had drawn increasingly adverse attention to someone who was locally well known and, in some circles, much hated. Pat Finucane had been killed just two days before. In the weeks leading up to Pat Finucane's death, government junior minister, Douglas Hogg, made an 'unjustifiable' (and unsubstantiated) complaint to the House of Commons of 'solicitors ... unduly sympathetic to the IRA'.[2] Based on an RUC briefing that reflected a 'mind-set' within the organisation 'against solicitors representing republican paramilitaries', Hogg's speech (SDLP MP Seamus Mallon declared at the time) helped ensure that some lawyers could 'become targets for assassin's [sic] bullets'. Months earlier, Mid-Ulster DUP MP (and local councillor) William McCrea used parliamentary privilege to go much further. Denouncing Davey as an IRA 'Godfather', McCrea accused him of being an 'active terrorist', directly involved in a 1986 killing.[3] This brought threats 'closer to home', says Davey's daughter Pauline Davey-Kennedy (herself later a Sinn Fein councillor), and was something the family took 'very seriously'. Indeed, John Davey was taking a legal case against McCrea at the time of his death.[4] According to John's wife Mary, like him a lifelong republican, being named in parliament 'signed John's death warrant ... after that our life became one of anticipation'.[5]

The night before his last journey home, John and Mary stayed with family overnight, following several threatening and abusive phone calls.[6] The day before that (as Pat Finucane was killed in his Belfast home), they had been stopped by a UDR patrol, one of whom implied that John Davey would soon be dead. In itself, this was not so unusual. A catalogue of threats, over several years, not least from UDR members, reinforced the family's sense of a shadow hanging over them. It was, says Pauline, 'an intense, really unreal, abnormal situation'. As a high-profile republican, denied the personal weapons or bodyguards available to other politicians, returning from publicly known, scheduled council meetings always generated anxiety. 'You felt hopeless, helpless and totally exposed, with nobody to protect you', Pauline would recall. So, John Davey would have been extremely cautious as he arrived home – not least as he had narrowly escaped death, in virtually the same spot, just over a year before. That is why his family suspect he would not have stopped his car in the driveway unless he had met what he took to be a police or UDR patrol. Whether or not they were in uniform, loyalists lay in wait, and killed John Davey sitting in his car, making good their escape before the alarm was raised.

This was the first of a spate of killings of Sinn Fein members, workers and political representatives that formed a distinct feature of loyalist killings in Mid-Ulster. While the upsurge of loyalist violence, here as elsewhere, was often characterised by blatant sectarianism, there is also a death toll of Sinn Fein activists that contrasts with other areas.[7] Twenty-five Sinn Fein members or representatives died during the three decades of the conflict.[8] Of these 14 (56 per cent of the total) were killed in the five years from 1989 to 1993, and half of those were Mid-Ulster victims. As well as John Davey, they included another member of Magherafelt Council, Bernard O'Hagan, shot dead by the UFF in broad daylight outside his workplace in September 1991. This came just a few months after the UFF killed Eddie Fullerton, a Sinn Fein councillor over the border in Donegal.

Also killed in Mid-Ulster were party workers, among them Tommy Casey, shot by the UVF in October 1990. While not strictly in the Mid-Ulster area, Patrick Shanaghan was killed near his West Tyrone home in August 1991. Danny Cassidy (shot dead in April 1992) was neither in Sinn Fein nor the IRA, but RUC harassment suggested he was, and likely sealed his fate. Others were also former prisoners, including Tommy Donaghy, killed in August 1991, and Malachy Carey, shot in December 1992 (who also stood for a council seat in 1989). There are parallels with other cases – such as the killing of Sam Marshall in Lurgan in 1990 – but in Mid-Ulster, at this time, the death toll of Sinn Fein members and officials is striking, and included one in four of all Sinn Fein members killed anywhere during the entire conflict. This was particularly notable in South Derry, which saw five deaths in an area where conflict was not generally as fierce as elsewhere.[9] Aside from Tommy Casey and John Davey, Mid-Ulster Sinn Fein victims died in a particularly intense period in 1991-2 – part of a wider pattern, apparent at the time, and not only to republicans. The 'same gang' who killed John Davey, noted the BBC, may have been responsible for 'five gun attacks in the Mid-Ulster area in the previous three months'.[10] They included an attack, in his home, on Johnny Rush, 'a Sinn Fein election worker in Stewartstown a few miles away', and the killing of Phelim McNally the previous November. Recent weeks had seen two gun attacks on the same night in nearby Moneymore, including one against the home of a brother of a Cookstown Sinn Fein councillor.[11]

Endgame Politics

The balance of politics and violence, of dialogue and coercion, that moved the North towards the conflict's endgame, is much disputed. Interpretations are often politically loaded, intent on drawing competing, contradictory 'lessons' for conflict resolution elsewhere.[12] In response to 'orthodox' perspectives, which focus on the primacy of political negotiation, hawkish, neo-conservative views valorise the part played by intelligence-led coercive force and counterinsurgency violence in reshaping the political terrain. Here, an 'irregular' or 'intelligence' war essentially defeated the IRA and made possible a political settlement on that basis.[13] It is a view echoed by others (from a very different political standpoint) for whom the compromises of modern Irish republicanism are the 'product of British state strategies'.[14] The former tend also to endorse the logic of British (and other) counterinsurgency thinking, where the application of military power is 'always a means to achieve a wider political purpose'.[15] Hawkish interpretations are similarly likely to follow British counterinsurgency thinkers in validating the state's adherence to the rule of law in the conduct of a 'dirty war', stressing its effectiveness while generally sidestepping critical, political, ethical or moral evaluation.

All actors in the conflict attempted to reforge the political terrain to their advantage. For republicans, this took shape, first, in the 'armalite and ballot box' approach, followed by an emerging, overlapping (and in some senses competing) 'peace strategy' by the end of the 1980s. If affected by state strategies, Sinn Fein electoralism also had a political dynamic of its own. The 'armalite and ballot box' strategy, coming in the wake of the 1981 hunger strike, sought to combine the 'cutting edge' of the ongoing IRA campaign with the politics of a 'resistance community' and developing organisational culture of Sinn Fein.[16] Initially it met with considerable success in European, Westminster and local council elections. The latter, in particular, brought local republican leaders into the public domain, and to public attention, as never before. Given the hostile reaction of unionists, it also made council chambers sites of intense, often bitter and sometimes violent confrontation.

However, tensions inherent in the 'armalite and ballot box' strategy also soon became apparent. Sinn Fein could rely on a core of support within traditional republican and Catholic working-class communities, either behind (or at least not dissuaded by) the IRA armed campaign. Yet, the party's ability to attract a wider constituency was limited by that self-same violence. Reaction to IRA attacks, such as the Remembrance Day bombing in Enniskillen in 1987, which left twelve people dead, only served to emphasise the fact. Sinn Fein's electoral success in the North ebbed, flowed, but essentially plateaued by the end of the decade. Two-thirds of nationalist votes continued to go the way of the SDLP. The party also failed entirely to make political inroads in the South, despite the contentious and divisive decision to drop its policy of abstention from the Dáil in 1986. Electoralism made many of these contradictions inescapable and combined with the increasing sense of a military standstill and stalemate. If the British military could not defeat the IRA they had demonstrated a capacity to inflict significant damage, infiltrated its ranks and nullified key aspects of its campaign. The adoption of a 'peace strategy' was the outcome of these various factors.[17] Pursuing a 'peace agenda' was no easy step and a long drawn-out process for republicans; the very word 'peace' had become part of counterinsurgency policy. Taking this path would lead to rancorous debate and a legacy of distrust, for some, down to the present. However, by 1988 it saw Sinn Fein in talks with the nationalist SDLP, themselves disillusioned with the political logjam in the wake of the 1985 Anglo-Irish Agreement. Over the next few years, even as conflict continued, politics within nationalism became a 'battle for fresh allies', and of getting key actors to join the 'ranks of the persuaders', for broadly nationalist aims, that would help forge a foundation for the (often halting) peace process to come.[18]

This is what unionists and loyalists would come to denounce as the 'pan-nationalist front'. Some argue that unionism had already been 'traumatised' by the Anglo-Irish Agreement.[19] Certainly the agreement was met with a 'wave of Protestant rage' evident in mass demonstrations, council boycotts and a one-day general strike. Forms of protest redolent with historical symbolism gave vent to a sense of political betrayal. A resort to arms was also a longstanding tradition and now saw the creation of the DUP-inspired 'Third Force', the network of armed 'Ulster Clubs' and the new, mass, loyalist paramilitary organisation, Ulster Resistance. The last of these brought together paramilitary and political leaders, notably from the DUP. Yet this 'trauma' did not manifest itself in an immediate upsurge in loyalist violence. Indeed, 1985 saw the lowest number of loyalist killings (four) since 1969.[20] It was not until 1991 that loyalist killings increased dramatically. That year, loyalists killed 40 people, twice as many as the year before – a scale not seen since the dark days of the mid-1970s. In the five years after the signing of the Anglo-Irish Agreement, loyalists claimed 90 lives, but in the four that followed (1991–4), that figure almost doubled to 164. Anger with the Anglo-Irish Agreement cannot, alone, explain this lethal rise.

Paradoxically, this upsurge also coincided with a supposed shift in loyalist strategy. UFF leaders (it has been suggested) had come to see terrorising Catholics, through random assassination, as counterproductive.[21] The emphasis now would be on 'selective targeting'. One might expect that a move from 'softer' sectarian targets towards republicans (more conscious of the threat) would result in a decline in overall numbers. The opposite is true. In part, of course, this is because an end to sectarian killing was a chimera – as Greysteel, Loughinisland and other individual attacks readily testify. But the capacity of loyalists to target republicans, not least party workers and officials, did increase significantly. The question is how, and why? In another apparent paradox, this rise in loyalist attacks (long rationalised as a reaction to IRA violence) grew exponentially as republicans moved closer to a cessation. Cries of 'sell-out' gathered pace as the net of 'legitimate' targets expanded to ensnare the whole 'pan-nationalist front', resulting in increasing attacks on SDLP, as well as Sinn Fein, officials. This upsurge should have undermined 'big lie' official adherence to the 'loyalist-violence-as-reactive' narrative, which had long served to justify a counterinsurgency focus on republicans.[22] Woefully belated, it at least saw the UDA proscribed in 1992. Yet state rhetoric would continue to portray such violence as essentially reactive even after loyalists themselves declared they had gone on the offensive.

For the Thatcher government, political battle lines in the North had been clearly drawn since before coming to power. The failure of political initiatives (such as the short-lived Northern Ireland Assembly), and experience of the hunger strike period, reinforced a predilection for tough security measures and hard power politics. Already widely reviled by nationalists, Thatcher would equally become a hate figure for unionists for signing the Anglo-Irish Agreement. But she was an ardent supporter of the Union, her instincts 'profoundly Unionist', having the 'greatest sympathy' for unionists, and antipathetic towards nationalists.[23] The agreement for her was essentially designed to deliver Irish government support for an escalation of the war against the IRA. Her disappointment at the lack of tangible results only led the British government to pursue, all the more vigorously, a coercive counterinsurgency approach. Politically, this centred on measures to isolate and marginalise Sinn Fein, evidenced in attempts to exclude them from political office and ban them from the airwaves, and in the draconian policing of republican funerals.

Talks, intended to encourage rapprochement and cooperation between 'mainstream' nationalism and unionism, stumbled on intermittently, with little sign or hope of success, and from which Sinn Fein was expressly excluded. There may have been struggles within British policy circles between 'hawks' and 'doves' over the direction policy should take. The possibility of backchannel talks was an option promoted and pursued, by some, from 1990 onwards – re-engaging avenues and contacts first forged in the mid-1970s, but which had lain largely dormant after the 1981 hunger strikes.[24] However, these were years dominated by what one ardent supporter would describe as 'the continuation of a security strategy based on effective intelligence, counterinsurgency and containment' aimed at the 'effective defeat of terrorism'.[25] 'Hard power' wearing down of republicans was the basis of a political strategy predicated on the idea that 'terrorists should only be talked to once they have been defeated'.[26] For Thatcher, this was a perspective only reinforced by the 'deep personal grief' felt after the IRA killed Ian Gow in July 1990. Like Airey Neave, blown up by the INLA just before she came to power, Gow was a close friend and confidante, personal adviser on Northern Ireland policy and 'longstanding unionist sympathiser and outspoken critic' of the IRA.[27] Not until that view no longer held such overwhelming sway did the way open up for the Downing Street Declaration and the – again prolonged and torturous – path towards the Good Friday Agreement.

Local, Personal and Political

The rise in killings of Sinn Fein officials and party workers took place against this backdrop of endgame politics. On the ground, these wider antagonisms were played out locally, not least in and around council chambers. Proximity made broader political tension more tangible and personal. This could sharpen a 'doomsday mindset' that was evident within certain sections of unionist and loyalist opinion, shaped in places by an all-consuming sense of decline and the collapse of community infrastructure. For example, republican attacks on Orange Halls were seen as the destruction of vital social institutions.[28] In some border areas there was a widely held perception that republican violence was directed at removing the Protestant community from the local countryside.[29] Given its make-up, the deaths of members of the UDR and RUC in these (and other) areas were experienced by unionists as community losses.

This 'doomsday' outlook could be further fomented by a vitriolic brand of populist political rhetoric. Nowhere is this better illustrated than in the 'hour long tirade', showing the 'less attractive face of Democratic Unionists', during which William McCrea named John Davey as a 'terrorist'.[30] Having previously called for 'Libyan-style' air raids against 'republican strongholds', McCrea now demanded ever more draconian action, 'military measures' and the death penalty that (he argued) would achieve more, in smashing the existential threat of the 'pan-nationalist front', than sitting politicians round a 'little conference table'.[31] Calls for inquiries into army shootings were denounced as nothing but a 'great hullabaloo', in which the real victims were young British soldiers, whose names were 'pulled through the gutter' for making a 'mistake'.[32] Attempts by the Stalker Inquiry to make 'scapegoats' of RUC men ('lads, sent out to do a job') would lead others, he warned, none too cryptically, 'to tell the full story [about] the political leaders higher up the line who gave the instructions in the first place ... decisions [that] went into the higher reaches of the political arena'.[33]

Earlier described by his party leader, Ian Paisley, as the 'Godfathers of murderers', it was, however, the spectre of Sinn Fein councillors who exercised McCrea's ire the most.[34] Someone within the NIO, he confided, had told him that 'practically every Sinn Fein councillor came from the military wing of the IRA'.[35] Not only did the IRA have 'safe homes all over the place', he continued, blurring distinctions further, 'it was important not to forget that 100,000 people went to the ballot box and voted for Sinn Fein'.[36] 'I came to the conclusion at the end of his speech', a despondent Labour shadow undersecretary of state commented, that 'his arguments go beyond the bounds of logic ... his driving force was irrationality, not rationality'.[37] William McCrea was not alone in his outlook. 'There were some who were very, very hostile to republicans and nationalists being in the council', recalls Pauline Davey-Kennedy.[38] After his first electoral victory in 1985, John Davey was attacked and hit with a chair by unionist council members.[39] At the end of the council meeting on the night he was killed, say his family, one unionist councillor 'made some snide remarks about whether he would be around for the next election'.[40]

But local antagonism should not be divorced from wider political developments. These form a crucial backdrop to the upsurge of loyalist attacks on Sinn Fein people in Mid-Ulster in 1991–2. Loyalists had called a ceasefire in April 1991 for the duration of party talks (which excluded Sinn Fein).[41] Eddie Fullerton would be the only person killed by loyalists in the ten-week period that followed. However, the talks ended in failure in early July and immediately loyalists 'ordered attacks on republicans'.[42] Two of the first victims were Patrick Shanaghan and Tommy Donaghy. The UFF struck again a month later, killing Bernard O'Hagan, and another month on Sean Anderson was shot dead in East Tyrone. By then loyalists had killed 16 people since calling off their ceasefire, but almost all other attacks had been in Belfast and of a blatantly sectarian nature, including the killing of four Catholic taxi drivers.[43] Two other people were shot dead because they stocked copies of *Republican News* in their West Belfast shops.[44] Far from targeting known or high-profile republicans, these attacks were designed to instil fear in the wider nationalist population. Those in Tyrone, South Derry and Donegal, on the other hand, appear to have been more carefully planned, premeditated and directed.

The cold political rationale of such violence was to 'diminish support for Sinn Fein, to do whatever could be done to discourage anyone from either supporting Sinn Fein, being a Sinn Fein activist, standing as a Sinn Fein candidate'.[45] For veteran journalist Brian Feeney such logic was paralleled in the outlook of 'certain elements in the security forces', most likely British Army and intelligence, who had a 'wider agenda. That you took out members of Sinn Fein, who weren't IRA men, to discourage the others'. 'It certainly had an effect', he concluded. Likewise, Desmond de Silva would argue that state intelligence agencies were actively working at this time to make loyalists a 'sharper weapon' in targeting republicans, and placing ever greater pressure on increasingly fractured communities as a result. Nor was this all happening in a policy vacuum. The effects of measures taken would be felt at a local level. Policies such as the broadcasting ban were directed at stigmatising support for Sinn Fein and identifying Sinn Fein councillors as 'terrorists in local government'.[46] Similarly, just a month after John Davey was killed, an act was passed requiring local election candidates to make a 'declaration against terrorism'.[47] Failure to do so could result in disqualification. Not long before he was killed, efforts to do just that to Bernard O'Hagan followed a 'heated exchange' in the council chamber, during which William McCrea denounced him (and others) as 'mouthpieces of the IRA in the building'.[48] The families of Sinn Fein officials would therefore experience an 'upping of the ante' and an intensification in the actions of security forces at the same time, and as part of the same process.[49] House raids saw the drawing up of plans of people's homes, and driving licences were taken away at roadblocks and not returned, some ending up in loyalists' hands. When 'the UDR and the RUC would stop you', says Pauline Davey-Kennedy, 'and had no hesitation in telling you "you're going to be shot"', they were also increasingly likely to be believed.

Targeting John Davey

Loyalists had tried to kill John Davey before. In 1987 the RUC told him his details had been 'leaked' to loyalists.[50] Soon after, loyalist Michael Stone targeted Davey and other republicans whose 'names and details appeared in intelligence files'. Stone was given the 'very professional files' by 'UFF intelligence officers', FRU agent Brian Nelson chief among them, at a time when Nelson was 'running his assassination campaign at the instigation of the FRU'.[51] 'It was obvious', Stone wrote, that 'UFF intelligence officers had connections with the security forces'.[52] Stone discussed the files and targets with UDA leader John McMichael and Nelson. He viewed John Davey as an 'old-school ... high-profile republican', someone he could target (in a plan later carried out to deadly effect in the Milltown massacre) so as to 'lure his comrades to his funeral'.[53]

In February 1988 – armed with a handgun that had 'belonged to a member of the RUC' – Michael Stone tried to shoot John Davey as he left his home. The attack, organised jointly by the UFF and Ulster Resistance, bore many hallmarks of the later fatal shooting.[54] Indeed, one accomplice (Stone would claim) was the person responsible for John Davey's assassination a year later.[55] Despite the high level of state surveillance to which the Davey home was regularly subjected, Stone was able to lie in wait, armed and undetected, for several hours beforehand.[56] As John Davey's would-be assassins shot at, then pursued him, he escaped by scrambling over fields and ditches, and later said he had 'no doubt' he could hear security force personnel talk to one another by army radios.[57] Family suspicions of a British army presence were fuelled by their previous experiences of uncovering soldiers 'dug in, in a sort of fox hole, really well camouflaged, and judging by the amount of food cans, they had been there for quite a while', who were then 'whisked away swiftly by helicopter'.[58] 'We always knew we were being watched', says Pauline Davey-Kennedy, 'that is how close and intense it was'.

A few weeks later Stone would try, again unsuccessfully, to kill John Davey's brother-in-law – a Kilrea farmer with no republican links – using a grenade from the South African weapons shipment.[59] A week after that, armed with a South African-sourced gun provided by a leading figure in Ulster Resistance, Stone killed three people and injured 60 others when he attacked the funeral, at Milltown Cemetery, of three IRA Volunteers shot dead in a shoot-to-kill operation by the SAS in Gibraltar.[60] Suspicions of collusion, and the possible involvement of the FRU, have been raised over the Milltown massacre.[61] Indeed, given Nelson's role, Martin Dillon has argued that throughout this period Michael Stone was essentially an 'assassin run by British military intelligence, probably without his knowledge'.[62]

A year later, John Davey was shot dead at virtually the same spot as the earlier attack on him. That night, Mary Davey heard the shots and sounded a siren the family had installed to alert neighbours. Many quickly arrived from the nearby local Gaelic Athletics Association (GAA) clubhouse. A number testified that John Davey's car was stopped in the middle of the laneway, the lights still on, but the engine turned off and the handbrake on; suggesting he had been stopped by men who were part of (or posing as) a security force patrol.[63] If ambushed while still moving, it was argued, the car 'would have crashed'.[64] The family contend he 'would not have stopped for anyone else than a man in a British uniform' and that it must have been 'the UDR that stopped him'.

Eyewitnesses also said there were no other cars in the village at the time and no road blocks in place in and around the village.[65] An RUC chief inspector stated that vehicle checkpoints were 'already in operation' when he was told of the shooting and requested a helicopter to help catch the killers, but bad weather 'precluded flying'.[66] The Daveys and others say they were able to travel to and from Gulladuff after the attack without being stopped and that there 'was no sign of any security forces'.[67] They also accuse the RUC of failing to secure evidence at the scene. Spent cartridges were picked up the next day, and from the car when it was returned.[68] After the earlier attack only Michael Stone's post-Milltown arrest brought any contact with the RUC, a pattern repeated again. After taking Mary Davey's statement, says Pauline Davey-Kennedy, the police 'never darkened my mother's door'.[69] The inquest would reveal that the police found a getaway car two days after the shooting, near farm buildings on a rural road close to the Daveys' home.[70] It contained one of the AK47-type weapons imported from South Africa, a pistol, ammunition, gloves and clothing.[71] This area had, though, been searched the day before by the UDR – who found the vehicle's tax disc but failed to uncover the car itself. 'I think the judge thought it sounded peculiar', remembers Pauline.[72] Two men were later found guilty for bringing one of the weapons into the South Derry area. They included the son of a co-owner of the building contractors targeted in the attack in which William McCrea accused John Davey of being involved. His father was also killed by the IRA.[73] However, no one was charged or convicted for direct involvement in killing John Davey.

'My mother always blamed the British government at the highest level, and unionist politicians, for his death', says Pauline Davey-Kennedy, 'for us, the family, it is obvious it was sanctioned. It was so well stage-managed. It was about sending a message to an entire community, "you elect a Sinn Fein councillor and he will end up dead".'[74] The killing of John Davey, says Ed Moloney, 'began an open season on Sinn Fein councillors and activists'.[75] A year after his death, a cache of British security files was discovered in the hands of loyalists in Derry.[76] Included were photographs of John Davey and Eddie Fullerton, who would be killed a year later. Across the photos of both men were written the words 'dead as doornails'.

The Killing of Bernard O'Hagan

Pauline Davey-Kennedy was soon after elected to Magherafelt Council and worked alongside Bernard O'Hagan, himself killed by loyalists two years later. Originally from North Belfast, Bernard had become involved politically while studying to be a teacher at university in England.[77] He married and moved back to the North with his young family in 1986, settling in Swatragh, South Derry (near the home of his brother John), and taking up a lecturing post at the nearby Magherafelt FE College. He also became involved in Sinn Fein, for whom he won a council seat. He was shot dead in the car park of the college after arriving for work at around 9.00 am on the morning of 16 September 1991, in broad daylight and in front of dozens of students and staff. A lone gunman – who had been waiting for him, possibly for as long as 45 minutes, unmasked and posing as a student carrying a folder – then made good his escape.

Bernard's brother, John O'Hagan, with whom he was 'close in age and close in life', says becoming a Sinn Fein councillor made Bernard a target, not only for loyalists, but also for 'heightened RUC and British Army harassment'.[78] In 1989 a neighbour reported that a UDR patrol photographed the O'Hagan's home. Despite complaints this was not properly investigated, the RUC soon declared 'the matter now closed'.[79] It was, says John, the start of a campaign that 'set the tone for the permission to proceed with his murder'.[80] After that, a large cache of intelligence files were inadvertently found on a rubbish tip, left there for collection by loyalists. They included Bernard's personal details. But loyalists soon had state intelligence on Bernard O'Hagan in any case. Three months before he was killed the RUC informed Bernard that state files with his details were in loyalist hands.[81]

After John Davey's death, like other Sinn Fein families, the O'Hagans installed security shutters and drop bars in the family home. 'Bernard was very uneasy leading up to his death', remembers Pauline Davey-Kennedy, 'the real fear was going in and coming out of the council meetings. He would ask me what route I had taken. When things got very, very intense we would set off really early and take a route going all over the place.'[82] He also believed he was being followed and discussed this with family and friends in the weeks before he was killed.[83] Fears also centred on travelling to and from work. He had become unhappy teaching night classes and had asked fellow councillors, and his brother, to meet and travel with him when he finished teaching. 'It was scary', remembers

John, 'it was dark and you were looking over your shoulder'. On the morning he was killed 'he was actually going to see the principal to change the night classes, but never got the chance'. Even in the mornings Bernard O'Hagan would take 'four or five different routes' to get to work. Invariably, though, 'whatever route he took, he still had to go in through the college gates'.

The day before he was killed Bernard told his brother he thought a car had been following him every day for the previous two weeks and that the RUC were involved. As with John Davey, he had also been subject to sustained threats, some from unionist fellow councillors. Just before he was killed one 'came up and whispered in his ear "it'll not be long now. Your days are numbered"'.[84] 'That night he explained his fears to me', says John O'Hagan, 'he was not a religious man but he said he was going to head up to the holy hour at the chapel in Swatragh. Then he left and I never saw him again until he was lying beside the car.' The next morning, on arriving at work, Bernard was shot dead as he gathered books and files from his car. The gunman 'took the gun out of the folder' and ran towards him, shooting and shouting his name.[85] As he slumped on the ground the gunman fired several more times, killing Bernard instantly, then ran out the front entrance as stunned staff and students looked on.[86] Some students tried to follow at a distance, for fear of being shot, and saw (what they took to be) a getaway car, some 100 yards or so away from the college.[87] Such a public attack in the light of day by an unmasked attacker was highly unusual.

Questions have been raised over the movement of security force patrols and checkpoints prior to and after the shooting. Bernard's brother Paul, who lived and worked locally as a lorry driver, was among others who claimed to have seen an 'unusual' number of checkpoints on the main road into the town which then disappeared 'a short time later just prior to the killing'.[88] RUC foot or vehicle patrols, said always to be in place near or around the college each morning (a local building contractor that worked on military installations was close by) were 'not to be seen' that day.[89] Told by a neighbour that his brother had been shot, John O'Hagan rushed to the scene, and says he passed 'UDR Land Rovers, just sitting there. There was no checkpoint or anything; they were just standing up in their Land Rovers talking and laughing'. He arrived at the college about 45 minutes after Bernard had been killed.[90] 'There were no checkpoints around the Tech', says John, who passed through the police cordon to approach his brother's body before other family started to arrive: 'I can still see him lying there. It is vivid even now. Then a policeman came over, I was pretty unhappy at this stage, and he started to manhandle me; threatened to arrest me'. Bernard's widow, Fiona, arrived soon after and would also later claim that no checkpoints were in place, leading her to think, at first, that news of Bernard's death was untrue.[91] Given the highly public nature of the attack, says John O'Hagan, it is even more surprising that 'no getaway car was spotted or abandoned, no disguises or overalls were dumped. No weapon was ever recovered and no one was ever arrested or charged in relation to Bernard's murder.'

The UFF claimed responsibility for killing Bernard O'Hagan and that he was in the IRA, which both Sinn Fein and the family denied.[92] Gerry Adams would suggest that his death evidenced a 'restructured counterinsurgency strategy' designed to 'intimidate Sinn Fein and the nationalist community' against the backdrop of the continued exclusion of the party from 'inclusive dialogue'.[93] Local political tensions did not dissipate. His killing was condemned by most. William McCrea said merely, 'he who lives by the sword often dies by the sword' because Bernard O'Hagan had 'consistently failed to condemn terrorism [and] believed firmly in the right of the IRA to carry on its murderous deeds'.[94] Former DUP Mayor of Belfast Sammy Wilson added that the shooting was the 'inevitable consequence of the sectarian IRA murder campaign', and that the 'IRA and its political supporters have only themselves to blame when loyalists retaliate'.[95] A week later local unionist councillors initially refused to accept a motion of sympathy and the RUC removed Fiona O'Hagan from the chamber.[96] Even two decades on, when a memorial plaque to both Bernard O'Hagan and John Davey were placed in the Magherafelt Council office, protestors (led by victims' campaigner Willie Frazer) declared it to be a 'disgrace to the innocent victims' of the area.[97]

The O'Hagans were told little about the investigation into the death. Fiona O'Hagan's father (a retired, former long-serving CID officer in England) wrote to the RUC chief constable voicing concerns over a 'lack of investigation'.[98] Despite assurances, little changed afterward. 'It felt as if police inspectors were blocking us from finding anything out', says John O'Hagan.[99] Concerns also focused on the apparent failure to take statements from several eyewitnesses and the treatment of two girls who had seen the gunman. 'They were taken in two separate cars to an identity parade in Belfast', says John, and police told them 'they needed glasses. They were scaring them. One of the girls told us afterwards she became frightened and, in the end, she did not want to go through with it.'[100]

That the perpetrator was unmasked was not made public and a photofit was not released.[101] Police may also have failed to investigate whether two men, convicted of attempting to shoot a Catholic council worker in February 1992, with the same gun used to kill Bernard O'Hagan, were involved in his killing.[102] His brother's death left 'a big hole in my life', says John O'Hagan, who has little doubt, not only of systematic collusion, but that its intent was to 'discredit people and to scare them so they would not get involved in politics. A scare tactic to stop people joining Sinn Fein, stop them becoming councillors. It was a way of saying: "if you get involved you are going to get shot".'[103]

The Shootings of Tommy Casey and Sean Anderson

Sinn Fein councillors were not the only party members to die in Mid-Ulster at the hands of loyalists. Father of eleven, 57-year-old Tommy Casey from Kildress, Co. Tyrone, never held political office (despite some newspaper reports and Police Service of Northern Ireland (PSNI) letters suggesting otherwise) but had worked for various republican organisations for years.[104] A painter and handyman by trade, living in and around Cookstown all his life, he had worked for Bernadette McAliskey on several election campaigns, particularly during the hunger strikes. Both he and his wife, Kathleen, were then active for many years in fundraising for republican prisoners and providing support and doing various jobs for their families.[105] Long involvement with republicanism had led to a series of threats and attacks.[106] In August 1990, Tommy Casey reported receiving a 'specific death threat from an RUC detective in Cookstown'.[107] A month later, shots were fired at the Casey home. One of an isolated row of terraced houses, this came after a neighbour's house (belonging to former Cookstown Sinn Fein Councillor Tony Driscoll) came under a well-planned attack, launched by several gunmen.[108] One group came across backfields and tried to sledgehammer their way into the Driscoll home. Only an upstairs security door (recently installed following the attack that left Phelim McNally dead) saved the Driscoll family, as dozens of shots were fired. Another group of gunmen, who had driven to the front of the house, then fired a dozen more shots before turning to spray the Casey's home with gunfire.[109] The downstairs rooms were 'riddled with upwards of two dozen shots' as the Casey's fled and escaped injury upstairs.[110]

Tony Driscoll reported receiving numerous death threats from the RUC and UDR, and loyalists had an RUC file with his details.[111] Both families suspected members of the security forces of involvement in this shooting. Two weeks later, two of Tommy Casey's grown-up daughters say they were stopped by a 'carload of CID men in plain clothes', one of whom pulled out a gun and said '"See this? We missed your da the other night but we'll get him and we're going to shoot him with this. After that, you two are next".[112] A week later the two sisters moved to London. A week after that, an early morning raid by armed police was how they found out their father had been shot dead.

At around 9.00 pm on 26 October 1991, Tommy and Kathleen Casey drove to the isolated farmhouse of a neighbour to fix a lock on the back door.[113] As Tommy walked towards the house he was shot eleven times, in the head and body, dying instantly.[114] The weapon used was one of those imported from South Africa. 'There was a terrible rattle of shots', Kathleen Casey would later recall, 'glass came in around me and I was struck by something on the head, either glass or a bullet fragment'. She watched as her husband stood with 'his hands above his head' by the backdoor just before he was killed and saw him 'fall back on to the ground'.[115] 'The next thing I knew', continued Kathleen, 'a man was dragging me out of the car and screaming "get the fuck out of here". Three of them then got into our car and drove off leaving me lying in the road.'[116] A witness in the house, hiding at the sound of gunfire, said she 'heard someone laugh' in the backyard just after the shooting and before the car sped away.[117] The UVF later claimed responsibility. When the RUC learnt of (and responded to) the shooting is a matter of dispute.[118] Tommy Casey's body would, though, be left cordoned off for some five hours. When one of Tommy's daughters, Collette, arrived she and her sister Martina found 'a lot of soldiers standing around and one of them said "Oh, we got him now!" Martina never had anything to do with politics, but I had to hold her back.'[119] 'Even with everything that had happened', says Janet Casey, 'you still never thought that they would actually have done it and killed him'.[120]

Republicans quickly accused the UDR and RUC of collusion in Tommy Casey's killing. 'There can be no doubt', Gerry Adams declared, given the record of death threats, that those involved were either from the security forces or 'acting on information received from those sources'.[121] However, suggestions that Tommy Casey may not have been the intended victim soon emerged – although if anything they reinforced the collusion allegations. It seems no one could have known the Caseys were due at the house that evening. They were not expected, nor do they appear to have been followed.[122] In the words of the local priest at the funeral, Tommy may have been 'in the wrong place at the wrong time'.[123] Yet the attack does appear to have been well planned. The house phone had been cut.[124] Two days before, a woman living in the house saw two figures, believed to be British soldiers carrying out surveillance, clambering over a low roof at the back of the house.[125]

The intended targets were likely two men, then dating the house owner's daughters, due to visit that evening. One was the brother of an IRA Volunteer killed in the Loughgall ambush. The other was Sean Anderson, recently released after serving a sentence for IRA membership and arms possession, who himself would soon be shot dead. Two weeks after Tommy Casey was killed, loyalists waited for over an hour at the same house in another ambush bid. When no one appeared they set the house on fire.[126] Sean Anderson was shot dead by gunmen in an ambush near his Pomeroy home almost exactly a year later.[127] Asked if there were any connections between the deaths of Tommy Casey and Sean Anderson, an RUC inspector simply noted that the latter 'was a frequent caller at the Mulgrew household'.[128] 'They were supposed to be there waiting for Sean Anderson', says Tommy Casey's daughter Janet, 'then when Daddy pulled up unexpectedly they probably panicked. But they also probably recognised Daddy and he was a target for them too. That's what I think happened.'[129] In October 1991 a planned unveiling of a monument to Tommy Casey in Kildress was cancelled when news came through of the killing of Sean Anderson.[130]

No one was convicted for killing Tommy Casey. The controversial book *The Committee* claimed that Tommy Casey was killed by Billy Wright and Robin Jackson.[131] At the time the RUC said it would 'prejudice' their investigations to confirm whether the weapon used to kill Tommy Casey was also used to shoot Sean Anderson. It had, and was later linked to some 16 other killings in North Armagh and East Tyrone from 1988 to 1994, suggesting these formed part of a distinct pattern.[132] Three years later Tommy Casey's name was found on a loyalist death list after an East Belfast loyalist was found in possession of British Army intelligence files.[133] There were more immediate, devastating and lethal repercussions. The East Tyrone IRA claimed they knew who was involved in killing Tommy Casey and would 'attack at every opportunity' those they suspected.[134] True or not, less than a week later the IRA killed a local part-time UDR man, Sergeant-Major Albert Cooper.[135] In reprisal the UVF shot dead Malachy McIvor, in similar circumstances to those of Albert Cooper, a few days later, using another of the South African weapons linked to so many other killings in the area.[136]

Inquests for Tommy Casey and Sean Anderson were held simultaneously.[137] In Tommy Casey's hearing the coroner ruled he would not allow questions to be raised about several other cars seen in the area at the time, because 'there was no evidence with regard to collusion'.[138] The Caseys long claimed that a local man saw a police car lead another on a 'dummy run' into the area, but was later threatened by members of the UDR and became afraid to make a statement.[139] This formed part of the investigation carried out by the Historical Enquiries Team (HET), a police unit set up to investigate unsolved conflict-related deaths. Their report confirmed an eyewitness said that he saw five RUC cars – and overheard on his car phone someone say 'there's fog in Moveagh, the roads are clear, do a good job tonight boys'.[140] Only in 2017 was it revealed that four members of the UDR were questioned about Tommy Casey's killing shortly after the attack. Records of what they were asked were among many destroyed at Gough Barracks in 1998. Later intelligence suggested that three of the UDR men had links to the UFF and UVF in Portadown.

The inquest also revealed that while the Casey's car, in which the gunmen made their getaway, had been found intact and not burnt out three hours after the shooting, no significant forensic evidence was apparently found.[141] Later reports have suggested that some forensic evidence in the case went missing.[142] It was unusual, in any case, for loyalists not to have their own means of escape. The car had been dumped close to where a local UDR man, Raymond Nicol, had been shot dead by the IRA in 1988.[143] This may have been symbolic. Another recent report suggests that a UVF unit, one of two operating in Mid-Ulster at the time – and including several UDR members – decided on a 'killing spree' after the death of Raymond Nicol. Their victims included not only Tommy Casey and Sean Anderson, but also Liam Ryan and Michael Devlin at the Battery Bar. It is claimed this UVF-UDR unit only ceased after calling a meeting with local republicans, in the wake of one of their own members being killed by the IRA, some time later.

The Killing of Patrick Shanaghan

On 11 August 1991, Patrick Shanaghan celebrated his 33rd birthday while working on the family farm in Aghnadoo, near the village of Killen, in a remote and isolated part of West Tyrone close to the border with Donegal.[144] The eldest of three, he now shared the large farmhouse only with his mother Mary, widowed six years earlier. He also worked at a local Department of the Environment depot, driving there and back in a distinctive yellow transit van.[145] Spare time was taken up crossing the hills behind the farm into Donegal on his motorbike, usually to pursue his abiding passion, Irish dancing. Never a player of Irish music, says his sister Anna, 'he took the dancing very seriously, set dancing, solo dancing, Sean-Nós; he knew all the dances'.[146] A year before he toured Norway with a local dancing group. 'He loved the warmness and friendship of ceilidhs', adds his other sister Mary Bogues, 'I remember waltzing with him; he was lovely waltzing'.[147] Patrick Shanaghan became a member of Sinn Fein in the wake of the hunger strikes, though the Shanaghans were not a republican family.[148] 'There was always a political side to him', says Mary, 'but he was always very calm, had his view and could back it up'.[149] He sometimes sold the republican newspaper, *An Phoblacht*, outside the local chapel on a Sunday, 'where the men would stand at the wall having a yarn'.[150] He also did some work around election times for Sinn Fein, in and around nearby Castletown, 'sticking up a few posters, knocking on a few doors, low-key stuff', says his brother-in-law Martin, 'Patrick would have gone along for the chat'.[151]

The morning after his birthday Patrick left for work as usual. At around 8.30 am, a masked gunman, waiting in a gateway two miles from the Shanaghan farm, fired 20 shots at the yellow van as it drove past. The gun was one of the South African shipment semi-automatic weapons.[152] Patrick was mortally wounded and declared dead by an RUC inspector shortly after. The van had crashed at the roadside and a hedge blocked the passenger door, so the RUC officer lent precariously in through a window to feel for a pulse, at first seeing no life-threatening injuries.[153] However, the police then (twice) prevented a local doctor – quickly on the scene – and a priest, from attending to Patrick.[154] There is evidence he was still alive. Eyewitnesses testified they saw his head and arm move, and that the RUC therefore wanted him left unattended to die from his wounds.[155] In addition, despite phone calls to the police initially describing the attack as a shooting, 'no ambulance was ever called to the crime scene'.[156] Only an hour later was a doctor allowed to see Patrick and officially pronounce him dead.[157]

The response and deployment of RUC officers after the shooting would raise concerns too. Several off-duty officers arrived, 'in their own car and in their own clothes', mere minutes later.[158] One RUC man recorded arriving at the scene 20 minutes *before* the shooting actually happened.[159] Nor, when they approached the body, did they appear to take standard precautions for fear of booby traps.[160] 'They just dashed in', says Mary, 'they tried to say they rushed to the scene because they thought it might have been another policeman who was shot. But if they thought it was a policeman the first thing they would have done was to phone an ambulance. Wouldn't they have got a helicopter? Can anyone in their right mind imagine they would have done anything else? But no ambulance ever came, and no helicopter. I am convinced they knew exactly what they were going to.'[161] Human rights groups also questioned the RUC's handling of the crime scene and forensic material.[162] The only eyewitness to the attack (the driver of a car who saw the shooting in his rear view mirror) was interviewed shortly after the attack, while still in shock. The RUC never contacted him again.[163]

These suspicions are rooted in the record of RUC threats and harassment to which Patrick Shanaghan had previously been subjected. They clearly seem to have thought he was something more than a sometime Sinn Fein worker. After claiming responsibility, the UFF said Patrick was in the IRA and involved with Eddie Fullerton in the killing of a Castlederg man months earlier – things the family fiercely deny. When asked by the Shanaghans to declare Patrick an innocent victim, the RUC refused.[164] For many years he had been regularly arrested, interrogated and harassed by the RUC and UDR. The Shanaghan farmhouse stood on a hill, at the end of a lane a quarter of a mile long, with the farm's fields on either side, off a quiet country road. He was sometimes stopped, held and searched as many as three times, by separate security force patrols, travelling the length of the lane.[165] Driving through the small town of Castlederg he was stopped three times by different RUC and UDR units.[166] Sometimes checkpoint stops lasted hours. The British Army and UDR patrolled round the farmhouse and would 'lay about the farm for several hours [sometimes] the whole day'.[167] The family home was searched 16 times between April 1985 and his death.[168] Nothing illegal was ever found. These searches, says Mary Bogues, were 'shocking, the stuff of nightmares; knocked out of bed with battering at the doors at six in the morning, then them rushing up the stairs. I don't know how my mum survived.'[169] The last raid came a month before Patrick was shot dead. The police photographed various rooms and the layout of the house.[170]

Between 1985 and 1991 Patrick Shanaghan was arrested and questioned by the RUC ten times, detained for a total of 42 days and, on six occasions, interrogated for four days or more.[171] Other prisoners knew he was in a neighbouring cell 'because they would have heard him doing his dancing, they could hear him doing his steps!'[172] He lodged several formal complaints against the RUC for threats, mistreatment and 'unlawful arrest'.[173] His statements record his having been physically abused, kicked, beaten and forced to stand in stress positions for 'hours on end'.[174] One interrogator told him 'an SAS type person [is] looking at you through the peep-hole this morning', another that 'loyalists in Castlederg know you now and they will get you'.[175] Witnesses testified to a catalogue of abuse and threats levelled against Patrick Shanaghan when in custody.[176] Others, that after he was killed, interrogators 'gloated over Paddy's death', using it as a form of intimidation. Former republican prisoner Sean McPeake (whose sister Kathleen O'Hagan was killed by loyalists in 1994) said one detective told him he would 'end up in a body bag' and they had 'set up Paddy Shanaghan [because] it was futile arresting him and dragging him in here continuously'.[177] Another said that interrogators, showing 'an extreme hate' for Patrick, told him they had him set up and 'a man of military experience … a crack shot' killed him, threatening his own details would be given to loyalists. His files later went 'missing'.[178]

Patrick Shanaghan tried to shield his family from the impact the raids and arrests had on him, but it took its toll on them all.[179] 'Each incident came and you just survived it', says Mary, 'Mummy could just about cope with things most of the time but whenever he had been arrested she literally just sat in the armchair and her whole body just shook; she was so nervous until he got home'.[180] The family also felt a growing sense that Patrick was being targeted. They were not alone. Worried about their own families, some friends became wary of contact.[181] A work colleague later recalled, 'nobody apart from myself was prepared to work with him, for fear of being shot'.[182] At the very least, this pattern of public harassment was marking out Patrick Shanaghan as a republican, isolating him from others and making him a target. There had already been an attempt to kill him. Eight shots were fired at him as he left his home one evening in 1989. He then watched 'a car travelling slowly away from the house'.[183] Although unhurt, Patrick considered moving away, in the end deciding to stay because 'he had done nothing wrong'.[184] 'He knew it was a possibility that something might happen', says Mary Bogues, 'he was calm, but it was just a horrible way to live'. Special Branch interrogators later threatened, 'we won't miss next time'.[185] The isolation of the farmhouse made any unfamiliar cars suspicious. The night before his death, a 'lovely day with good weather' spent bailing, his sister Mary and a neighbour were working with Patrick in a field when they spotted a car and heard a noise. 'One minute Paddy was beside me', says Mary, 'the next he had hopped over a ditch and in behind it. He just said "keep down" and I thought "what kind of life is this?"'[186]

In December 1990 the RUC told Patrick that 'security force documentation, containing information about him, including a photographic montage had accidentally fallen out of the back of an army vehicle'.[187] His solicitors tried to gain more information but heard nothing more until long after his death, and then merely that the intelligence file 'had been accidentally lost by the Army'.[188] Later again, and after European Court intervention, it emerged a British Army officer's combat jacket 'fell out of the rear doors' of a patrol vehicle, containing intelligence montages, including photos of Patrick Shanaghan. The jacket was not recovered. The officer was not disciplined.[189] As the European Court of Human Rights judgement noted, a situation where 'Patrick Shanaghan was shot and killed after photographs identifying him fell off the back of a lorry ... to borrow the words of the domestic courts, cries out for an explanation'.[190] In April 1991 the RUC told Patrick Shanaghan 'he was being targeted by loyalists'.[191] However, such warnings often 'look more like threats than any attempt to protect the victim'.[192] Indeed, it emerged at the inquest that the RUC officer who had delivered this warning, far from advising him on steps for his safety, stopped and searched Patrick Shanaghan in his van only half an hour later.[193]

The severe limits placed on inquests to investigate controversial killings were exacerbated by lengthy delays.[194] Such was the case after the death of Patrick Shanaghan, which was only fuelled further by an RUC attitude towards the family that was evident in their heavy-handed policing of the funeral and lack of contact thereafter.[195] Waiting five years before the inquest began left the Shanaghans 'with a sense of helplessness'.[196] When it finally was held, witness testimony of RUC threats was rejected, or in one case stopped, along with an independent forensic report, after an RUC appeal to a higher court. The appeal judgement reinforced the inquest's narrow remit to ask only 'by what means' death had occurred.[197] RUC death threats were judged 'not germane to the question of his death'. After lawyers questioned why doctors had been prevented from accessing the body, and why no ambulance had been called, a late police witness was belatedly produced, testifying that he had already checked and found Patrick dead. The court was filled with policemen. 'They were behind you, around you, it all became intimidating', says Anna Shanaghan, 'it would have been a great piece of theatre if it was not all so awful'.[198] The family withdrew when cross-questioning of police testimony was refused.[199] 'The whole thing was just terrible for the family', says Mary, 'when we found out the priest had been turned away that was really hard, that was really important to Mummy'.[200]

A complaint to the Independent Commission for Police Complaints followed. Despite 'rhetoric to the contrary', the much criticised police complaints system had changed little.[201] Effectively the RUC investigated itself. Making complaints was generally viewed as futile, but of those lodged the majority concerned counterinsurgency policing. Very few were upheld. Between 1979 and 1990 only 1 per cent of allegations of RUC harassment were 'substantiated'.[202] Reviewing police investigations fared little better. Despite this, the Shanaghan family formally questioned the investigation. They were left disappointed by its findings. The director of public prosecutions brought no prosecutions.[203] 'We never expected anything from the police', says Anna, 'in that at least we were not disappointed'.[204] But the family had many supporters, and in 1996 an unofficial international public inquiry, chaired by a US judge, was held, hearing testimony refused at the inquest. It concluded that Patrick Shanaghan had been killed 'with the collusion of the police' and called for the indictment of 'members of the Royal Ulster Constabulary from top to bottom'.[205] The Shanaghans would later take their case to the European Court of Human Rights in Strasbourg, which found against the British government under Article 2 ('the right to life') of the Human Rights Convention, casting an international light on the shadowy world of collusion. 'We knew the police had conspired against him', says Anna Shanaghan, 'and I want the truth about the awful things that happened to come out. But the important thing is to get the real, positive flavour of Patrick. I also want to show what a big, soft heart he had; what a gorgeous, optimistic, positive guy he was. That's how he got through all the dark days he had with the Army and the RUC.'[206]

The Killings of Tommy Donaghy and Malachy Carey

Loyalist killing of Sinn Fein workers as well as elected representatives was even more evident in South Derry. It also involved targeting former IRA prisoners. Just four days after the killing of Patrick Shanaghan, 38-year-old Tommy Donaghy was shot dead by the UFF as he arrived for work at the Portna Eel Fishery, near Kilrea in South Derry. He had joined the IRA in 1971, when just 18, and had been interned, released and returned to the IRA before turning 21. Sometime after that, after he was warned 'in a roundabout way' by a soldier during a house raid that 'the police had him marked down to be killed', he went 'on the run'.[207] In 1977 he was captured following a shoot-out with a British Army patrol near Slaughtneil. After his arrest he was severely beaten, then taken to Maghera police station. 'The police there asked the Army to take him back out to the spot he had been caught and shoot him', says Tommy's brother, Johnny – 'when they said they would not do that the police were fighting with each other to get at him. They called police in from other areas too, so even before he went to Castlereagh, they half-slaughtered him in the barracks'.[208] He was sentenced to 19 years for possession of weapons, IRA membership and attempting to kill members of the security forces, serving eleven years in the H-blocks before his release in late 1988.[209] After prison, Tommy Donaghy returned to the rural family home near Kilrea and his father found him work at the nearby fishery, on the banks of the Bann. Soon after, he and his girlfriend had a child, born just three months before he was killed. They moved in together in Kilrea, 'because he felt safer living in the midst of the town than driving back and forward in the country'.[210] Well recognised as a republican in the South Derry area, Tommy Donaghy also worked for Sinn Fein following his release.

The Donaghy family home was long subject to security force surveillance but, says Johnny Donaghy, in the lead-up to Tommy's death it was 'very, very heavy … genuinely never-ending'.[211] This involved raids into the farmyard by heavily armed special police units (DMSUs) and UDR roadblocks placed either side of the house; 'that went on more or less right up until he was killed'. On one occasion, while out walking his dog, Tommy uncovered British soldiers working on a surveillance camera. 'They were changing the batteries', says Johnny, 'when Tommy came up they held him at gunpoint till a helicopter came out from Kilrea and lifted them away'. On another, a UDR soldier took photos of Tommy

Donaghy after stopping him at a checkpoint. There were also death threats. 'In Castlereagh they said they would "put him in the way" of loyalists', says Johnny Donaghy, 'they said the same thing at roadblocks. A lot of people were getting that, so you did not always take it seriously, but if someone says they are going to be killed, and they are killed, then you realise they got them killed.' Much of the attention, says Johnny, was because the security forces had an 'exaggerated idea about Tommy that probably came from the police. That he was a dangerous character with arms and explosives at his workplace, which he hadn't. A few ordinary British soldiers said to him "weren't you the fella in the shoot-out with the SAS?"'

However, the pattern of surveillance changed in the few weeks prior to the shooting. There were far fewer roadblocks around the house. The RUC, army and UDR 'just completely stopped bothering him', says Johnny, 'as if he didn't exist at all. It may have made Tommy a bit off his guard'. At the same time, the family say, there was an intensification of security force operations that 'saturated' the area as a whole, with regular helicopter patrols and road blocks in and around Kilrea and neighbouring villages. To such an extent, continues Johnny, it was something he talked over with his brother the night before he was shot. 'We had been to a Sinn Fein meeting', he says, 'and he was dropping me off and we were discussing it, sitting wondering who was going to be killed. I know from someone this security "blitz" round the area all ended around midnight that night. Then, at 8.00 am the next morning, Tommy was shot dead. So we have always tied the two things in together.'[212]

According to eyewitnesses, that morning a distinctive 'vintage model' Rover car containing three men drove from Rasharkin, parking in a laneway near the fishery. Two men then crossed a footbridge over the river Bann and hid in a derelict house. When Tommy Donaghy drove his car into the works car park the gunmen emerged and shot him dead with a shotgun and revolver.[213] One witness said the gunmen then ran 'fairly hard' from the scene, though another is said to have watched them walking away, 'kind of laughing and joking'.[214] Another saw them, unrushed, get into a car and drive through Rasharkin. The car is said to have stopped near a crossroads as a 'long package' (possibly the weapons) was passed to someone waiting in a field.[215] The killing itself seems well planned. Four days earlier, a workman reportedly saw three men around the derelict building and the footbridge. Tommy Donaghy tended to arrive before anyone else, so usually there would have been no witnesses.[216]

News reports claimed the RUC set up 'road blocks on both sides of the river [Bann] shortly after the shooting'.[217] A Coleraine RUC inspector said he requested checkpoints on all routes, but the decision on where they were placed was taken by the RUC in Magherafelt.[218] The family believe no road blocks were established on the side of the river, or route, taken by the gunmen, or 'if they were, it was a long time after the event'.[219] Rather, they say, the only checkpoint established immediately was on the Derry bank of the river on a road in 'the complete opposite direction, the last way the gunmen would be going', heading towards the 'very nationalist area' of Swatragh. Johnny Donaghy was informed by the RUC of his brother's death and then went to the scene to identify him. 'That was a tough one', says Johnny, 'something you don't forget. Some of the police that were there would have been ones who would have been involved with the threats, so with that too, that was not easy.'[220] He later called publicly for no 'tit-for-tat' killings and condemned the targeting of all former prisoners, both 'Catholic and Protestant. You don't go about shooting somebody because he is a former prisoner or because of his religion. That to me is murder and serves no cause.'[221] The death of his brother, Johnny would later say, 'was like a sword going through the family'.

The RUC did not contact the Donaghys again. At the inquest in 1994, begun the same day as Bernard O'Hagan's, the coroner would not admit evidence of security force threats, while the Magherafelt head of CID added a handwritten note to his statement saying he was 'not aware of any threats to Mr Donaghy's life by members of the security forces'.[222] Even as this was taking place, say the family, a relative who lived across the road from the family home witnessed 'a police car stopping briefly outside our house and fire three rifle shots into the air, then it drove off towards Garvagh'.[223] Other issues emerged. Tommy's name had been found by the RUC on a loyalist death list in North Antrim in February 1991, but he received no warning.[224] There have also been allegations that several loyalists involved in the Castlerock and Greysteel shootings were seen regularly in and around Kilrea just before the killings of both Tommy Donaghy and Danny Cassidy. Some, it is alleged, were RUC informers. The weapons used to kill Tommy Donaghy were also employed in other killings, including the Castlerock massacre.

Malachy Carey was also a former republican prisoner and, at the time of his death in 1992, was a member of both Sinn Fein and the IRA. Early on the evening of 13 December 1992, he was waiting in the centre of Ballymoney for his girlfriend to finish work when two gunmen approached him. As he struggled with one of them, the gunman fired five shots, wounding Malachy, who died the next day. Brought up on a small hill farm in the remote area around Loughguile (a small nationalist rural enclave surrounded by unionist areas in North Antrim, close to the border with South Derry), he was arrested for arms possession and sent to the H-blocks in 1978 – though not before he got 'a real hiding from the local Constabulary at Ballymoney barracks', says his brother, Danny, 'and they took him to Castlereagh where things didn't get much better'.[225] In jail he spent three years on the blanket protest, until it was ended following the 1981 hunger strike.[226] For much of that time he shared a cell with Bobby Sands, OC of the IRA within the prison before he died on hunger strike. Malachy gained the nickname 'the suitcase' for his ability to smuggle items and communications to his cellmate inside his body.[227]

Released in 1987, Malachy Carey 'immediately re-joined the ranks of the IRA' and, as a well-known republican, also became active in Sinn Fein.[228] He stood in the 1989 local elections and, while unsuccessful, helped increase the party's strength locally. Security forces also suspected him of involvement in IRA attacks in the area, including the killing of two RUC men in a landmine attack about a year before his death. Threats of retribution followed. His mother was stopped by an RUC patrol and told he was 'on borrowed time' because of the killing of the two policemen.[229] Other family members were told the same. Shortly before he was killed, the RUC informed Malachy that his name was on a loyalist death list. There are some suggestions that Robin Jackson was one of the gunmen involved in the killing of Malachy Carey. Whatever the truth, the gun was the same as that used to kill Bernard O'Hagan. Unusually there was a conviction in this case. The getaway car driver received a life sentence for 'aiding and abetting' the shooting and was the first person convicted of UDA membership after it was very belatedly proscribed. Held on the Loyalist Volunteer Force (LVF) wing of the H-blocks, he was released under the Good Friday Agreement in 1998 and went on to become a development officer of the official agency charged with promoting Ulster-Scots culture and language. By then he was already a DUP party official in Ballymoney, even as the party continued to refuse to talk to Sinn Fein as 'unreconstructed terrorists'.[230]

The Shooting of Danny Cassidy

Like that of Patrick Shanaghan, Danny Cassidy's death came in the wake of a campaign of RUC public harassment that readily (and wrongly) identified him as a republican, and so potential loyalist target. He was shot dead on the afternoon of 2 April 1992. He had spent the day at his home in Kilrea, cutting logs then going to and fro delivering them locally.[231] He was sitting in his car chatting to a neighbour, only 200 yards from his home, when a car pulled up beside him. It contained four men dressed in boiler suits and balaclavas. They fired several shots, killing Danny Cassidy instantly. His son Nicholas was just returning from school. Seeing a crowd around his father's car, he ran home to tell his mother there had been an 'accident'. Danny's wife Emmanuelle knew things were worse as two neighbours came to their door. Rushing to the scene, she found her husband's face covered with a coat. Danny Cassidy was 40 years old at the time of his death, and left a widow and four children, aged between four and ten.

The UFF claimed responsibility shortly after, and that Danny Cassidy was in the IRA. This was immediately rejected by the family and others. Indeed, Emmanuelle Cassidy denies he was even in Sinn Fein. In the early 1980s Danny had been one of seven people charged for IRA-related activity on the evidence of the 'supergrass' Charles Dillon.[232] Held in Crumlin Road Gaol, he was released after Dillon retracted his statement. The case never went to trial. In February 1990 he was arrested along with Tommy Donaghy and taken for interrogation to Castlereagh. Again, no charges followed. However, a sustained campaign of harassment by the RUC did. In the wake of his death, Bishop Edward Daly (an ardent critic of the IRA) described the 'harassment that he suffered by the police [as] unjust and unfair', pointing to the 'danger of this kind of public harassment of an individual'.[233] Such 'special treatment by some units of the police', he continued, 'where he was publicly searched and spread-eagled on different occasions [was] irresponsible and wrong' and put his life in 'mortal danger'. Emmanuelle also complained that being 'regularly stopped by members of an RUC Mobile Divisional Support Unit (DMSU)' contributed to her husband's death.

These concerns were voiced even before Danny Cassidy was killed. He was threatened a couple of days before his death and, only a week earlier, local SDLP councillor John Dallat complained to the RUC of the 'continual harassment' of Danny Cassidy 'over a long period of time

[and] mostly in public places, especially the Diamond in Kilrea'. He also blamed DMSUs who 'visited the town on a regular basis' and gave Danny Cassidy 'undue attention'.[234] This level of police harassment, another source noted, meant that even though he was not in the IRA or Sinn Fein 'a lot of Protestants must have been convinced he was'.[235] Some suggested that a particular member of a DMSU was 'mistakenly convinced' Danny Cassidy was 'an important IRA player'. Reluctantly, the RUC agreed to investigate. Their findings were never published.

Several months later, in an echo of the circumstances surrounding the death of Loughlin Maginn, state intelligence photos of 20 republicans were sent to a local newspaper with the words 'UVF' written across them.[236] Among them was a photo of Danny Cassidy, leading to calls for an independent inquiry. Although Emmanuelle Cassidy had little faith in a process when 'it's obvious there has been collusion between my husband's murderers and the security forces [and] it's the RUC investigating the RUC'. Equally troubling was evidence that emerged at the inquest of an off-duty RUC man at the scene when the shooting happened. While accepting that he was present at the time, the RUC officer denied rumours he was following the route of the killers or had any involvement in the shooting.[237] The family was questioned about the killing in its immediate aftermath. The RUC also conducted a reconstruction ten days later. However, the Cassidys heard nothing about the investigation after that. When Danny's car was returned, after forensic tests had been carried out, they found a bullet still embedded. They handed it to the RUC. The guns used were, though, recovered, and found to have been employed before – in the attack on Tommy Donaghy. After their seizure, two UDR men were initially arrested, but soon released. No one was ever charged for killing Danny Cassidy.

Collusion and the Case of Eddie Fullerton

While not killed in Mid-Ulster, much connects the death of Donegal Sinn Fein councillor Eddie Fullerton with those that were – not least the fact that one of the weapons used to kill him was later used to shoot dead Danny Cassidy. Another was also used in the killing of Tommy Donaghy, and used again in both the Castlerock and Greysteel massacres.[238] Despite that, those later convicted for both Greysteel and Castlerock were never questioned about Eddie Fullerton's death. This was one of a catalogue of complaints the Fullerton family have made about the Gardaí investigation.[239] Likewise, if UVF units dominated the killings that took place in East Tyrone, victims in South Derry more often died at the hands of the UFF, as was the case with Eddie Fullerton. His death was also linked to that of Patrick Shanaghan a few months later. Both were accused of involvement in the killing of Castlederg man Ian Sproule, something denied by the Fullertons and the Shanaghans. Eddie was alleged to have passed a Gardaí intelligence file on Sproule to the IRA – an accusation the Gardaí themselves deny.[240] The killing of Eddie Fullerton is also linked to others in the Mid-Ulster area because, in many ways, this is one of the starkest and most striking cases of collusion involving the death of an elected member of Sinn Fein.

In the early hours of 25 May 1991, four gunmen broke into the Fullerton home in Buncrana, a seaside town a few miles over the border from Derry.[241] Reminiscent of the killing two years before of Gerard Casey, they sledgehammered the door as Eddie and his wife Diana lay in bed. Eddie had not long returned from a late-night meeting, so the gunmen likely had the home under surveillance.[242] They also appeared to know the layout of the house, heading straight for the bedroom. Despite having received death threats, given the apparent relative safety of Donegal the Fullertons had not installed the gates and bars that were, by now, common in the homes of Sinn Fein officials in the North. However, awoken by the noise, Eddie Fullerton came onto the landing to confront the gunmen. In the ensuing struggle he was shot five times. Diana remembered hearing five or six shots, but the last 'stuck in her mind. There was like a silence and somebody said "come on" and then there was two shots.'[243] The gunmen then fled. When Diana came out of the bedroom 'Eddie was lying on the floor … blood everywhere'. In the immediate aftermath, current DUP MP Sammy Wilson, then a Belfast city councillor, called for the council to offer it's congratulations to 'those who had done a good job on two sides of the border' after the killing of Eddie Fullerton.[244]

Aged 56, and married with six grown-up children, Eddie Fullerton had been a councillor for twelve years, seen by Sinn Fein as a 'stalwart … who created the organisation in Inishowen'.[245] Originally from Donegal, the builder and businessman had spent many years working in England before moving back with his family from Birmingham to Buncrana in 1976. His electoral support had always come from campaigning on social and economic, as well as political, issues. He long worked to improve local water supplies through the building a new dam – approved shortly before, and constructed after, his death – that now bears his name.

Several features of Eddie Fullerton's death were highly unusual. First, it was the only loyalist killing during a ten-week-long ceasefire. Even more striking, it required loyalists making an extremely rare venture across the border into the Republic to carry out a targeted lethal attack. Nothing quite like it happened before or after. Certainly, it was a pattern alien to the usual activities of Derry-based loyalists. A month later the IRA would, however, shoot dead Cecil McKnight, a leading UDA member in Derry, who they said was responsible for organising Eddie Fullerton's killing. Another Derry loyalist, Gary Lynch, was killed by the IRA in the city the following August.[246] A year before, Eddie Fullerton had received a tarot card death threat from the 'Maiden City Action Force'; a cover name for the UDA in the city. However, whatever the involvement of Derry city loyalism, Eddie Fullerton's killing was a far from local affair. Evidence suggests many of the UFF gunmen came from much further afield. It had the hallmarks of an extremely well-planned attack, carried out by people with skill and knowledge. Their ability to get in and out of Donegal without being detected caused the greatest suspicion of collusion. So too did their apparently detailed knowledge of the local area and the Fullerton home.

A leading UDA man from South Belfast was long suspected of directing the killing, as well as being an MI5 agent.[247] Another, believed to have been one of the gunmen, was a senior South Belfast loyalist known as the 'gravedigger'. There are suggestions Billy Wright was also involved. A fourth, identified as Ned Greer, is said to have worked for the FRU, brought into the UDA by John McMichael (like Brian Nelson) to become a leading figure of loyalism in Lisburn.[248] After being seen driving into an army base in December 1993, Greer would be 'spirited away in the dead of night' by his FRU handlers. In the early hours, removal vans took away all he owned, as he and his family were 'taken to an unknown destination across the Irish Sea' – not, however, before he is believed to have been party to the shooting of Eddie Fullerton. While not directly involved, he was 'fully aware' of the attack and 'all the players sent to Donegal for the killing'. As Brian Nelson provided intelligence to the UFF in North and West Belfast, so Greer is said to have given 'information gleaned from his own FRU handlers' to the UDA in South Belfast.[249] Along with detail provide by the UDR, such intelligence is also believed to have been used in targeting Patrick Shanaghan two months later.

The attack itself was carried out with a 'level of professionalism' untypical of many UFF killings, amid allegation they were helped by the security forces.[250] Four masked men, dressed in clothing that would 'leave no forensic trace', held the owners of a nearby B&B hostage in the lead-up to the attack.[251] It is believed the UFF unit had earlier been transported across the Foyle into Donegal in two high-speed dinghies, before being driven in two cars to Buncrana. Afterwards, they were taken out, again at high speed, in two different directions. An eyewitness would later testify they saw 'three people behaving suspiciously dressed in paramilitary type attire', in the early hours of the morning, close to where one getaway car was found burnt out near the border.[252] The three were then 'picked up' in an 'RUC unmarked car', before being 'driven in the direction of a British Army checkpoint on its way into Derry city'. The police on both sides of the border would take little notice of this testimony. The considerable failings of the Gardaí inquiry and subsequent investigations, as well as a lack of cooperation by the PSNI, have ensured that a number of key suspects, including those convicted for their part in the Castlerock and Greysteel killings, cannot now be charged.[253] 'At best', says Eddie Fullerton's daughter Amanda, 'this was total Gardaí incompetence, but at worst there was Gardaí collusion in the cover-up of my father's murder'.[254] No one has ever been convicted for killing Eddie Fullerton.

7
Instilling Fear: Targeting Republican Families and Communities

It was like it was even better for them to get family members, to kill a brother or a nephew, because it had even more impact.[1]

'See No Evil' and 'Breakfast Table' Collusion

Just after 10.00 pm on 18 June 1994, two masked, armed UVF gunmen entered the Heights Bar in the small townland of Loughinisland in Co. Down. The tiny, rural pub was packed with locals, their eyes glued to the television watching what proved to be the Republic of Ireland's historic win over Italy in the opening game of the football World Cup at the Giants Stadium in New Jersey. Given its location the gunmen could be assured that most (if not all) of those inside would be Catholics. The attackers opened fire, one with an automatic rifle, shooting dead six men and seriously injuring five others, leaving behind a scene of utter carnage. 'There were bodies piled on top of each other', one eyewitness recounted, 'It was like a dream; a nightmare'.[2] Those killed, mostly middle-aged family men (the youngest, father-of-two Adrian Rogan, was 34; the eldest, Barney Green, was 87), were all from in and around Loughinisland, a village that had seen little enough of the Troubles.[3] None had any political or paramilitary connections.

The Loughinisland massacre was one of a wave of loyalist bar attacks and mass killings that rose even as the IRA moved towards a ceasefire, declared just two months later, and Northern Ireland embarked upon the peace process that would ultimately see an end to 30 years of conflict. For the first time in decades, the year leading up to the Loughinisland attack had seen loyalists kill more people than anyone else – due in no small part to the substantial rearming of loyalism.[4] The recent, damning Police Ombudsman report into Loughinisland has found substantial evidence of widespread collusion in the massacre.[5] One of the weapons used was part of the 1987 South African arms shipment. The report is scathing in its criticism of the role played by British intelligence and RUC Special Branch in allowing these weapons to get into loyalist hands. More immediately, the desire of the local RUC to protect informants impacted on 'policing activity' and 'undermined the police investigation' into Loughinisland itself.[6] An 'intelligence mind-set' deferred or stopped criminal investigation and demonstrated a 'disregard for the suffering of the families involved at the hands of loyalist paramilitary gangs'.[7] Evidence of an increasingly active UVF unit operating in the Co. Down area was all but ignored by the local RUC, whose attention remained 'almost entirely' fixed on the IRA.[8] As a direct result, the nationalist community faced a 'heightened risk' of attack.[9] Republicanism was the enemy; loyalism, at the very least, far less so.

Worse, both the RUC and the UDR in the area had been 'compromised', through either 'direct involvement with loyalist paramilitaries, associations or sympathies'.[10] At least three members of the UVF unit involved in the Loughinisland massacre were members of the UDR.[11] Another, identified years earlier as an 'active loyalist terrorist' and the 'main organiser and planner' of attacks, was a former member of the UDR who had previously provided UDR files and photo montages and was suspected of involvement in earlier loyalist attacks. He continued in the UDR for several months after this came to light, attending 'RUC/UDR briefings', before resigning.[12] Such things were not unknown to the RUC or its senior officers. Several local UVF members were identified as having 'connections to the security forces' on the eve of the Loughinisland attack.[13] This included having 'close family members' working within the RUC.[14]

The police investigation into the massacre was a catalogue of catastrophes.[15] 'Corrupt' relations led to a 'leak' by a police officer of the imminent arrest of members of the South Down UVF in the wake of the Loughinisland killings, followed by an 'inexcusable' decision never to investigate the leak.[16] Several men suspected of involvement within hours of the attack were not questioned until weeks, months, sometimes years later.[17] The former UDR man reported as being a key UVF organiser in South Down was identified as a suspect within a day of the massacre, yet was not arrested for questioning until over two months later.[18] Within hours the getaway car was found abandoned close to his home and that of another key suspect. Other houses in the area were 'visited' but, inexplicably, theirs were not.[19] And so it goes on. Such delays ensured that any opportunities to find the culprits responsible for the Loughinisland attack were lost. Up to the present, no one has ever been charged or convicted for direct involvement in the Loughinisland killings. Their connections to the security forces likely afforded protection to some. Some of the loyalists involved in carrying out the Loughinisland massacre may also have been protected as police informers. Despite their supposed role in aiding the police in preventing such violence, senior loyalist 'sources' were not pressed to find out what they could about the killings, in case they implicated themselves in wrongdoing.[20] Suspected involvement in the gunning down of six innocent men did not bar someone from working on behalf of the state afterward. One 'legitimate suspect' continued to act as an RUC informer for many years to come.[21]

This was a social milieu where collusion appears to have been an endemic feature of policing – and one not only conditioned by the logic of counterinsurgency and the 'grey zone' of handling informers. It also stemmed from the long-term sectarianised character of state and society in the North; not least in the countryside. Most analyses of sectarian division and segregation (and its relationship to conflict and violence) have focused on the major cities of Belfast and Derry.[22] However, such divisions, deeply rooted in a history of conquest, appropriation and settlement, have always been just as stark and real in many rural areas of the North, if often all but invisible to those less attuned to the signs, signals and local social knowledge of the sectarian habitus.[23] Nor were they simply the product of 30 years of conflict. A complex of segregated social and kinship networks, and the everyday negotiation of interactions and distance between religiously defined communities of 'neighbours' and 'strangers', was a feature of life in the pre-conflict rural North.[24] These separate worlds found institutional expression in the pivotal communal role of various churches, social institutions (like the Orange Order and the GAA) and local political loyalties, fostered to cut across divisions of status and class. Nor have such divisions disappeared. Despite important changes, for many a contemporary landscape of spatial, social and institutional separation in rural areas is a 'continuing legacy of the troubles'.[25]

During the conflict such divisions were all the more acute and relations tense. A study of two villages – one overwhelmingly Catholic the other Protestant – in Co. Armagh in the 1990s, demonstrated the everyday lack of contact and avoidance of people from the other community – the tendency to 'stick to your own', and how this had been accentuated by the 'devastating impact' of the conflict.[26] The social make-up of loyalist paramilitaries in rural areas often differed from urban areas. The UVF in small towns and villages often came from the very same 'respectable' rural social groups, classes and family networks as were the members of the RUC and UDR. For veteran Tyrone-based political activist Bernadette McAliskey, victim of the loyalist attack in 1981, this was a recipe for 'breakfast table' collusion.[27] Where loyalists and the RUC and UDR were drawn from 'the same population, the same communities, the same families' the social order of sectarianism and the structure of locally recruited security forces could meld together. Such socially embedded networks of family and community, of separation and division, could be mobilised in the organisation and conduct of campaigns of violence. This was as true of the family trees that branched through and bound together the UVF in border areas like East Tyrone and South Armagh, as it did the IRA in those self-same places. They were also, though, defined by the broader organisation of social and political power and their relationship to the institutions of the northern state. After partition (indeed even before) these social divisions were replicated and reflected in the political order and in policing.

Wars of Attrition

Loyalists happily declared that their campaign of attacks on nationalist communities (even more so republican families) was designed to instil fear. What relationship this had to the logic of state counterinsurgency is less obvious. Counterinsurgency conforms to what Elaine Scarry understands as the essential aim of war: not simply military victory but the 'unmaking of the world' of the 'other'. In other words, to employ power and violence to reverse the other's self-image of acting in the world and undermine the enemy will to resist.[28] 'Terrorism', in turn (though a fraught, ideologically-loaded term), if anything, involves inflicting harm on 'innocents', and instilling fear in others, as a violent political tactic.[29] This can be as true of the actions of states as of non-state groups.[30] Loyalist killings, whether in terms of pub massacres such as Loughinisland, or of attacks targeted at republican families, were undoubtedly intended to undermine a 'will to resist'. However, they were also, of course, demonstrably and unarguably unlawful. 'Set-piece' legal fictions had little legitimacy where 'non-combatants' were deliberately targeted – not least because the principle of 'non-combatant immunity' is enshrined in the laws of war, and its breach is also a definition of 'terrorism'.[31] If nationalist communities, or republican families, were the target of loyalist attack, any state support, connivance or collusion had therefore to be all the more readily deniable.

In the late 1980s and early 1990s loyalists undoubtedly targeted a broad swathe of nationalists and republican families in Mid-Ulster. Allegations of collusion surround many such deaths. The apparent logic was precisely to wear down morale, instil fear and isolate republicans within their own communities. In relatively remote rural areas, associating with republicans and their families came to be seen as an increasingly dangerous affair; the focus, then, was as much on the social and psychological reverberations of violence as the act itself. At the very least, this is hardly alien to counterinsurgency thinking, though ensuring that the issue of adherence to the rule of law once more takes centre stage. In several cases (it should be said) where republican family members died, the primary target may have been republican combatants or political representatives. So, for example, when Phelim McNally was shot dead in 1988, he was in the house of his brother, a Sinn Fein councillor. Likewise, when Frank Hughes was abducted in his taxi in 1990, it may have been instead of his republican son, Eamonn. After shooting dead the seven-month-pregnant Kathleen O'Hagan in her home in front of her children, her killers declared that if her (republican ex-prisoner) husband Paddy had been there, 'they'd also have killed him'. Jimmy Kelly, one of four men shot dead at Castlerock, was a leading IRA man in South Derry.

Yet these cases show, too, that if assassinating a republican was not possible a dead relative would do. Phelim McNally was shot on the ground to ensure he was dead. Frank Hughes' innocence did not stop him being killed and his body left in his burnt-out car. Kathleen O'Hagan's assassins had no compunction in shooting her as she sat, terrified, in a corner of the room. Indeed, the killing of Kathleen O'Hagan shows much more besides. As the last republican family victim in this period, her death is the endpoint of a rising tide of attritional violence – a killing that touched a 'raw nerve' and 'shocked the unshockable', coming less than two months after the Loughinisland massacre.[32] Around midnight on the night of 7 August 1994, UVF gunmen broke into the O'Hagan's isolated home on a country road near Greencastle, Co. Tyrone. They shot Kathleen multiple times in her bedroom.[33] Her heavily pregnant body slumped dead beside the cot of her 15-month-old son. The wall above the cot was riddled with bullets. The other four children (all under eight) were found a short time later by their father, huddled around her, hiding under bedclothes, too terrified to raise the alarm. 'Bad boys were here and broke the glass', Paddy recalled one of his sons saying, 'Mummy's shot and she's in heaven'.[34] Damian O'Hagan, then seven, would remember the sound of his mother begging for her life just before she was killed.[35] It was 'mayhem, a scene from hell', says Kathleen's sister-in-law Charity McPeake, 'so Paddy bundled the kids in the car and took them away. He was afraid they were going to come back and kill them all'.[36]

Kathleen was from a well-known republican family, the McPeakes, from Ballynease, near Bellaghy, South Derry. This likely made her a loyalist target in her own right. Her brother Sean lost a leg in 1976 when transporting an IRA bomb (alongside future hunger striker Thomas McElwee) that exploded prematurely. She met her husband-to-be Paddy O'Hagan while visiting Sean in jail. The two men shared a cell during the blanket protest. When Paddy got out of jail, the couple married and set up home in a remote part of Tyrone, where Paddy's own family lived. After receiving a series of threats they had shutters installed on the windows and a heavy grille placed across the stairs in case of attack. On the night of the shooting, Paddy O'Hagan went to a local pub for a family party, only leaving the house around 11.00 pm. Several British Army checkpoints around the area, in place earlier, had now gone. 'They had the whole area sealed off. Then they were all lifted around the time the shooting happened', says Sean McPeake.[37] After the attack, Paddy took the children back to the pub where he had been and phoned the police at around 1.30 am. The police did not then arrive until 4.00 am. The gunmen were long gone, a burnt-out getaway car not found until much later and by local people. An army helicopter had failed to see the car alight a mile from the O'Hagan's home.[38] No one was ever arrested or convicted for killing Kathleen O'Hagan. There are allegations the attack was set up by Billy Wright and outstanding calls for security force collusion in her death to be properly investigated.

The UVF claimed Kathleen's killing was in retaliation for the Teebane massacre in which they said she had been involved, something her family vehemently deny. 'She was not involved in anything like that', says Charity McPeake, 'she had too many babies to look after'.[39] 'Shooting her, there', adds Sean McPeake, 'they got at us, her family, and Paddy both. Letting us all know. There were a lot of bad shootings like that around the area then; building up pressure on a lot of families.'[40] If the attritional intent behind the killing of Kathleen O'Hagan was to intensify a sense of widespread fear against the backdrop of the emerging peace process – the IRA ceasefire was called just three weeks later – it achieved its end. Bernie McKearney, who had recently lost both her husband and parents to loyalist attacks, would recall, in the wake of Kathleen's death, feeling genuinely afraid for the first time throughout the Troubles.[41] 'I remember thinking to myself', said Bernie, 'well if they kill women now, why would they not kill me, here on my own, with the children?'

In many cases relatives were clearly the intended target. That was so when Bernie's husband Kevin and his uncle Jack McKearney were shot dead in the family butcher's shop in Moy, and when loyalists went into the home of her aged parents, Charlie and Teresa Fox. Here, killing relatives was the point, instilling fear the unadorned purpose. Indeed, the effect of killing the relative of a republican could be even greater, often leaving a legacy of deep-seated remorse, guilt and shame. Others died, not as family members, but because they kept company with republicans. The men killed alongside Jimmy Kelly at Castlerock were shot as his fellow workers. 'There was a lot of guilt by association', says Poilin Quinn, people were told 'by the RUC and UDR "if you're going to hang around with them we're going to give you a hard time too". It was a policy to try to isolate people.'[42] The net of collective, communal culpability could be spread wider still. The 1997 LVF shooting in South Derry of Sean Brown – a prominent community figure, a GAA man, but no 'republican' – came in the wake of a local Sinn Fein electoral victory.[43]

The killing of republican family members was particularly acute in East Tyrone. Journalist Ed Moloney has argued that this was, in part, the result of a 'new, restrained retaliation policy' on the part of the IRA, limiting their ability to respond in kind. In turn, he argues, this followed the damage done to Sinn Fein's electoral strategy, amid the angry public response to the 1987 IRA bombing of the Remembrance Day ceremony in Enniskillen.[44] Sinn Fein's 'concentric circle' strategy to expand support was dealt a 'body blow'. So, preventing attacks seen as sectarian became a greater political priority.[45] Reprisals for the deaths of republican relatives, it is argued, had now to involve targeting the loyalists directly responsible. The IRA in East Tyrone, it is suggested, was then less effective in deterring attacks, their families increasingly vulnerable as a result. Here too, says one senior local republican, while 'the SAS went for IRA members, the UVF went for their families'.[46]

There is much that links these attacks with those targeting republican combatants and political representatives. Not least in terms of who may have been involved and the weapons used. For example, the gun used to kill Phelim McNally was used again a year later to shoot dead Michael Devlin and Liam Ryan in nearby Ardboe. Much such evidence has only latterly come to light, even if the weapons had often been recovered by the police decades earlier.[47] Certainly a sense of threat felt by Mid-Ulster republican families seems to have grown considerably during this time. 'You definitely had a sense it was becoming a family thing', says Malcolm Nugent's sister Siobhan, 'it was like it was even better for them to get family members, to kill a brother or a nephew, because it had even more impact'.[48]

The Shooting of Phelim McNally

The first such killing of a republican relative in East Tyrone was that of 28-year-old Phelim McNally on the night of 24 November 1988. While his family were republican, says his brother Henry, Phelim 'wasn't interested in politics'.[49] A 'very good musician, a good singer', the local accordion band to which he belonged provided the Honour Guard at Phelim's funeral. He was also a devoted family man, raising his five children in the village of Moortown, on the banks of Lough Neagh. All his children were under nine years old and, on the night of his death, Phelim was on his way back to the local hospital, where his wife Pauline was expecting their sixth child. He had only left around 9.30 pm to drop back home and check all was well, intending to return later. On the way he stopped briefly to light a candle in a local chapel and then visit his brother, Francie, at his recently built home, on a country road near Coagh, Co. Tyrone.[50]

Francie McNally was a well-known local republican and Sinn Fein councillor. Another brother, Lawrence, was a senior member of the IRA, close to Jim Lynagh, who would be killed along with two others in an SAS ambush in Coagh in 1991.[51] Tensions locally had been running high and there was a 'lot of tit-for-tat. In the area at that time it was really like it was between two families. People more or less knew who was doing what and what was happening.'[52] This was a starkly divided area. The nearby village of Coagh was overwhelmingly unionist – the surrounding area, nationalist. Violence was increasing too. Only 24 hours earlier, an IRA bomb, planted outside the RUC station in the small village of Benburb, killed 67-year-old Barney Lavery and his 13-year-old granddaughter.[53] Several months before, local man Ned Gibson, married with a three-year-old daughter and part-time member of the UDR, had been shot dead while on his round as a refuse collector. The suspicion was that Francie McNally – believed by the police to be the leader of the IRA in the area – used his role on the council to know where Ned Gibson would be.[54] 'The Troubles were really bad at that time around our area', says Henry McNally, and Ned Gibson's death 'was the start of the whole thing. Ordinary people were being targeted but key figures like Sinn Fein councillors, like Francie, were definitely targets. There were boiling points in the way things were going round here.'[55] When Ned Gibson's name was mentioned, continues Henry, 'I remember Phelim saying "he was another woman's child". That was his answer; he had no interest in politics.'

Francie McNally would later state that he had received death threats numerous times from UDR soldiers at checkpoints, and while detained and interrogated in Gough Barracks.[56] One RUC officer was under investigation for an alleged death threat at the time Phelim was shot. Earlier that day, UDR patrols had twice passed Francie McNally's home, apparently staking out the house, and spent 'several hours searching around outside'.[57] The suspicion is they were 'clearing the area in preparation for an attack'.[58] Francie McNally was stopped several times at UDR checkpoints throughout the day. When stopped again, outside the police station in Cookstown, he says that a senior RUC officer 'asked me was I going home ... I was taken out of the car three times and asked the same question again ... was I sure I was going home'.[59] Francie would be in little doubt that 'it was me they were going for' when his brother was killed, and that the UDR was involved.[60]

Phelim arrived at Francie's home just after 10.00 pm.[61] 'He and I were just sitting chatting in the kitchen', says Francie McNally. Phelim had been playing the accordion, then 'I heard a slight tapping on the kitchen door'.[62] Given previous threats, Francie had precautions in place. 'The back door and the front door would be locked', says Henry McNally, 'so you had to knock and give a signal to get in. He would have all the windows closed. There was just one window open that night, the kitchen window, at the gable of the house'.[63] Getting up to switch off the light, Francie saw 'a figure crouched down' moving towards the front of the house. He switched on lights outside and saw 'the car with a driver sitting in it wearing a balaclava'. 'Phelim had put down the accordion and got up to see out the window what was going on', says Henry McNally, 'just a normal instinct'.[64] At that point Francie heard shooting. 'Before I had time to shout or say anything to Phelim', Francie told reporters, 'I heard what sounded like two bursts of heavy automatic fire, then I saw my brother lying on the floor'.[65] 'He was taking his last breaths as I reached him', he later remembered, 'the next day I actually picked up empty shells which were lying below the window. I believe one of the two gunmen had leaned in through the window to finish Phelim off as he lay dying in the kitchen.'[66] He had been shot seven times.[67]

An ambulance and local doctor arrived within minutes, the RUC not till some three hours later, blaming the delay on heavy fog and fear of IRA attack.[68] 'If you were in a police patrol', says Henry McNally, 'you would know everything inside 30 seconds, but it took three hours. The RUC sergeant in Coagh, two miles away, got word soon after the shooting but didn't get to Francie's house until ten to one.'[69] The inquest papers confirm the timings.[70] The RUC in Cookstown received a call at 10.30 pm and, at Coagh, five minutes later, but 'security precautions' prevented their arrival till 12.45 am.[71] As Phelim's son, Kevin McNally, wryly comments, 'that was some brave security situation they were going through before they got there'.[72] A nearby RUC mobile patrol, notified within minutes, did not arrive to 'commence the scene log' until over two and a half hours later.[73] Nor is there any evidence of vehicle checkpoints being put in place, which was standard procedure following a shooting. 'It's not as if they had to drive from one end of Belfast to the other', adds another son, Lawrence. 'This is rural Tyrone. Usually they would have been there within seconds. Even if they were taking security measures, getting back up from Cookstown, that is only ten minutes away. If you look at other shootings in the area, there is no way it takes them that long.'[74] At the same time, Henry McNally was told of his brother's shooting within minutes. He immediately drove to Francie's house but was 'stopped by the UDR three times coming down the road from Ardboe. My place was saturated with UDR, so they had no problems going there.'[75]

By then, the gunmen had made their getaway.[76] Twenty minutes before the shooting, three armed men had taken a car near Coagh, one telling the courting couple inside, in a calm measured tone, 'not to move for an hour'.[77] It was found the next morning parked outside Coagh Orange Hall, the lodge to which Ned Gibson had belonged.[78] The RUC found 'nothing to link the car with the murder'.[79] Empty bullet shells were missed at the McNally house.[80] The revolver used in the shooting (and later of Michael Devlin and Liam Ryan) was a UDR weapon. 'The guy with the revolver shot him while he was lying on the ground', says Kevin

McNally, 'the way he did it was saying "you know who's done this". It was a signal, with a UDR gun. Everybody in the parish knew who walked in and did it because they were from not far away.'[81]

Both the Mid-Antrim UDA and the 'Protestant Action Force' claimed responsibility for the killing.[82] The latter was a *nom-de-guerre* sometimes used by the UVF including, notoriously, by the Glennane Gang in the 1970s and the Mid-Ulster UVF under the leadership of Robin Jackson and Billy Wright, including after the killing of Frank Hughes in October 1990.[83] As in the case of Gerard Casey, neither call claiming responsibility could provide a recognised code word.[84] No arrests or convictions followed. The inquest refused to look at the issue of death threats or collusion allegations.[85] The British Army would not comment on allegations of UDR threats because 'the matter was under police investigation'. The RUC in turn would not discuss the movement of security force patrols.[86] Nothing then happened. The only contact the family had with any investigation was when Henry McNally had to identify his brother's body.[87] When asked to go to Cookstown police station, the policemen on the gate 'burst out laughing' when he told them he was there about his dead brother. The eight-year-old Kevin McNally found out his father was dead in the early hours of the morning, not long after his uncle had identified his body in one local hospital.[88] In another, a few miles away and a couple of hours later, Pauline McNally gave birth to their youngest son, Christopher. Only afterwards was she told Phelim was dead.[89] 'With a baby still in the hospital and five bits of weans to rear', one relative asked, 'what does she do now?'[90]

The Killing of Frank Hughes

Sixty-one-year-old Frank 'Francie' Hughes was not a member of any political organisation. Like most of his family he was not even a republican, though his son Eamonn was 'an IRA Volunteer for most of his adult life'.[91] Frank Hughes was killed because he was Eamonn's father. 'Frank wouldn't have had any political allegiance at all', says Eamonn's wife Eileen, 'I suppose he had his own beliefs, but whatever they were he kept them very much to himself. He was just a big, quiet, inoffensive man.'[92] Frank Hughes worked as a stonemason, carving headstones, and ran a small taxi and wedding car business with his two sons in his native Dungannon. 'He was always a very hardworking man', continues Eileen, 'always had a lot of regular customers, a good clientele. He used to taxi for both sides.'[93] At around 10.30 pm on the night of 23 October 1990, Frank Hughes went to pick up a woman who had booked a cab from a local hotel, calling herself Mary Fox.[94] A week earlier, someone giving the same name had tried to book a cab from a nearby pub, but the Hugheses had been too busy.[95] This time Frank Hughes picked up the fare. He was never seen alive again.

A few hours later the family learnt Frank was missing. Eamonn was at home and got a call to take a regular taxi run when his father failed to turn up.[96] Around 2.00 am his mother, Norah, phoned to say Frank had still not returned. Eamonn and his brother John began to search the route of his suspected last fare, thinking he may have had an accident. An increasingly frantic Eamonn Hughes tried to contact his father on the two-way radio. There was no response.[97] He began to suspect something terrible had happened. At 3.00 am the brothers contacted the RUC. When he entered the local police station Eamonn would later recall the 'colour draining from the face' of the duty officer as if 'taken aback' to see him alive, and then 'apathetic and dismissive' in dealing with the news of Frank's disappearance.[98] The brothers waited there for several hours but no news came that night.[99] Along with neighbours, they continued the search, 'covering the same ground in daylight as we had covered in darkness', but found no trace.[100] The family hoped, in vein, that Frank's taxi had been hijacked for a bomb attack.[101] At 9.30 am the next morning Frank's car was found, burnt out and smouldering, near derelict farm buildings on a rural road just off the motorway between Dungannon and Portadown.[102] It had been seen alight at 11.00 pm the night before. An hour after being alerted, a lone plain clothes RUC officer arrived and found the badly burnt body inside. A further hour later, a crime scene was finally formally established.[103]

It appears Frank Hughes had picked up 'Mary Fox' and then driven the 13 miles to where his body was later found. His assailants lay in wait and shot him, before setting the car alight with Frank (possibly still alive) inside. His body was only identified by his watch and door key.[104] The Hughes family first found out through a phone call from a local newspaper that afternoon. Only after were they contacted by the RUC.[105] By then, the 'Tyrone Protestant Action Force' said they had shot Frank Hughes, claiming it was in retaliation for an IRA killing of a Protestant taxi driver and UVF member in West Belfast that day.[106] They also claimed their victim was a 'well-known republican'.[107] Reports linked it to other recent, nearby deaths, some carried out by the 'Protestant Action

Force', in which Billy Wright was believed to have been involved.[108] This dominant retaliatory narrative was, however, countered by the efforts of 'Mary Fox' to have booked a taxi many days earlier.[109] Rather, the original aim was likely to lure Eamonn Hughes to his death. However, as with 'a number of other murders where the intended victim was not present', said the HET report into Frank's killing, 'another person was murdered'.

Although never convicted, the RUC long suspected Eamonn Hughes of being in the IRA and, as well as the target of death threats, he feared his details had been 'leaked' to loyalists. The RUC may also have had prior intelligence of a specific threat against him, though this was withheld.[110] Eamonn Hughes had used his father's car on the day of the attack, before they swapped back again. He suspected security forces may have passed on information that it would be him in the car that evening.[111] While first denied, evidence later emerged that RUC men in an unmarked car were in the hotel car park when Frank picked up 'Mary Fox'.[112] The RUC then stated they had been on routine patrol, while the officers themselves, claiming they had 'forgotten they were there', were never questioned.[113] This was a pattern of coincidence paralleled in other killings, including those of Kevin and Jack McKearney in Moy and Danny Cassidy in Kilrea. Indeed, Eamonn Hughes long believed a second RUC car was present at the time, although the HET investigation found no record of other RUC or UDR personnel in the area.[114] There were also claims a researcher for the documentary *The Committee* was told that Frank Hughes had driven past a UDR patrol after being in the hotel car park. The patrol (it was claimed) then radioed the waiting UVF unit that it was not Eamonn Hughes in the car, but was told 'let him come on anyway'.[115] Eamonn Hughes similarly said that a senior investigating RUC man told him the car had been stopped and searched at a checkpoint. The officer would, however, refuse to cooperate with the HET, which, in turn, found no record of any such checkpoint.[116] Likewise, they were unable to contact *The Committee* researcher. Other bravura loyalist claims made in the programme have proven illusory.[117]

While the HET concluded that the RUC investigation was conducted methodically and professionally, it has long been the subject of considerable concern.[118] RUC contact with the Hughes family was minimal, brusque and at times offensive, including with Frank's widow Norah.[119] The first RUC officer on the scene, unusually on his own while 'on plain clothes patrol' in an unmarked car, approached on foot as a 'precautionary tactic' for fear it was a 'come on ... to lure RUC officers' into an ambush.[120]

Given that, one might wonder why a lone policeman would approach such a scene at all, or that no others were sent to investigate when reports indicated the car was likely a taxi. All local RUC had already been alerted that there were 'concerns for Frank's welfare'.[121] There were also claims the car may have been left unattended for some time after the RUC man 'saw the remains of what he thought was a human body', and suspicions, too, over the timings of some of the movements of police officers coming to and from Dungannon station.[122] Unusually, the RUC later never made public a photofit of 'Mary Fox', giving the excuse, said Eamonn Hughes, that 'it would endanger the suspect's life'.[123] Three female suspects, with strong links both to the UVF and the security forces, were questioned, but 'informal identification parades' proved inconclusive.[124] Questions were raised, too, over the forensics conducted at the scene, the actions of certain RUC officers and the way several suspects were dealt with.[125] The pistol used to kill Frank Hughes was found in an arms cache in an Orange Hall in February 1993. It had been used in ten killings and other attacks carried out by the UVF against Catholics throughout Armagh and Tyrone, including the death of Patrick Boyle and the wounding of his two sons a few months before Frank Hughes was killed.[126] While the HET found his death was 'linked to a number of murders in Armagh and Tyrone', no one was ever charged or convicted for killing Frank Hughes.[127] Two retired police officers concluded for a BBC documentary that 'all roads seem to point to Billy Wright and [his close associate] "Swinger" Fulton' in Frank's case.[128]

Eamonn Hughes would continue to be threatened. On one occasion, a joint British Army/RUC patrol taunted that his father had 'his own wee barbeque a wee while before', and that Eamonn was 'a dead man walking'.[129] The death had a devastating effect on the Hughes family, particularly Frank's widow Norah and on Eamonn himself. He could 'never come to terms' with the horror of his father's death and that he was the real target.[130] 'Eamonn sort of took the blame on to himself', says Eileen, 'and that was said to him many times after too; "only for you, they got the wrong man". It was hard. It just really ate Eamonn up'. Haunted by grief, loss and guilt, Eamonn Hughes would be driven (until his own untimely death in 2008) to search for the truth.[131] 'The sense of blame Eamonn felt is what started him doing the work', says his widow Eileen, 'we knew there was collusion but the problem was trying to prove it. We knew from the start that no one was ever going to be charged for it. It was more to say "look, there was collusion here. This man was murdered even though they knew they had gotten the wrong man." He was murdered to teach the family a lesson, to teach Eamonn a lesson.'[132]

Killings in the Moy

The small village of Moy (population 2,000) is both historic and picturesque. Its tree-lined centre, with its elegant, early Georgian architecture, was laid out in the mid-eighteenth century, modelled on an Italian renaissance square. Yet its beauty belies deeply rooted social and spatial divisions. 'Moy is a rural interface', says republican former prisoner Tommy McKearney, 'and this was a place where there would have been considerable sensitivity for political unionism. They would have been very aware of the population balance and sectarian demographic of a village like the Moy'.[133] The Moy sits on the Tyrone-Armagh border, between the predominantly nationalist town of Dungannon to the west and unionist majority Portadown to the east. Five miles down the road lies Loughgall, not just the site of the 1987 ambush, but symbolically important, too, as the founding place of the Orange Order. 'When I was growing up the whole ethos of Moy would have been unionist', says Tommy, an 'imposed normality' ensured that 'the sectarian balance didn't change. Catholics were fairly modest, well-behaved and discrete.'[134] That changed with the outbreak of the conflict and, as a 'frontier village', Moy would see more than its fair share of the violence that followed.

In the 1970s Moy lay at the heart of the 'murder triangle'. In August 1973, Francis and Bernadette Mullan were brutally killed in their home a mile from Moy. Their two-year-old son, wounded four times, was found lying across his dead mother's head. These were the first of 26 sectarian loyalist killings within a ten-mile radius of the Moy in the next six years, many at the hands of the Glennane Gang.[135] 'The failure to arrest or intern a single suspect' in the Mullan killings, wrote Denis Faul and Raymond Murray, 'made the Catholic people realise that the RUC and the British Army had no interest in stopping the sectarian assassinations, which were serving a useful purpose'.[136] When the elderly couple Peter and Jenny McKearney were killed in 1975, four 'recognised UVF members' were stopped in a car shortly after, a UDR soldier among them. Two tested positive for handling firearms but were not charged – the UDR man because he was legally entitled to handle weapons, a 'get-out-of-jail-free card for UDR men and their associates'.[137] One was later convicted for the 1976 Hillcrest pub bombing in Dungannon that left four dead, including two 13-year-old boys.[138] The RUC said Peter and Jenny McKearney were targeted in the mistaken belief they were part of a 'well-known republican family'.[139]

The IRA was responsible for many deaths in this area too, including that of Protestant civilians, as well as members of the UDR, RUC and reservists of both.[140] One of the first RUC men killed anywhere during the conflict was Roy Leslie, a native of Moy, shot dead in Strabane in 1971.[141] In 1976, two brothers, Thomas and Robert Dobson, were killed in Moy, two days after loyalists shot dead four Catholics in bar attacks in the nearby village of Charlemont.[142] Thomas Dobson was due to pick up his wife and newborn baby from hospital that day. Former 'B' Special and UDR soldier Fred Irwin was killed by the IRA in 1979, with a gun later recovered from a cache of weapons after the SAS ambush of the unarmed Brian Campbell and Colm McGirr in 1983.[143] In 1980, former UDR man and local unionist party official William Elliott was shot dead by the IRA, as he attended a cattle market in Monaghan.[144] His brother-in-law, Jack Donnelly, also a local unionist party figure and UDR member since its formation, was shot dead by the INLA in a bar in Moy a year later.[145] This was, then, an area in which violence had been visited on communities and families starkly divided along political and sectarian lines.

Then, in December 1991, a member of the INLA shot dead 19-year-old Robin Farmer in his father's outdoor sports shop, just off the Moy's main square. Home from university in Glasgow, Robin had been helping out in the store.[146] When the gunman entered he 'shouted, pushing his father out of the way', and was shot four times. The attacker's likely target, who worked in the shop and survived a failed IRA bomb attack weeks earlier, was the son of a local loyalist jailed for his part in the 1976 Charlemont attacks, while an RUC Reservist.[147] An alarm door trapped the INLA man, who was later given a life sentence.

In the wake of Robin Farmer's death, fears and rumours abounded of possible retaliatory attacks on Catholics.[148] This was particularly so for the McKearneys, well-known locally as a family long steeped in republican tradition. At that time, Tommy McKearney was in jail. Convicted in 1977 for the killing of Stanley Adams, a postman and part-time UDR member, he eventually served 16 years. In 1980 Tommy McKearney took part in the first republican hunger strike. Both his grandfathers had been senior figures in the IRA in the War of Independence.[149] One elder brother, Sean, was killed transporting an IRA bomb in 1974.[150] Another, Padraig, was one of those killed at Loughgall in 1987.[151] His sister, Margaret, spent many years in exile. However, not all the family were active republicans. The McKearneys had owned and run a family butcher shop on the main square in Moy for many years. It was now co-managed by Tommy's siblings, Kevin and Angela. 'Like thousands of others, Kevin would have voted Sinn Fein', says Tommy, 'but he had neither the inclination nor the desire to be actively involved. Not by any stretch of the imagination could you call him politically active, much less in the IRA.'[152] Rather, Kevin McKearney was 'very focused on his family. Quite quiet and introverted, his only interest was bringing up his children'. Kevin had married Bernadette Fox when young and the couple had four children, 'so there wasn't much spare time, money or energy for much else'. In December 1991 the eldest was just ten, the youngest two, so 'all of them would just have been waiting for Santa Claus'.

Threats of an attack began to take a more focused and definite form. Kevin's mother, Maura, received a phone call in late December, warning 'three bastards with white coats [a reference to the family butchers] [would be] lying in Moy Square next Friday'.[153] Given the atmosphere, the family took this seriously. They closed the shop for several days. Kevin's wife, Bernie, would recall 'a gut feeling, deep down, something was going to happen'. Some suggested the family should move across the border for a while, but 'Kevin said nobody was going to drive him out. This was where he had made his home for his family. So we stayed'.[154] Via a local councillor, the family received assurances that the RUC would 'put something in place' to watch the shop.[155] Attempts were also made to get local unionist MP (and former UDR major) Ken Maginnis to help reduce local tensions, but to no avail.

Five other families who received death threats were given security advice by the RUC – not, though, the McKearneys. Indeed, the RUC did not 'formally record or investigate the reported death threat' against the McKearneys.[156] As Desmond de Silva found, loyalist threats were often not recorded or acted upon.[157] Those whom the RUC considered a 'thorn in the side', he concluded, 'were not provided with protection during this period of the troubles'. For the McKearneys, this was so even after Special Branch ordered Moy 'out of bounds' to uniformed officers on 31 December, following intelligence a loyalist attack was imminent.[158] The local chief inspector then said there would be a 'visible presence to instil public confidence'. Yet, on 3 January 1992, the day of the attack, there was no record of either uniformed patrols or a Special Branch 'out-of-bounds' order in place.[159] This, despite Angela McKearney remembering how secure she felt, working in the shop that afternoon, the windows still decked with Christmas decorations, through which she could see a marked RUC car parked in the square.[160] It left around 4.30 pm.

A short time later Kevin McKearney was standing behind the counter of the shop. His 70-year-old uncle, Jack, was standing beside him. Contrary to reports, Jack did not work in the shop.[161] A 'typical rural bachelor farmer', he was 'of that generation that got by with very little, farmed his modest bit of land, was never too far from home, smoked his pipe and drank a few bottles of stout in the local pub'.[162] Still a 'big, powerful man', he shared the family home with his two elderly sisters, one suffering from multiple sclerosis. That day he had dropped in, as he often did, for a 'regular yarn' with his brother, Kevin senior. Just before 5.00 pm a UVF gunman entered the McKearneys shop. He shot Kevin McKearney with a pistol. It would be used later in several other killings.[163] As Kevin fell to the ground, the gunman walked towards him and fired more rounds. Jack McKearney may have tried to protect his nephew. The gunman shot him in the chest.[164] Angela McKearney came out from the back of the shop to see Jack fall. She held Kevin's body until the ambulance arrived and as an off-duty ambulance man, who had been in the square, tried to give first aid.[165] Kevin was confirmed dead on arrival at hospital. Jack McKearney died from his wounds three months later.

The gunman ran to a getaway car waiting outside. Before getting in, he crouched in 'a steady firing position' and shot into a car just behind containing a woman and three children, wounding a ten-year-old in the chest.[166] It may be that the gunman thought it was Bernadette McKearney and her children in the car.[167] The getaway car then sped away, to be found on fire, a couple of miles distant, half an hour later. The following day the UVF claimed responsibility, saying Kevin's and Jack's deaths were the 'price' paid for what they called a 'campaign of genocide against the Protestant people'.[168] Within minutes of the shooting, the RUC had set up four checkpoints covering several main roads out of Moy.[169] The route taken by the UVF unit was not among them. Small roads gave access to the nearby motorway, but no checkpoint was placed there.[170] The absence of the RUC in the village compounded the time it took to set up checkpoints, though manpower was available.[171] Less than five miles away 15 officers were deployed on road speed traps. Instead of 'sealing off' Moy the RUC 'allocated resources to traffic control'.[172] There was no apparent British Army response at all.[173]

Six well-known Mid-Ulster loyalists were arrested as part of the subsequent investigation – others followed. However, only one was charged, found in possession of weapons (including one of the South African guns) used in the shooting dead of three Catholic workmen a couple of months before.[174] While Billy Wright was implicated in this attack he was not arrested as a result.[175] What questions were asked of the loyalists taken in following the McKearney killings is not known. The interview records were among the vast cache of files deliberately destroyed at Gough Barracks in 1998, allegedly because of exposure to asbestos.[176] No copies were made. This lack of detailed records is a 'barrier' to future prosecutions.[177] Important forensic evidence has also been destroyed. The getaway car was discovered while still alight and several items recovered. They included a 'partially burnt green parka', like that witnesses saw the gunman wearing.[178] Sent to a forensic lab the jacket was then either 'lost' or destroyed, something that 'cannot be explained' and may have been 'deliberately removed to frustrate' investigation.[179] The impact of this loss cannot be underestimated, removing any chance of identifying its wearer through new DNA tests. This alone meant the HET could not allay suspicions of collusion and 'possibly denied the McKearney family the chance of justice'.[180] 'The loss of the jacket was crucial', says Tommy McKearney, 'how can you have a situation where someone can just walk in and take it? When there is also a pattern of things being "lost" you have to say once is a misfortune. Twice is no longer a mistake. Then three, four times?'[181]

There are allegations, too, of an undercover intelligence presence in Moy Square at the time of the shooting.[182] Immediately afterwards witnesses phoned the police from the shop, giving an incorrect car registration number. When shouted out, another witness wrote this wrong number down. The paper with the wrong number was discovered by the phone days later.[183] Yet, just a couple of minutes after the witness call was made, the RUC received another from an 'unidentified Special Branch officer' giving the same wrong car number.[184] Lauded by the HET for raising the alarm, this raises other questions. Not least, how a Special Branch officer had this information three minutes after the shooting? The HET proposed he might have received another call from the scene. There is no evidence that was so. The other possibility was it came 'from a covert police operation in Moy'.[185] Much suggests that someone in direct contact with Special Branch was in Moy Square when the attack happened. Suspicion has fallen on a British Telecom (BT) technician and his van. The technician was remembered by several witnesses, who saw him wiring a phone box.[186] BT had no record of any of their workers there that day. It would not have been the first time intelligence units used the cover of telephone vans during operations.[187] Yet, there are also no records of a covert operation at the time either. As things stand, the identity of the BT technician remains a mystery. The HET therefore found that it could not 'allay family suspicions that a covert operation' was in place at the time, or their 'concerns … of collusion by security forces in the murders of Kevin and Jack'.[188] There are parallels here, again, with other cases of an 'inadvertent' police presence (as in that of Frank Hughes) or undercover surveillance in place (of Roseann Mallon) at the time the killings took place. This was one of eight areas the HET identified where circumstances were unexplained and collusion allegations (at least) not disproved, including that state intelligence and photomontages may have been used to target the McKearneys.[189]

The muted HET conclusion, that the RUC were 'derelict in their duty' by not putting measures in place to prevent Kevin and Jack being killed, was still met with ferocious condemnation by (among others) former local MP Ken Maginnis.[190] Decrying the investigation as lacking logic, with 'slovenly and speculative conclusions', this was the result, he said, of 'republican revisionism'. Just as it was the 'McKearneys' IRA family connections' that had 'set the scene' for the 'carnage Moy village had to endure'. 'It is the weight of evidence that indicates the degree of culpability', says Tommy McKearney, 'then you place that against the backdrop of other cases, other patterns and the broader context of other counterinsurgency and colonial campaigns. Is it credible the British military, uniquely, decided not to employ those tactics here? With the evidence we have I think that stretches credulity. And Tyrone was a republican powerhouse, and maybe a block on the peace process. These shootings showed the IRA could not protect their own and the police would not protect you. For the state that made sense in military terms. It terrorised the republican base.'[191]

The Killing of Charlie and Teresa Fox

For Kevin McKearney's widow Bernadette, conflict-inflicted loss did not end there. A mere seven months later, on 6 September, her elderly mother and father, Charlie and Teresa 'Tess' Fox, were killed by the UVF in their own home. Both were lifelong republicans, born into republican families.

Charlie Fox had been jailed during the 1950s IRA border campaign for having republican leaflets.[192] Under the Special Powers Act, it was an offence to circulate anything advocating 'republican ideals'.[193] The Foxes were one of a small number of families in the local area – alongside the McKearneys and the Grews – known to be republicans. The family lived close to Moy, in the small Tyrone townland of Listamlet. Less than half a mile long, it includes only a handful of houses. Communal division here was stark. The Fox home lay on an all-but-invisible boundary – the 'last Catholic household on the road' – with the neighbouring Protestant townland of Killyman.[194] In microcosm this was the social world of 'neighbours' and 'strangers'.[195] Here too, long before the outbreak of the Troubles, was a history of strained relations with the state and the police. 'Growing up, I can't think of any circumstance where you would have called the police', remembers Paddy Fox, one of Charlie and Teresa's sons and himself a republican former prisoner.[196] 'In a way', he continues, 'it was like you were autonomous from the state, like it didn't exist at all'. After the start of the conflict, the IRA launched deadly attacks in and around the area. Listamlet also sat at the heart of the 'Murder Triangle' and so, again, saw more than its share of violence from the 1970s onward. Including the Foxes, as many as eight people were shot in the space of less than half a mile, including wider family members. Among others were Peter and Jenny McKearney and, in 1993, Tommy Molloy, who was shot dead in his own living room – alleged to have been mistakenly identified as the relative of a local Sinn Fein councillor. He was not, nor was he involved with any political or armed organisation.[197]

A week before Charlie and Teresa Fox were killed, Paddy Fox was jailed for transporting a large IRA bomb in Dungannon. On the Sunday evening of her death Tess Fox was at the house of her daughter, Bernadette. For months after Kevin McKearney was shot dead, she regularly visited her daughter and grandchildren 'to make sure everything was alright'.[198] Afterwards Bernadette drove her home – it was the last time she would see her mother alive. Just before 11.00 pm Charlie and Tess were preparing to go to bed. A UVF gunman broke in through a kitchen window and Charlie went to investigate the noise. He was shot four times. Tess Fox heard the shots from the back of the house. The gunman shot her five times as she ran through the scullery. Both died instantly, killed with one of the Czech-made South African imported weapons.[199] Minutes later, the getaway car was set on fire a mile away. It was Bernadette and her sister Teresa who found the bodies the next morning, having been alerted when their parents did not appear to give a regular lift to work.[200] Just after 8.30 am the sisters arrived to find the back door lying open. Then Bernadette heard her sister 'squealing her head off. All I could see was Mummy lying in the scullery and Daddy lying up in the kitchen in his pyjamas.' The attackers had cut the telephone lines so they phoned for help from a neighbour's house.[201] The RUC prevented other family members, who quickly arrived, from going into the house, and a local priest (distressingly for the family) from performing the last rites.[202] The UVF claimed responsibility for the killings later that day.

The HET suggested the failure of the police or British Army to visit the scene of the burnt-out getaway car until the next day (though discovered within minutes of the shooting) was a 'matter of routine', for fear of attack.[203] Nor were several photofit descriptions, distributed among intelligence officers, made public. Some arrests and a conviction did, though, follow. A Portadown loyalist was caught, a month later, storing guns, including that used to kill Charlie and Tess. He pleaded guilty to conspiring in five killings (including the McKearneys) though not that of the Foxes.[204] However, he also admitted holding the weapons for Billy Wright, who was not questioned until some time later, and then faced no charges. Another loyalist named in the same confession, believed to have been the gunman who killed the Foxes, also faced no charges.

In May 1993, loyalist Laurence Maguire pleaded guilty to being the getaway driver when Charlie and Tess were killed, after he and two others were caught in possession of weapons.[205] Maguire confessed to involvement in several other killings. They included those of Pat and Diarmuid Shields in January that year, targeted because Pat Shields was said by the UVF (wrongly) to be a member of Sinn Fein. It showed, said Cardinal Cahal Daly at the Shields' funeral, that loyalists had dropped the pretence of attacking so-called 'legitimate targets'.[206] As head of the UVF in Lisburn, Maguire was also the first person convicted of the new offence of 'directing terrorism'. However, it was Billy Wright, says the HET, who sanctioned specific attacks and controlled the UVF throughout Mid-Ulster.[207] Other notable suspects were not questioned, including Wright's close ally Mark Fulton and another man, believed to have been directly involved in killing Charlie and Tess. This failure was a 'lost opportunity to gather information or forensic evidence'.[208] Records of interrogations that did happen were also lost, destroyed at Gough Barracks.[209] The HET named several people (including Wright and Fulton) as likely involved in the attack, but stopped short of finding proof of collusion. The Fox family continue to contest that claim, not least because it was in large part based on ballistic evidence that has since been discredited.[210]

The Foxes also point to the movement of the security forces in the area prior to the shootings. The HET did find 'abnormal patterns' of RUC and British Army patrols.[211] Two units of the Royal Irish Regiment were 'patrolling a large area, including Moy' throughout the day and night, though 'focussed on Armagh'. However, there were no RUC checkpoints or patrols in place in the area at the time the Foxes were killed. A Moy-based RUC unit finished its patrols at 4.00 pm. This was unusual. Normally such patrols continued much later, often into the early hours of the morning. In the two months prior to the attack on the Foxes only once before were there no RUC road checkpoints operating around Moy at 11.00 pm. Just the night before, three RUC units (including two specialist mobile support units) were on patrol, one through till 2.00 am. On the previous two Sundays the RUC had checkpoints in place at 11.00 pm.[212] It therefore seems likely that the loyalists who shot the couple dead had prior knowledge of a complete absence of RUC patrols, and virtually no security force presence, in the area at the time of their attack.

Maguire also told the HET that he 'attended numerous meetings of the UVF where photomontages were available from which he and others could select targets'.[213] As a result, UVF victims in Mid-Ulster were 'sometimes identified from intelligence ... from security force photographs of people considered members of the IRA or *supporters of the republican cause* [my italics]'.[214] These photographs 'most likely' came from members of the security forces and this 'sharing of confidential intelligence with loyalist terrorists amounts to collusion on their behalf'.[215] The Foxes long believed that such material was used in the attack on Charlie and Tess – fears the HET could not allay. Indeed, the day after the shooting, the Foxes said they had been the subject of numerous threats and that the RUC told Charlie Fox a file on his son Paddy 'was in the hands of loyalists'.[216] Even before the shooting, Paddy Fox made public that Special Branch had mixed threats with financial inducements for him to turn informer. Afterwards, he said that 'on more than one occasion' a member of the UDR and RUC threatened 'they would set my family up to be killed by the UVF' if he refused.[217] There have been allegations, too, that the man suspected of being the gunman was a police informant – a 'protected species' – and someone close to Robin Jackson.[218] This was raised with the Police Ombudsman in 2010 (as was the claim that Billy Wright was a state agent), but was met merely with a 'neither confirm nor deny' response. Everything, concludes Bernie McKearney, says there was 'definitely collusion in my mother and father's case'.[219]

The UVF would claim that Tess Fox was shot 'in the confusion' and their aim had been to 'kill a number of IRA personnel in the house'.[220] If the couple's sons were the intended victims (though it was 'inconceivable' the UVF were not aware of Paddy Fox's much publicised imprisonment), the gunmen in any case 'callously shot their parents dead'.[221] The family have argued that the UVF claim was simply a cover for their actions, and that the real purpose of the attack was to instil fear and demoralisation within the local republican community and push the IRA towards a ceasefire. His parents' killing, says Paddy Fox, was designed to 'up the ante, put pressure on the IRA to divert attention to getting loyalists. People were afraid and it put them on the back foot. When the ceasefire came in 1994, people in Tyrone were begging for it.'[222]

The Castlerock Massacre

Attacks targeting republicans and those associated with them were not restricted to East Tyrone, or to family members. On the morning of 25 March 1993, the UFF shot dead four Catholic workmen as they arrived for work in the small, quiet town of Castlerock on the Co. Derry coast. Among them was 25-year-old Jimmy Kelly, a member of the South Derry IRA. The three other men, Gerry Dalrymple, Noel O'Kane and James McKenna, were not. In claiming responsibility, the UFF declared that all 'the victims were republicans', and this was a blow against the 'pan-nationalist front'. Such violence would continue 'so long as the IRA and Sinn Fein act as the military wing of Irish nationalism' and the SDLP 'exercise a veto on political progress ... courtesy of PIRA violence'.[223] It was an attack, said SDLP MP Seamus Mallon, 'decidedly done in such a way as to terrorise a whole community'.[224] The Castlerock massacre came during an upsurge of loyalist violence. The day before it happened another Catholic workman was killed, arriving for work in West Belfast. The day before that, the house of a Sinn Fein councillor in North Belfast was attacked and a grenade thrown at the home of another, in the west of the city – evidence the UFF was 'intensifying its violent campaign against the republican party'.[225] And it was not only members of Sinn Fein who were targeted. The same night, incendiary bombs were thrown at the homes of two SDLP councillors in Banbridge, Co. Down. On the day of the Castlerock killings, Catholic teenager Damien Walsh was shot dead (again arriving for work) at a West Belfast shopping centre.[226] Collusion has now been identified as a key feature of this killing too.[227] This includes the presence of a British Army undercover unit, which had the workplace under surveillance at the time Damien Walsh was killed – not revealed until a HET investigation in 2010.[228] The IRA bombing of Warrington a week earlier, killing two young boys, caused widespread revulsion. Damien Walsh's uncle, a university professor, contrasted the wave of emotion he shared following the Warrington bomb deaths, with the muted, negligible public reaction to the killing of his nephew.[229] 'This week', a UFF spokesman said, 'has been a success'.[230]

Jimmy Kelly had joined the IRA a year after his 16-year-old brother died in a suspected sectarian killing.[231] By the time of his death, the RUC said he was a senior figure in the South Derry IRA, the 'mastermind' behind several attacks.[232] During interrogations in Castlereagh, say his family, he was threatened and told that his details would be passed to loyalists. 'He would get phone calls from Special Branch', says his father Neecie, 'I heard them myself. They tried to get him to become an informer. They said they would give his name to loyalists who would sort him out. Or tell the Provos he was an informer anyway.'[233] Threats were made at checkpoints too, often placed just outside the family home. 'They would kick the sides of the house, banging it with their rifles', says Neecie, and the UDR and British Army kept the house under covert surveillance; 'then the fellas he was working with started getting the same treatment too'.[234]

For some time Jimmy Kelly had worked for a local building firm. The work team regularly travelled to worksites together. Among them was James McKenna – 52 years old, the married father of two sons and two daughters, who lived near Maghera. Twenty-one-year-old Noel O'Kane was from Upperlands, near the village of Swatragh, one of ten children. Gerry Dalrymple was 58, married with six children, and from Rasharkin. He was, said his son Joe, 'an honest, hardworking man who hadn't a bad word to say about anybody. Catholics and Protestants were all the same [to him]. It was always the innocent who suffered.'[235] The foreman was Gerry McEldowney, one of two workmen to survive the attack. Gerry says that in the weeks and months leading up to the shooting tensions rose. They were regularly stopped by the RUC, the 'police were giving us hassle every worksite'. The police would drive in 'two or three times a week' and told Jimmy Kelly 'umpteen times it was only a matter of time before they got him. That they were going to set him up to be killed by the UVF or UDA. He would not last till Christmas. It created a bit of fear in us all.'[236]

The team began work in Castlerock, renovating houses, several weeks earlier. One day his workmates shouted to Jimmy to flee when they saw a man get out of a car 'reaching inside his jacket for what looked like a gun'.[237] Others claimed a former UDR soldier, later killed by the IRA (who said he was a leading UFF man – something denied by his family), kept watch on the workmen.[238] Fear was growing. Noel O'Kane's sister, Donna Martin, says there were 'a few things that worried him', and he told a family member of 'a couple of things that really scared him'. At some point, Donna continues, 'they obviously decided to just get the lot of them'.[239] The other survivor of the attack was Declan Mullan who also remembered that the fear was increased by the actions of the RUC. A week before, he followed a car containing 'two men in civilian clothes' that had been parked outside his home, and which then drove into a local police station.[240] Earlier, the RUC stopped Gerry McEldowney and James McKenna leaving the worksite and questioned them about when they arrived for work and where the team were picked up in the morning.[241] 'We were being stopped [by the RUC] in the morning and coming home in the evenings', says Gerry McEldowney, 'sometimes, more than once, they'd throw the tools in the road'. The evening before, RUC 'roadblocks all around' meant they 'could hardly get out of the street'. 'It was obvious the men were being set up', says Declan Mullan.[242]

But then, on the morning itself, there were 'no cops around at all'.[243] Declan Mullan drove separately to where the men were then working in Castlerock. He arrived first, at around 8.15 am. As he waited in his car a local man (claimed to have loyalist connections) asked him if his colleagues were late. The others in the van were on the way but stopped off to collect building supplies first. The van arrived just before 9.00 am. A transit van then drove up 'at top speed' and blocked the van in. Two masked men 'yelling and shouting' got out. 'A well-built man, wearing a blue boiler suit and a mask, came up to the window of the van and produced a revolver', remembers Gerry McEldowney, 'he put it tight up against the window and started to shoot indiscriminately, I was in total shock'. Gerry watched as the windscreen glass shattered in front of him and turned to see Jimmy Kelly 'lying back with blood streaming down his face'. Another gunman slid open the side door and fired inside, as Gerry desperately scrambled for cover. The gunmen 'sprayed the van with gunfire' as Declan Mullan sat, horrified. One turned towards him, before turning back and 'continued to fire at the workers in the van'.[244] The gunmen then got back into their van and drove away 'at a leisurely pace, in no rush'. Then there was 'no noise whatsoever', remembers Gerry. As he got out, Declan Mullan tried to comfort him, but Gerry 'was so scared and going off my rocker a bit at that stage'.[245] They both then dived under the van as the killers drove back towards them, 'at a crawl, looking for signs of life. The driver raised a clenched fist out of the window and shouted "Up the UFF" then drove away.'[246] The burning van would be found two miles away shortly after.

Declan Mullan called for help, then comforted the others.[247] In shock, Gerry started to walk down the road 'shouting and roaring ... adrenalin was just pumping through my body'. Shot in the leg and head, blood was coming out of his shoe, covering his face and soaking his jumper. He asked a woman who came to his aid if he was going to die. As he lay on the ground, she said an act of contrition in his ear. 'She stayed with me and held my hand', says Gerry, 'that helped me so much, to know that somebody cares'.[248] By then, an ambulance and officers from the nearby RUC station had arrived. Jimmy Kelly and James McKenna were already dead. Gerry Dalrymple lay on the ground, 'rolling about the footpath in pain ... asking for a drink of water'.[249] He would die shortly after arriving at hospital. Noel O'Kane survived longer, but died from his wounds that evening.[250] As he lay on a hospital trolley the families asked Gerry what had happened, but he 'couldn't answer them. That was the worst thing.'[251]

There have been suspicions that some of those involved in carrying out the Castlerock massacre were former members of the UDR, or working as agents or informers for RUC Special Branch.[252] Several local loyalists were arrested, questioned and then released. They included Torrens Knight, a known loyalist who would confess to taking part in the Greysteel massacre several months later.[253] Shouting 'trick or treat', loyalists killed eight people and injured many more firing into the crowded Rising Sun pub in Greysteel on Halloween night, a week after the IRA Shankill Road bomb.[254] Knight also confessed to being the driver at Castlerock. As a result, his case never came to trial and he was led away laughing and shouting sectarian obscenities. Knight was released under the Good Friday Agreement in 2000.[255] Soon after, it is claimed, he withdrew a 'large amount of money' from a local bank account into which £50,000 was deposited each year. The bank contacted the RUC, fearing this was a money laundering scheme, but were assured nothing was wrong. The account was then 'hastily closed down' shortly after.[256] Allegations that this showed Knight was a Special Branch informer were met by a routine 'neither confirm nor deny' response.[257] Police Ombudsman Nuala O'Loan said that deciding whether or not Knight was an agent 'was not within her remit'.[258]

Earlier, local SDLP councillor John Dallat claimed he had passed on information about an arms cache to the RUC between the Castlerock and Greysteel attacks.[259] He later said a security force member told him these guns were moved by 'a member of Special Branch who was protecting Knight'. One gun was used at Greysteel. The RUC would state they had 'no record of any information received from Mr Dallat' and three (now retired) RUC officers had 'no recollection' of it either.[260] The RUC did, though, find some weapons used at Greysteel soon after. One gun had been used in the shootings of Donegal Sinn Fein councillor Eddie Fullerton and Tommy Donaghy in Kilrea.[261] Another was a UDR pistol, left by a soldier in a bag in his unlocked car, which had then been 'stolen' when he went drinking.[262] The RUC did not investigate further and the soldier was merely fined by the army. 'The veracity of the soldier's account' for the loss of a gun used to carry out the Castlerock massacre, said the HET, was 'dubious at best'.

'I have no doubt there was collusion', says Neecie Kelly, 'the ones who did it knew where the boys would be and the only place they would have got that information was the RUC.'[263] The day after Jimmy Kelly's funeral, says Neecie, four policemen drove past the family home 'holding up four fingers, signalling 4-0'.[264] 'The dogs in the street know there was collusion', says Gerry McEldowney, 'but the truth would open a can of worms. We can prise that tin open but I don't know if it will ever be emptied out. The implications are too big, too biting.'[265] For Oonagh Martin, another sister of young Noel O'Kane, regret is greater given how close the deaths came to the 1994 ceasefires. There was 'already talk of peace', remembers Oonagh, 'and when the Agreement was signed, you couldn't help feeling cross and thinking "why could that not have happened a bit earlier"'.[266]

The Killing of Roseann Mallon

Roseann Mallon was a 'quiet, very caring, very gentle, loving person, who just devoted herself to her family, her nephews and nieces and their children. They were her life really.'[267] She lived all her life in the same part of rural Tyrone, a few miles south of Dungannon. Never married, Roseann lived simply, working the small family farm and taking care of her parents until they died in old age, then dividing her time between looking after others in her extended close-knit family, who lived close by, and regularly attending mass. Her brother had established a successful engineering works in the mid-1950s and raised his family next door. Growing up, Roseann was 'like a second mother to us', says her nephew Martin Mallon, 'she liked to cook, bake, was always a very capable, straightforward, very religious person. Her whole life was looking after our families.'[268] Martin and his brother were well-known local republicans, though their father and others were not. Rather, Roseann was 'totally against violence of any description.' 'They were most certainly not republicans', says Martin, 'it would be wrong to portray her and others in my family in that way. If ever there was an innocent victim, it was Roseann.'[269] On the night of 8 May 1994, UVF gunmen shot 76-year-old Roseann Mallon in what, for many reasons, is a symbol of the story of collusion.

Martin Mallon, a former republican prisoner and prominent figure in Sinn Fein in East Tyrone, had for some time been receiving death threats.[270] A month before he had been stopped in his car by an RUC Special Branch unit. After waiting 20 minutes, another car pulled up in front of him. Martin Mallon claims the well-known loyalist Tony McNeill was driving and, beside him, Billy Wright. 'They were chatting to the Special cops', says Martin, 'then the cop said "Get out of the car" and said to Billy Wright and McNeill, "this is Martin Mallon". Martin got back into his car and as he drove past Wright 'had his neck stuck up and he was shouting "you Fenian bastard!" There was a vein down his neck like forked lightning. He was roaring and shouting. I just went "alright Billy, how are you doing?" By now the cop was saying "come on, move on, move on". Wright was going plain mad.'[271] Martin Mallon recorded what happened with a local solicitor and Amnesty International, before Roseann was killed.[272]

Around the same time he was taken into Gough Barracks. After a couple of days a senior British intelligence officer came into the interrogation room. He was 'very, very well dressed, spick and span', recalls Martin, 'in a pin-striped suit, polished shoes and had a perfect, Oxford English accent. He said he was there from the British government to negotiate with me, on behalf of MI5.'[273] He offered Martin and his family the chance to move to America. 'He said "I know you don't speak in here'", says Martin, "'but if you are prepared to negotiate, just nod or wink". I thought "is this candid camera? Are these boys winding me up?" I couldn't believe it and just sort of laughed.' But then, he continues, 'and I will never forget this', the intelligence officer stood up and 'stamped his feet and saluted. Then he says "At our convenience, we'll kill you or a member of your family". That's just the simple, God's honest truth, that's what happened. Then he walked out through the door and I was released after another couple of hours. I'd say Roseann was dead just three or four weeks later.'

Martin's brother, Christie, was also receiving threats. About to park his car in his mother's driveway one night, another car dramatically pulled up behind.[274] Three RUC men got out. "'I thought it was the UVF", Christie said. "Sure we are all the one Christie" came the policeman's reply'. 'You need to understand we were being harassed all the time', says Martin Mallon, 'they took you in, tried to recruit you. Then threaten you and your family. Things were hot and heavy in Tyrone then. It was continual. You wouldn't let the children or your wife travel in the car with you. It was too dangerous, simple as that. At night, you'd have been lying on mattresses in their rooms, because you were afraid of them coming in through the window. That's the way it was.' The logic behind it, he says, was political. 'There was an element in Special Branch and people like them that did not want the peace process to progress, for negotiations between the IRA and the Government.' Rather, he argues, 'their aim was to defeat the IRA and Sinn Fein, they wanted them crushed'.

The day before Roseann was killed, several armed men, dressed in military combats, were reportedly sighted close to the Mallon home by two local children playing by some disused sheds. One of the children was a relative of the Mallons. Several of the men in military garb were inside a shed, with guns propped against the wall. Another was in a nearby hedge. Scared, the children ran, telling their parents, the Mallons and then the RUC. When there was no response, 'no helicopters, no police cars', says Martin, they thought it must have been the British Army. Having made statements, the RUC pressured the children to change them. There were later, wider attempts to discredit their story, as suspicions rose (in the wake of Roseann's death) that they had stumbled on her UVF killers. Only when other circumstances came to light did an RUC inspector state they had, in fact, come across members of an 'unidentified regiment of the British Army, which meant an undercover unit'.[275]

Roseann Mallon spent the night of 8 May with her sister-in-law Bridie, visiting her niece, Paula, who lived across the road.[276] Around midnight, Paula watched them go home, but as they went into Bridie's house she saw another car pull up, containing three men. Suspicious, she called her mother, as two of the men made their way up the side of the house. Bridie shouted to Roseann that something was wrong but, as she tried to get out of her chair, the gunmen fired several bursts of automatic gunfire through the window. Roseann was shot five times. Bridie was also wounded, the phone dangling from her hand as her daughter listened to what happened. The UVF would claim Martin and Christie were their targets, but they could see into the room – they 'knew that they were shooting an old woman', said Bridie Mallon.[277] 'Gaping holes in the walls' showed they 'must have raked the whole place', Cardinal Cahal Daly would later add, 'the object was to kill anyone there'.[278] The plan, concludes journalist Paul Larkin, was to 'wipe out as many of the Mallon family as possible'.[279] The gunmen's getaway car was later found a mile away and one gun discovered in a disused house in Dungannon. Several loyalists, including Billy Wright, were briefly questioned, then released. News reports emphasised the sectarian nature of the killing.[280] Much more was to come.

As she was shot dead, the house Roseann was in was under surveillance by a covert British Army unit, mere metres away. They were part of a major operation, involving anything up to 50 British soldiers under the control of the TCG, which would have required approval at the highest military and political levels.[281] At first, this was all kept secret, even from the RUC investigating the shooting. Things only came to light weeks later, after a neighbour inadvertently found a military surveillance camera in a hedge near the Mallon home. As the Mallons hid the camera 'three helicopters were coming in, two of them out wide. Like something you would see on TV!'[282] The area was 'sealed off by cars with no number plates, boys with trench coats; about 20 of them within less than half an hour, but only one policeman in a uniform'. As cover, the authorities told neighbours they were defusing a non-existent IRA bomb. Sometime later the Mallons returned the camera.

There is dispute as to whether the camera was on at the time of the shooting. The MoD claim it was not because it lacked night vision – though quite why cameras, intending to surveil the activities of suspected members of the IRA in rural East Tyrone, would not be able to see what they were doing after dark remains something of a mystery. 'Given the sophistication of the equipment the British army use', says Martin Mallon, 'and night-time being when most things would happen, the daftest thing they could do in a rural area like this would be to put in a camera that doesn't work at night'.[283] The MoD also said the camera lacked a zoom and, from its position, was unable to see the killers approach the house. Before returning the camera, the Mallons had it tested by technical staff at UTV, who found it included 'one small camera with a wide angled lens and another camera with a powerful telephoto lens'.[284] Recordings show it could zoom in on faces and car registration numbers, and was able to pan across 'picking up on the people walking up to the house. They could see the cars on the road and they could see people coming to and down the side of my mother's house'.[285] There was also more than one camera. Another had a full view of the road and was able to track and record all vehicles travelling past the house. Evidence suggests that a UVF team was outside the home earlier in the day, so they, and their car, could have been seen, recorded and identified. 'You were not coming in', says Martin, 'if the British military did not want you to'.[286]

None of this had been revealed to the CID team investigating Roseann's death, the result of Special Branch's 'no downward dissemination' or 'slow waltz' practices.[287] Indeed, at first the British Army continued to deny the camera was theirs and kept secret the existence of taped recordings. When eventually these tapes were handed over it was (very unusually) not to CID, but initially to the chief inspector of Special Branch for the area.[288] The military liaison officer, who apparently knew nothing about the tapes being removed from the surveillance posts, admitted that in this process Special Branch may have 'bypassed procedures'.[289] CID eventually received the tapes for the three-week period before Roseann's death. Only those for the day she was killed were missing, uniquely (and unbelievably) reported destroyed after being taped over unintentionally.

The secrecy around the surveillance operation (sanctioned at senior police and military levels) – and the wiping of the tapes – fundamentally undermined the police investigation. There were other problems. Reports that known loyalists (including Billy Wright) had been seen, unusually, at a bar half a mile from the Mallon house, were not acted upon. This was at the time in the afternoon when other UVF men were outside the Mallon house. The HET argued that Wright, while 'orchestrating the murders attributed to the Mid-Ulster UVF', was here likely acting as a decoy, to 'divert attention and disrupt an investigation'.[290] Other evidence suggests otherwise – not least, that Wright was one of three loyalists arrested nearby soon after the shooting, in a car matching one seen earlier where the getaway car was found burnt out.[291] However, all three were soon released – and without forensic tests being taken of their clothes. Other suspects were never followed up.[292] No one has ever been convicted for killing Roseann Mallon.

The spy cameras in place when Roseann was killed transmitted pictures directly to a senior British Army officer overseeing the surveillance in an operations room in Mahon Barracks.[293] They formed only part of a much wider, sophisticated surveillance operation. British soldiers had been dug into the fields around the Mallon house and workshop for months, and continued to be so until the hidden camera was discovered. So, as Roseann was shot dead, six covert British soldiers less than 100 yards away listened and watched. Heavily redacted military radio logs show the soldiers heard the gunfire, knew the attack was happening and immediately relayed this to the senior officer. They were ordered 'not to react to the situation and that the RUC would be informed'. When Roseann Mallon lay dying, and her killers fled, British soldiers, mere yards away, did nothing. The RUC did not prevent the UVF men escaping. 'The soldiers were there for quick response', says Martin Mallon, 'if an IRA gunman was identified they were going to be shot. And lo and behold, two gunmen and another man drive right into the middle of the plot, hop out of the car, dander round the back of the house, shoot Roseann, dander back, and drive right through the whole lot. You don't have to be a genius to work out these people weren't going to be shot.'[294] Kathleen O'Hagan, the last Mid-Ulster republican relative killed, was shot dead three months later. The IRA ceasefire followed just three weeks after that.

Conclusion:
Collusion, Truth and Justice

I'm not saying this is my position, I'm saying that there would be some who argue that in the prosecution of a campaign against paramilitaries that you have to infiltrate [to obtain information to prevent death] … and then you get into a whole grey area … if those individuals, whether they were placed there or were turned, are engaging in acts of terrorism. Does that equal collusion? What we need to look at is what equals collusion. And one man's collusion is another man's counterinsurgency.[1]

They adopted the same tactic, sending squads in to shoot people in order to apply pressure. So they need to come clean about it. All we are asking is 'tell us what happened'. Let's have closure on it. We are surely in a situation for that today. We don't want our grandchildren growing up and thinking 'God, who was Roseann, what happened to her and why?' What has happened has happened. All that's over, we're not asking for prosecutions. All we want is closure in the case so that we can go on with our lives. And we've been denied that from day one.[2]

Dealing With the Past

On 30 January 1972, a then youthful Captain Mike Jackson was second in command of Support Company of the Parachute Regiment, colloquially called 'Kitson's private army'.[3] This was the unit responsible for killing 13 innocent civilians in Derry that day, soon known around the world as Bloody Sunday. A fourteenth victim would later die of his wounds. On return to their Belfast barracks, Jackson later recalled, his commanding officer, Derek Wilford, was met by counterinsurgency guru Kitson. The latter, while 'generally supportive', had only one point of criticism about the Paras' actions, asking 'why, having got that far in [to the no-go area of the Bogside] you didn't go on and sort the whole bloody mess out'?[4] For Jackson, Kitson may have been 'brusque' and expressed himself 'brutally' but he 'knew his soldiering' and 'had a point'. Jackson's own chief concern was the charge the Paras had 'run amok', given that the British 'Army is very proud of professionalism'.[5] So the events of Bloody Sunday were remembered over three decades later by (now General Sir) Mike Jackson. In his 2002 evidence to the Saville Inquiry, Kitson would still describe those responsible for Bloody Sunday as a 'jolly good' unit.[6] He also denied that any of the counterinsurgency tactics he developed, such as counter-gangs, had been used in the North.[7]

The Saville Inquiry was set up in 1998 in the wake of the Good Friday Agreement to re-examine the events of Bloody Sunday. It became the longest inquiry of its kind, only reporting in 2010. Saville then completely overturned the 'whitewash' findings of the earlier Widgery Inquiry to declare the victims entirely innocent and the actions of the British soldiers 'unjustified and unjustifiable'. Subsequent police investigations have been met by a virulent, high-profile campaign to prevent prosecution of the British soldiers involved. It is an echo of what has gone before. Contrary to current claims of a witch-hunt aimed at British soldiers for past crimes (the killers of Bloody Sunday chief among them), the record rather suggests a long-term *de facto* immunity and *a priori* amnesty for military wrongdoing.[8] Here too a practical, instrumental logic of 'necessity' was at play. (Mostly) young men sent to kill and maim may be less inclined to do so if potentially liable to criminal culpability at some unknown later date; something of which military hierarchies are all too aware. It required bending and subverting the law. In fact, only four British soldiers were convicted for murder in the North of Ireland, for a handful of the over 300 people directly killed by the British Army during the conflict, mostly civilians from the nationalist community.[9] In each case campaigns demanding the convicted soldiers release were spearheaded by the right-wing British press and a raft of figures from the political and military establishment. In each case too, the soldier in question served less than three years in jail before being released and returned to the ranks of the British Army. At least one, decorated for his service to the Parachute Regiment, was part of the British occupying forces in Afghanistan.[10]

Throughout its long years accumulating evidence and since, the Bloody Sunday Inquiry sharply divided opinion; a lightning rod for conflicting attitudes on how to deal with the past in the North. Over two decades, how to get to the truth or find justice as part of a transition away from violent social division has been more politically contentious than any other issue left in the conflict's wake. This has been nowhere more so than when state violence and collusion have been under scrutiny. Unlike many other societies emerging from conflict or authoritarian rule, the North has seen no comprehensive truth recovery process, such as a truth commission. Rather, there have been various, disparate legal and investigative mechanisms put in place to deal with specific issues or events, some successfully, others anything but. The result has been a 'piecemeal approach' (and 'package of measures') that has often allowed for the state management of truth recovery.[11] Though rare, there have been full-blown inquiries, such as that into Bloody Sunday. Special units have been created, like the HET, to investigate all unresolved conflict deaths. It was wound up amid considerable controversy before completing its task. There have also been investigations by the Office of the Police Ombudsman for Northern Ireland, a body set up to enhance accountability as part of the post-conflict transition. An innovative and largely successful independent commission was created to help find the remains of the 'disappeared', victims (mostly of the IRA) whose bodies had until then never been found. Inquests have been reopened, often decades after the deaths under investigation. While there have been many important revelations for victims' families this complex of processes has often felt like a tangled, impenetrable maze – something not helped by the considerable institutional resistance often encountered from the police, military and intelligence services.

Dealing with the past remains politically contentious and in a fraught, unsettled state of limbo. Even the definition of who counts as a victim is contested. That anyone injured or bereaved in the conflict should be seen as a victim, whatever their background or status or that of those they lost, is hotly disputed.[12] It is the mark of an ideological battle, much to do with replaying divisions of the war itself. It likewise reflects and shapes public consciousness of whose lost lives are grievable.[13] There have been efforts to establish a more coherent and comprehensive response. However, the 2009 report of an independent Consultative Group on the Past was shot down almost before it was announced.[14] Its many positive and progressive recommendations did, though, form much of the basis of later talks.[15] In 2014, agreement was reached between the British government and main political parties of the North on a range of issues, including how to deal with the past.[16] The Stormont House Agreement (SHA) included provision for a range of bodies to be set up, including an oral history archive, services for victims, a new Historical Investigative Unit and an Independent Commission on Information Retrieval.[17]

Able to offer limited immunity from prosecution, the last of these is envisaged as a means for 'victims and survivors to seek and privately receive information about the deaths of their next of kin'. However, despite earlier apparent consensus, unionist political opposition has ensured that these measures have not yet been implemented. In 2017, the minority Conservative government struck a deal with the DUP to keep itself in power. It included a joint statement opposing what they called an unfair focus on the police and the army in 'legacy' matters.[18] They also both affirmed their 'debt of gratitude' to the police and military in 'upholding democracy and the rule of law' throughout the conflict. Despite earlier agreement, in May 2018 the British government then announced a consultation process on the legacy provisions contained in the SHA.[19] It garnered over 15,000 responses and was met with a wave of opposition to the SHA measures from a chorus of right-wing commentators, unionist newspapers and former senior British military figures.[20] The whole process seems likely to do little other than defer ever longer (if not entirely derail) the implementation of a comprehensive means of dealing with the past. That may well be its purpose. Going hand in hand with calls to enshrine state impunity in law by introducing an amnesty in all but name, solely for former members of the security forces, the same chorus of right-wing voices continues to denounce a supposed 'disproportionate focus' in legacy investigations on killings where the perpetrators were members of the British Army or RUC.[21] Worryingly (if unsurprising), it is a view echoed by British government officials, including Prime Minister Theresa May and Secretary of State Karen Bradley in statements to the House of Commons.[22] The only problem with the 'disproportionate focus' argument is that it just happens to be completely untrue; as evidenced by official records directly refuting such claims and fact-girded denials of any 'unfair bias' from (among others) the Northern Ireland Victims' Commissioner and head of the PSNI.[23]

Investigating Collusion

Many of the most difficult and contested legacy investigations have had collusion at their core. Like Bloody Sunday, revealing the truth about collusion has been a touchstone in the difficult, divisive debate about dealing with the past. There have been several official inquiries into collusion, going back to the Stevens Inquiries from the 1990s onwards. His 2003 report (though never fully published) was instrumental in establishing that collusion had been widespread and extended 'to the extreme of agents being involved in murder'.[24] It has been followed by others but the road has been anything but straightforward. Judge Cory found extensive evidence of collusion in the several cases he was asked to investigate, including those of human rights lawyers Pat Finucane and Rosemary Nelson. Cory called for full public inquiries to follow.[25] The British government subsequently substantially changed the rules for inquiries, undermining confidence in their impartiality, independence and rigour. After the Finucane family refused an inquiry under these skewed conditions a review was set up, led by Desmond de Silva.[26] It painted a bleak, devastating picture of state complicity and collusion in the killing of Pat Finucane and beyond. Yet it was also limited– not least as it could not examine patterns of collusion after Brian Nelson's arrest (when many of the victims in Mid-Ulster were shot dead). Many of the inquiries that were held confirmed fears. They included a deeply flawed investigation into the 1997 killing of Mid-Ulster loyalist leader Billy Wright. His own possible role in collusion was not even under consideration. Efforts to discover whether or not Wright worked as an informer or state agent have been consistently stymied and blocked. Raised as an issue with Special Branch witnesses during the Roseann Mallon inquest in 2013, the question was met with the now commonplace 'neither confirm nor deny' response. When the coroner pressed further the inquest was once more delayed. To date, the answers given have proven anything but satisfactory. As in many other legacy inquests, the court has severely criticised the police for the slow release of material in dribs and drabs; to say nothing of the evidence mislaid, lost or disappeared.[27] As of late 2018, we still await the coroner's conclusions and ruling in the killing of Roseann Mallon. The exact part played by state agents within Mid-Ulster loyalism remains one of the great 'unknowns' of the Troubles.[28]

Other investigations by the HET and Police Ombudsman have examined cases of collusion. Some have sought to look at the links and patterns of cases, with varying degrees of success. It was its handling of cases of state killings that prematurely ended the work of the HET amid great rancour and criticism.[29] A legacy unit within the reformed PSNI is currently undertaking this work. Grave concerns remain about its independence and ability to circumvent barriers of secrecy and institutional memory within policing. Retired RUC officers have been to the fore in campaigns against investigations into collusion. For some, it is part of the 'Ulsterisation of blame'. It is tellingly depressing, long after the conflict's end, that former RUC and Special Branch officers 'just accepted as a matter of fact' that Pat Finucane and Rosemary Nelson 'were fronts for the IRA and knowingly acted on their behalf'.[30] Criticism of Special Branch was seen as 'part of an orchestrated campaign against it by the terrorists'.[31] One former Special Branch officer recently denounced the entire peace process as 'appeasement' in which republicans 'concocted' collusion to justify themselves and soothe the conscience of those who withheld support from the police.[32] The latter include, among others, republicans, nationalists, the SDLP, successive Irish governments, human rights groups, the Catholic Church, 'left wing socialists and bleeding heart liberals'.[33] There is an echo here of wider contentious historical arguments, readily damning and dismissing critiques of state actions as 'republican revisionism'. There is a need for a different social space within which to talk about these important issues. Collusion should not become a mere pivot around which vying ideological narratives of culpability and blame turn.

Successive Police Ombudsmen have turned a light on collusion with wildly different results. Investigations have revealed patterns of collusion between Special Branch and loyalists that extended beyond the years of the conflict and included agents being directly involved in killing.[34] Others were deeply criticised for a lack of rigour and caving in to institutional interests in sidelining evidence of collusion.[35] The report of the current Ombudsman into the Loughinisland massacre exposed a culture of collusion that helped lead to the death of six innocent men and to a cover-up in its aftermath.[36] It promises much for his current inquiry into collusion in Mid-Ulster, although it may not be complete before his term of office comes to an end. If so, its fate is less clear. In any case, the hurdles will be considerable. Many avenues of inquiry have been starved of the resources needed to do their work. Over 60 legacy inquests, many into state killings and collusion, have been delayed time and again. The result is a stultifying backlog, stalling and petrifying progress. This remains the case to the present day. Inquests have, though, provided some important information. Links between many of the killings in Mid-Ulster have been belatedly confirmed by evidence presented in coroners' courts. The gun used to kill Roseann Mallon, for example, had been used in some two dozen killings and attempted killings.[37] They included the attack in Cappagh and the shooting of Charlie and Teresa Fox. Uncovered shortly after Roseann was killed, it was 'misidentified' by a specialist forensics unit of Special Branch so these vital links were not made until some two decades later.[38] At the time, it has now been revealed, someone in Special Branch may have 'tampered' with the gun in a 'deliberate attempt to hinder the identification process'.[39]

Although long denied, collusion happened – institutional in character, widespread in scale. Inevitably, in looking at aspects of the 'dirty war', evidence in individual cases is often elusive, fragmentary and shrouded in secrecy and deliberate obfuscation. Nowhere is this more evident than when agents and informers were involved. When head of the FRU, Gordon Kerr, complained that successive British governments had 'wilfully failed to address' the 'armchair rules' in place for handling informers he bitterly noted they had still reaped 'the political rewards of FRU's work'.[40] Like other FRU operatives he went on to serve in a senior intelligence role 'recruiting double agents' in Iraq.[41] In many ways the story of collusion provides a bridge between campaigns of colonial counterinsurgency in the past and the imperial interventionism of the present. These are concerns that go beyond the conflict in the North. In sum the relationship of the British counterinsurgency tradition to the rule of law comes down to this; given the ends in mind, where circumstances permit the law might be adapted but where they dictated otherwise, it might rather be circumvented, subverted or rendered all but immaterial. If the story of collusion reveals anything it is that, in the context of counterinsurgency, the classic Latin proverb 'necessity has no law' holds considerable sway.

Revealing what agents and informers were allowed and asked to do is crucial to understanding the nature of collusion as counterinsurgency practice. Much stands in the way. The mantra of 'neither confirm nor deny' and defence of state security and national interest considerably hamper the ability to get to the truth. The limitations, failings and lack of independence of processes like the HET, setbacks with long drawn-out court cases, some spanning decades, have made many relatives, understandably, highly sceptical. The long years of trying to discover the truth have taken a toll, emotionally and physically. Time passing has seen relatives age; some have died. Yet often the search for truth has been taken up by a new, younger generation. For families, the legacy of conflict, collusion and loss never goes away. They have been central in campaigns for truth and justice throughout and continue to be so today.[42] Much of what has been revealed about the death of Roseann Mallon has only been the result of long years of campaigning and legal work undertaken by her family. At one point they received vital files that had been hidden for years, after a 'civil servant got a letter and released documents he was never supposed to release'.[43] 'If it wasn't for that blunder', says Martin Mallon, 'a lot of people would say "what a load of republican propaganda"'. Roseann's case is not unique. There is just a better paper trail. All victims of the conflict matter. This is not an issue that is going to disappear.

Postscript: What Proves Collusion?

On 7 January 2019 (as this book went to press), Justice Weir, the coroner in the inquest into the shooting of Roseann Mallon, finally delivered his verdict.[44] Coming over three years after the court's hearings concluded, and nearly a quarter of a century since the actual shooting, it made for much delayed, depressing (if also depressingly familiar) reading. While providing some answers, it raised as many questions. Chief among them: what burden of proof needs to be met, what weight of evidence established, for a British court to rule that state collusion in a conflict killing took place? That is because, despite testifying to a litany of 'failings' in terms of 'acts and omissions' on the part of the police investigation and actions of state agents surrounding the killing, the coroner ultimately concluded he nevertheless could not find 'direct or indirect evidence of collusion'.[45]

The court ruled it was not British soldiers who had been seen in the old mill days before the shooting.[46] It also accepted the argument of the British Army that its highly trained covert soldiers, dug in near the Mallon property, could not see, properly hear or respond to the lethal shooting and that the order from their officer they should not intervene was justified.[47] If the six undercover soldiers were there as a 'Quick Reaction Force', said the military, this was only if there was a 'risk of compromise to the camera'; though also claiming they were 500 yards away and (at the same time) that it would have taken them 'some 20 to 25 minutes' to reach the camera. The coroner similarly accepted the official explanation that the surveillance cameras ('whatever the family had been told by the civilian "expert"') could not film at night.[48]

A considerable body of evidence was presented to support these claims. Yet the question must surely still arise as to what it is this complex and costly covert operation was there to do, after dark, supposedly stalking the lethal force of the IRA, amid the blackened fields of East Tyrone? The post-dusk ineffectiveness of the military's surveillance, the camera's supposed lack of a zoom capability, its capacity to pan part of the route toward the house taken by the killers, as well as the general character of the covert operation, are all matters that continue to be fiercely contested by the Mallon family. 'To those of you who think we, as nationalists or republicans, will get justice in a British court from a British judge', declared Martin Mallon in response, 'read this judgement'.

Judge Weir noted his conclusions were based on 'the evidence which has been brought before me'.[49] At the same time he confirmed that (potentially important) evidence had not been provided, disappeared, been lost, tampered with or destroyed by the police – including suspect interview notes, police officers' notebooks, and last, but by no means least, the wiped video footage taken from the covert British post on the day of the killing. Much here is focused on the role of RUC Special Branch. Senior figures in the 'force within a force', it was found, had taken a decision not to provide the original murder investigation team with information, knowledge of the covert surveillance or (at any stage) the tapes showing the cars present during the day outside the Mallon home.[50] A list of registration numbers they eventually provided also contained unexplained 'discrepancies'.[51] An eyewitness who said he could identify the person to whom he had sold the getaway car was never invited back to take part in an ID parade.[52] There was no explanation either as to why Special Branch had not handed over various other tapes and logs to the murder inquiry, or why, apparently even before some of them may have been viewed, SB informed the CID officers investigating Roseann's murder this material held 'nothing of evidential value'.[53] The 'apparent despatch' with which some army logs were destroyed similarly struck the coroner as 'odd'. The later absence of police notebooks for the coroner to view was 'unhelpful'.[54] The destruction of the interview notes of the interrogation of Billy Wright and two other suspects, part of the large tranche of documents destroyed at Gough Barracks, was 'very surprising' and 'casual in the extreme'.[55] Getting to the truth was also hindered by the refusal of some former policemen, servants of the law, to cooperate with the court and the lengthy, drawn-out battles to overcome official barriers put in the way of disclosure.

Yet, the coroner drew no inference from this destruction of evidence and record of obstructionism (as has happened in other cases), declaring instead he could not find sufficient proof of collusion. Indeed, far from taking such destruction as itself evidence of collusion, because it was unseen (having been destroyed), the judge was even unwilling to say whether the lost evidence might have materially affected the original police investigation; something of a pirouette of legal logic that should provide little comfort to anyone – aside from those with a predilection for making evidence disappear.[56]

As important are the range of questions the coroner did not, in some instances could not, consider. That starts with what he understood collusion to be, which went undefined. While explaining away as 'entirely innocent' the official misrecognition of the gun used in the shooting, he also noted it was part of a loyalist 'consignment received into Northern Ireland'.[57] However, the role of British intelligence in the South African arms importation was not something he was ever going to explore. The record of threats made against Martin Mallon prior to the attack, both by Billy Wright and by state officials while held in custody, was not considered by the court. Even though he had himself earlier raised the question (with no little display of intent) as to whether or not Wright, or any others potentially involved in the killing, were agents and informers, that vital, overriding issue ultimately formed no part of the coroner's final verdict. A striking absence which therefore ensured (among other things) that a motive for official wrongdoing was always lacking. And, of course, the 'surprising', 'unexplained' and 'odd' events surrounding the death and investigation could not be seen in the light of similar patterns evident in other cases in East Tyrone and elsewhere, because that is not what an inquest is designed to do. All of which only serves to reinforce, again, the need for a comprehensive process truly capable of getting beyond the denials and cover-ups of the counterinsurgency role of collusion in the North's 'dirty war'.

Notes

Introduction

1. Ivan Little, *UTV Live at Six* (6 January 2004).
2. Allison Morris, 'Relatives of Mid-Ulster victims of UVF welcome Ombudsman's collective inquiry', *Irish News*, 16 November 2016.
3. Al Hutchinson, *Public Statement by the Police Ombudsman Relating to the Complaint by the Relatives of the Victims of the Bombing of McGurk's Bar, Belfast on 4 December 1971* (Belfast: PONI, 2011); Al Hutchinson, *Public Statement by the Police Ombudsman Relating to the Murders at the Heights Bar, Loughinisland on 18 June 1994* (Belfast: PONI, 2011); Al Hutchinson, *Public Statement by the Police Ombudsman Relating to the RUC Investigation of the Alleged Involvement of the Late Father James Chesney in the Bombing of Claudy on 31 July 1972* (Belfast: PONI, 2010); Lord Ranald MacLean, *The Billy Wright Inquiry Report* (London: HMSO, 2010).
4. Graham Ellison and Jim Smyth, *The Crowned Harp: Policing in Northern Ireland* (London: Pluto Press, 2000), p. 134.
5. Relatives for Justice, *Collusion 1990–1994: Loyalist Paramilitary Murders in North of Ireland* (Belfast: Relatives for Justice, 1995), p. 1.
6. Sir John Stevens, *Stevens Enquiry 3: Overview and Recommendations* (17 April 2003), p. 3.
7. Judge Peter Cory, *Cory Collusion Inquiry Report: Patrick Finucane* (London: HMSO, 2004), p. 21.
8. Mark McGovern, 'Inquiring into collusion? Collusion, the state and the management of truth recovery in Northern Ireland', *State Crime*, 2:1 (2013), pp. 4–29. See also Committee on the Administration of Justice, *Mapping the Rollback? Human Rights Provisions of the Belfast/Good Friday Agreement 15 Years On* (Belfast: CAJ, 2013); Committee on the Administration of Justice, *Human Rights and Dealing with Historic Cases: A Review of the Office of the Police Ombudsman for Northern Ireland* (Belfast: CAJ, 2011); Hutchinson, *McGurk's Bar*; MacLean, *Billy Wright*.
9. CAJ, *Dealing with Historic Cases*. See also Sir Desmond de Silva QC, *The Report of the Patrick Finucane Review: Volumes I and II* (London: HMSO, 2012), p. 30; Hutchinson, *Bombing of Claudy*; Hutchinson, *McGurk's Bar*; Hutchinson, *Loughinisland*; Maclean, *Billy Wright*, p. 9; McGovern, *Inquiring into Collusion*.
10. Michael Maguire, *The Murders at the Heights Bar, Loughinisland, 18 June 1994* (Belfast: PONI, 2016); Judge Peter Smithwick, *Report of the Tribunal of Inquiry into Suggestions that Members of An Garda Síochána or other Employees of the State Colluded in the Fatal Shootings of RUC Chief Super-

intendent Harry Breen and RUC Superintendent Robert Buchanan on 20th March 1989 (Dublin: Stationary Office, 2013).
11. Mark McGovern, 'See no evil collusion in Northern Ireland', *Race and Class*, 58:3 (2017), pp. 46–63; Mark McGovern, 'Informers, agents and the liberal ideology of collusion in Northern Ireland', *Critical Studies on Terrorism*, 9:2 (2016), pp. 292–311; Mark McGovern, 'State violence and the colonial roots of collusion', *Race and Class*, 57:2 (2015), pp. 3–23; Mark McGovern, 'The dilemma of democracy: collusion and the state of exception', *Studies in Social Justice*, 5:2 (2011), pp. 213–30.
12. This definition of institutional racism was given by A. Sivanandan, former director of the Institute of Race Relations. See also Jenny Bourne, 'The life and times of institutional racism', *Race and Class*, 43:2 (2001), pp. 7–22, p. 9; A. Sivanandan, *Catching History on the Wing: Race, Culture and Globalisation* (London: Pluto Press, 2008).
13. Angelique Chrisafis, 'Mystery of Sinn Fein man who spied for British', *The Guardian*, 17 December 2005.
14. 'Transcript of a Telephone Conversation with General Sir John Wilsey being interviewed by "Jeremy Giles"', 14 April 2012. See also Martin Ingram and Greg Harkin, *Stakeknife: Britain's Secret Agents in Ireland* (Dublin: O'Brien Press, 2004).
15. David McKittrick, Seamus Kelters, Brian Feeney and Chris Thornton, *Lost Lives: The Stories of the Men, Women and Children Who Died as a Result of the Northern Ireland Troubles* (Edinburgh: Mainstream Publishing, 1999), pp. 1473–6.

Chapter 1

1. Sir Desmond de Silva QC, *The Report of the Patrick Finucane Review: Volumes I and II* (London: HMSO, 2012). See also Paddy Hillyard, 'Perfidious Albion: collusion and cover-up in Northern Ireland', *Statewatch*, 22:4 (2013), pp. 1–14; Justin O'Brien, *Killing Finucane: Murder in Defence of the Realm* (Dublin: Gill and Macmillan, 2005); Bill Rolston, '"An effective mask for terror": democracy, death squads and Northern Ireland', *Crime, Law and Social Change*, 44:2 (2005), pp. 181–203.
2. De Silva, *Patrick Finucane Review (I)*, p. 121.
3. Colin Crawford, *Inside the UDA: Volunteers and Violence* (London: Pluto Press, 2003), p. 44.
4. Mark McGovern, 'See no evil collusion in Northern Ireland', *Race and Class*, 58:3 (2017), pp. 46–63; Mark McGovern, 'Informers, agents and the liberal ideology of collusion in Northern Ireland', *Critical Studies on Terrorism*, 9:2 (2016), pp. 292–311.
5. Mark McGovern, 'State violence and the colonial roots of collusion', *Race and Class*, 57:2 (2015), pp. 3–23.
6. Ian Cobain, 'Northern Ireland loyalist shootings: one night of carnage, 18 years of silence', *The Guardian* (15 October 2012).

7. British Army, *British Army Field Manual Volume 1 Part 10: Counterinsurgency Army Code 71876* (London: Ministry of Defence, 2009), p. 1–6.
8. United States Army, *Counterinsurgency: Field Manual No. 3-24* (Washington, DC: Headquarters Department of the Army, 2006).
9. Thomas Rid, 'The nineteenth century origins of counterinsurgency doctrine', *Journal of Strategic Studies*, 33:5 (2010), pp. 727–58, p. 727.
10. David Petraeus, 'Foreword', in *Social Science Goes to War: The Human Terrain System in Iraq and Afghanistan*, ed. by Montgomery McFate and Janice H. Laurence (London: Hurst and Company, 2015), pp. vii–xi, p. ix.
11. David Kilcullen, 'Counterinsurgency: the state of a controversial art', in *The Routledge Handbook of Insurgency and Counterinsurgency*, ed. by Paul B. Rich and Isabelle Duyvesteyn (London: Routledge, 2014), pp. 128–53.
12. United States Army, *Psychological Operations: Field Manual No. 3-05.30* (Washington, DC: Headquarters Department of the Army, 2005).
13. British Army, *Field Manual*, pp. 1–7.
14. Kilcullen, 'Counterinsurgency', p. 144.
15. Brigadier Gavin Bulloch, 'Military doctrine and counter-insurgency: a British perspective', *Parameters: US Army War College Quarterly*, Summer (1996), pp. 4–16, p. 6.
16. Ibid., p. 11.
17. British Army, *Field Manual*, 1–13.
18. Rod Thornton, 'Historical origins of the British Army's counterinsurgency and counterterrorist techniques', in *Combatting Terrorism and its Implications for the Security Sector*, ed. by Theodor Winkler, Anja Ernöther and Mats Hanson (Stockholm: Swedish National Defence College, 2005), pp. 26–44, p. 26.
19. Ibid.; David A. Charters, 'Counter-insurgency intelligence: the evolution of British theory and practice', *Journal of Conflict Studies*, 29 (2009), pp. 55–74, p. 5.
20. General Sir Mike Jackson, 'The safety of the realm in retrospect and prospect: the future of land warfare', *RUSI Journal*, 148:4 (2003), pp. 55–9, p. 58; General Sir Mike Jackson, 'British counter-insurgency', *Journal of Strategic Studies*, 32:3 (2009), pp. 347–51, p. 347.
21. Jackson, 'British counter-insurgency', p. 349.
22. Ibid., 350.
23. M.L.R. Smith, 'A tradition that never was: critiquing the critique of British COIN', *Small Wars Journal* (9 August 2012).
24. Ibid.
25. Paul Dixon, '"Hearts and minds"? British counter-insurgency from Malaya to Iraq', *Journal of Strategic Studies*, 32:3 (2009), pp. 353–81; Matthew Hughes, 'Introduction: British ways of counterinsurgency', *Small Wars and Insurgencies*, 23:4–5 (2012), pp. 580–90; Bruno C. Reis, 'The myth of British minimum force in counterinsurgency campaigns during decolonisation', *Journal of Strategic Studies*, 34:2 (2011), pp. 245–79.
26. Colonel Charles E. Callwell, *Small Wars: Their Principle and Practice* (Lincoln NE: University of Nebraska Press, 1996, 3rd edn); Major-Gen-

eral Charles Gwynn, *Imperial Policing* (London: Macmillan, 1939, 3rd edn); Frank Kitson, *Bunch of Five* (London: Faber and Faber, 1977); Frank Kitson, *Low Intensity Operations: Subversion, Insurgency and Peacekeeping* (London: Faber and Faber, 1971); Frank Kitson, *Gangs and Counter-Gangs* (London: Barrie and Rockliff, 1960).

27. Alexander Alderson, 'Revising the British Army's counterinsurgency doctrine', *RUSI Journal*, 152:4 (2007), pp. 6–11, p. 10; Callwell, *Small Wars*.
28. T. R. Moreman. 'Callwell, Sir Charles Edward (1859–1928)', in *Oxford Dictionary of National Biography* (Oxford: Oxford University Press, 2004).
29. Jacqueline Genet, *The Big House in Ireland: Reality and Representation* (Cork: Brandon Press, 1991), p. 191, p. 17; Keith Jeffrey, *Field Marshall Sir Henry Wilson: A Political Soldier* (Oxford: Oxford University Press, 2006); Declan Kiberd, *Inventing Ireland: The Literature of the Modern Nation* (London: Jonathan Cape, 1995), pp. 69–82. The Callwell family estate in Ballycastle, Co. Antrim had been built by his grandfather, a Belfast banker. His mother was one of the Martins of Connemara, who lost their estate in 1872, and his aunt, Violet Florence Martin, writing under a pseudonym, formed one half of the popular 'Big House' and comic novel-writing duo Somerville and Ross.
30. Moreman, 'Callwell'.
31. In March 1914, British Army Officers at the Curragh, the military HQ in Ireland, indicated they would refuse government instructions to move against the armed UVF should the Irish Home Rule bill, then before Parliament, become law.
32. Bernard Ash, *The Lost Dictator: Field Marshal Sir Henry Wilson* (London: Cassels, 1968); A.T.Q. Stewart, *The Ulster Crisis: Resistance to Home Rule, 1912–14* (London: Faber and Faber, 1979); Charles Townsend, *Political Violence in Ireland: Government and Resistance Since 1948* (Oxford: Clarendon Press, 1983), pp. 268–73.
33. Alvin Jackson, 'Irish Unionism', in *The Making of Modern Irish History: Revisionism and the Revisionist Controversy*, ed. by D. George Boyce and Alan O'Day (London: Routledge, 1996), pp.120–40, p. 126.
34. Callwell, *Small Wars*, pp. 21–2; Andrew Mumford and Bruno C. Reis, 'Constructing and deconstructing warrior-scholars', in *The Theory and Practice of Counter-insurgency: Warrior Scholarship in Counter-insurgency*, ed. by Andrew Mumford and Bruno C. Reis (London: Routledge, 2014), pp. 4–17.
35. Callwell, *Small Wars*, p. 25, p. 80. See also Daniel Whittingham, '"Savage warfare": C.E. Callwell, the roots of counterinsurgency and the nineteenth century context', *Small Wars and Insurgencies*, 23:4–5 (2012), pp. 591–607.
36. Callwell, *Small Wars*, p. 80.
37. Ibid., pp. 72–6.
38. Ibid., p. 77.
39. Sven Lindqvist, *A History of Bombing* (London: Granta, 2001), para. 50; Sven Lindqvist, *Exterminate All the Brutes* (London: Granta, 1997).

40. Laleh Khalili, *Time in the Shadows: Confinement in Counterinsurgencies* (Stanford CA: Stanford University Press, 2013), p. 28.
41. Callwell, quoted in Whittingham, 'Savage Warfare', p. 601.
42. Callwell, *Small Wars*, pp. 146-9.
43. Georgina Sinclair, 'Gwynn, Sir Charles William (1870-1963)', in *Oxford Dictionary of National Biography*.
44. Gwynn's father was a Church of Ireland clergyman (later Professor of Divinity at Trinity College, Dublin), his maternal grandfather the Young Ireland Movement leader, William Smith O'Brien and his eldest brother the journalist, author and leading Home Rule MP Stephen Gwynn. See Henry Boylan, *A Dictionary of Irish Biography* (Dublin: Gill and Macmillan, 1988), p. 141; Louis McRedmond, *Modern Irish Lives: Dictionary of 20th Century Biography* (Dublin: Gill and Macmillan, 1998), p. 122.
45. Sinclair, 'Gwynn'.
46. Gwynn, *Imperial Policing*, p. 8.
47. Charters, 'Counter-insurgency intelligence', p. 11.
48. Gwynn, *Imperial Policing*, p. 14.
49. Ibid., p. v, pp. 367-70.
50. Ibid., pp. 375-80.
51. Richard Andrew Cahill, '"Going Berserk": "Black and Tans" in Palestine', *Jerusalem Quarterly*, 38 (2009); Ian Cobain, *Cruel Britannia: A Secret History of Torture* (London: Portebello Books, 2012), p. 77; Matthew Hughes, 'The banality of brutality: British armed forces and the repression of the Arab Revolt in Palestine', *English Historical Review*, 124:507 (2009), pp. 313-54, pp. 332-3.
52. Hughes, 'Banality of brutality', p. 347.
53. Gwynn, *Imperial Policing*, p. 376, Hughes, 'Banality of brutality', pp. 320-3, pp. 349-50.
54. Hughes, 'Banality of brutality', pp. 329-31.
55. Matthew Hughes, 'The practice and theory of British counterinsurgency: the histories of the atrocities at the Palestinian villages of al-Bassa and Halhul, 1938-1939', *Small Wars and Insurgencies*, 20:3-4 (2009), pp. 528-50, pp. 531-2.
56. Khalili, *Time in the Shadows*, p. 31.
57. Hughes, 'Banality of brutality', p. 350.
58. War Office, 1929, p. 255, quoted in Hughes, 'Banality of brutality', p. 317.
59. Hughes, 'Banality of brutality', pp. 317-18.
60. Gwynn, *Imperial Policing*, pp. 382-91.
61. Ibid., 24.
62. See for example William Matchett, *Secret Victory: The Intelligence War that Beat the IRA* (Belfast: Matchett, 2016), p. 34.
63. John Newsinger, *British Counter-insurgency: From Palestine to Northern Ireland* (Basingstoke: Palgrave, 2002), p. 170. See also Roger Faligot, *Britain's Military Strategy in Ireland: The Kitson Experiment* (London: Zed Books, 1983); John Newsinger, 'British security policy in Northern Ireland', *Race and Class*, 37:1 (1995), pp. 83-94; John Newsinger, 'From

counter-insurgency to internal security: Northern Ireland 1969–1992', *Small Wars and Insurgencies*, 6:1 (1995), pp. 88–111; John Newsinger, 'Minimum force, British counter-insurgency and the Mau Mau rebellion', *Small Wars and Insurgencies*, 3:1 (1992), pp. 47–57; John Newsinger, 'A counter-insurgency tale: Kitson in Kenya', *Race and Class*, 31:4 (1990), pp. 61–72.

64. Kitson, *Bunch of Five*, *Low-Intensity Operations* and *Gangs and Counter-Gangs*.
65. Newsinger, 'Kitson in Kenya', p. 61.
66. Newsinger, *British Counter-insurgency*, p. 168.
67. Bulloch in British Army, *Field Manual*, p. 1–5.
68. Kitson, *Gangs and Counter-gangs*.
69. Antony Anghie, *Imperialism, Sovereignty and the Making of International Law* (Cambridge: Cambridge University Press, 2005); Beau Grosscup, *Strategic Terror: The Politics and Ethics of Aerial Bombardment* (London: Zed Books, 2006); Khalili, *Time in the Shadows*, p. 60; Lindqvist, *History of Bombing*.
70. Kitson, *Bunch of Five*, p. 301.
71. Sir Robert Thompson, *Defeating Communist Insurgency: The Lessons of Malaya and Vietnam* (London: Praeger, 1966). See also David French, 'Nasty not nice: British counter-insurgency doctrine and practice', *Small Wars and Insurgencies*, 23:4–5 (2012), pp. 744–61, p. 745.
72. Huw Bennett, '"A very salutary effect": the counter-terror strategy in the early Malayan Emergency', *Journal of Strategic Studies*, 32:3 (2009), pp. 415–44; Paul Dixon, '"Hearts and minds"? British counter-insurgency from Malaya to Iraq', *Journal of Strategic Studies*, 32:3 (2009), pp. 353–81; Karl Hack, 'The Malayan Emergency as counter-insurgency paradigm', *Journal of Strategic Studies*, 32:3 (2009), pp. 383–414; Patricia Owens, *Economy of Force: Counterinsurgency and the Historical Rise of the Social* (Cambridge: Cambridge University Press, 2015).
73. Kitson, *Bunch of Five*.
74. Ibid., p. 302.
75. Ibid., p. xii.
76. Ibid., pp. 286–7, p. 291.
77. Ibid.
78. Huw Bennett and Rory Cormac, 'Low intensity operations in theory and practice: General Sir Frank Kitson as warrior scholar', in *The Theory and Practice of Irregular Warfare*, ed. by Andrew Mumford and Bruno C. Reis (London: Routledge, 2013), pp. 105–24, p. 119.
79. Kitson, *Low-Intensity Operations*, p. 69.
80. Newsinger, 'Kitson in Kenya', p. 63.
81. Kitson, *Low-Intensity Operations*, p. 69.
82. Kitson, *Bunch of Five*, pp. 289–90.
83. Matchett, *Secret Victory*, p. 34.
84. Owens, *Economy of Force*, p. 187.
85. Matchett, *Secret Victory*, p. 34.

86. Raymond Murray, *The SAS in Ireland* (Dublin: Mercier Press, 1990), p. 41.
87. Lawrence E. Cline, *Pseudo Operations and Counterinsurgency: Lessons from Other Countries* (Carlisle PA: Strategic Studies Institute, 2005); Daniel Branch, 'Footprints in the sand: colonial counterinsurgency and the war in Iraq', *Politics and Society*, 38:1 (2010), pp. 15–34.
88. Branch, 'Footprints in the sand', p. 24. See also Daniel Branch, 'The enemy within: loyalists and the war against the Mau Mau in Kenya', *Journal of African History*, 48:2 (2007), pp. 291–315.
89. Kitson, *Bunch of Five*, p. 59.
90. David Anderson, *Histories of the Hanged: Britain's Dirty War in Kenya and the End of Empire* (London: Weidenfeld and Nicholson, 2006); Cobain, *Cruel Britannia*; Caroline Elkins, *Britain's Gulag: The Brutal End of Empire in Kenya* (London: Jonathan Cape, 2005).
91. Bruce B. Campbell, 'Death squads: definitions, problems and historical context', in *Death Squads in Global Perspective: Murder with Deniability*, ed. by Bruce B. Campbell and Arthur D. Brenner (London: Palgrave, 2002), pp. 1–2.

Chapter 2

1. Ciarán MacAirt, *The McGurk's Bar Bombing: Collusion, Cover-up and a Campaign for Truth* (Edinburgh: Frontline Noir, 2012).
2. Al Hutchinson, *Public Statement by the Police Ombudsman Relating to the Complaint by the Relatives of the Victims of the Bombing of McGurk's Bar, Belfast on 4 December 1971* (Belfast: PONI, 2011), p. 70, p. 77.
3. Ibid., p. 69.
4. Colin Wallace, quoted in MacAirt, *McGurk's*, p. xi.
5. David McKittrick, quoted in David Miller, *Don't Mention the War: Northern Ireland, Propaganda and the Media* (London: Pluto, 1994), p. 79.
6. Gavin Bulloch, in British Army, *British Army Field Manual Volume 1 Part 10: Counterinsurgency Army Code 71876* (London: Ministry of Defence, 2009), pp. 1–5; Paul Foot, *Who Framed Colin Wallace?* (London: Macmillan, 1989), p. 16.
7. John Black, *Killing for Britain* (Scotland: Frontline Noir, 2008); MacAirt, *McGurk's*.
8. Mark Urban, *Big Boys' Rules: The Secret Struggle Against the IRA* (London: Faber and Faber, 1992), pp. 35–6.
9. Ibid., p. 35. The very name of the MRF was the subject of deliberate confusion, sometimes known as the Mobile Reconnaissance Force or the Military Reconnaissance Force.
10. David A. Charters, 'Professionalizing clandestine military intelligence in Northern Ireland: creating the Special Reconnaissance Unit', *Intelligence and National Security*, 33:1 (2018), pp. 130–8.
11. Ibid., p. 135.
12. Urban, *Big Boys' Rules*, p. 35.

13. Raymond Murray, *The SAS in Ireland* (Dublin: Mercier Press, 1990), pp. 41-5. See also Tony Geraghty, *The Irish War: The Military History of a Domestic Conflict* (London: HarperCollins, 1998), pp. 137-9.
14. BBC, 'Britain's secret terror force', *Panorama*, 21 November 2013; Murray, *SAS in Ireland*, pp. 45-8.
15. Quoted in Urban, *Big Boys' Rules*, p. 35.
16. Former MRF member, in BBC, 'Britain's secret terror force'.
17. Simon Cursey, *MRF Shadow Troop: The Untold Story of Top Secret British Military Intelligence Undercover Operations in Belfast, Northern Ireland, 1972-1974* (London: Thistle Publishing, 2013), p. i.
18. Major-General Charles Gwynn, *Imperial Policing* (London: Macmillan, 1939, 3rd edn), p. 8.
19. Keith Jeffrey, 'Intelligence and counter-insurgency operations: some reflections on the British experience', *Intelligence and National Security*, 2:1 (1987), pp. 118-49, p. 127.
20. D.M. Leeson, *The Black and Tans: British Police and Auxiliaries in the Irish War on Independence, 1920-1921* (Oxford: Oxford University Press, 2011), p. 1.
21. Ibid., pp. 2-3.
22. C.J.C. Street, *Ireland in 1921* (London: Phillip Allan and Co, 1922), p. 5.
23. Peter Hart, *The IRA at War, 1916-1923* (Oxford: Oxford University Press, 2003); Peter Hart, *The IRA and Its Enemies: Violence and Community in Cork, 1916-1923* (Oxford: Oxford University Press, 1998).
24. I.O., *The Administration of Ireland, 1920* (London: Phillip Allan and Co, 1921), p. 300; Street, *Ireland in 1921*, p. 5.
25. I.O., *Administration of Ireland*, p. 299, p. 311.
26. Hart, *The IRA at War*, p. 79.
27. Charles Townsend, *Political Violence in Ireland: Government and Resistance Since 1948* (Oxford: Clarendon Press, 1983), p. 352.
28. Sir Henry Wilson, Wilson's Diary, 7 July 1920, quoted in Charles Townshend, *The British Campaign in Ireland 1919-1921: The Development of Political and Military Policies* (Oxford: Oxford University Press, 1978), p. 100; Bernard Ash, *The Lost Dictator: Field Marshal Sir Henry Wilson* (London: Cassels, 1968), p. 276.
29. Winston Churchill, quoted in Townshend, *Political Violence*, p. 352.
30. Sir Henry Wilson, Wilson's Diary, 23 September 1920, quoted in Townshend, *British Campaign in Ireland*, p. 116.
31. Townshend, *British Campaign in Ireland*, p. 100.
32. Sir Henry Wilson, quoted in Keith Jeffrey, *Field Marshall Sir Henry Wilson: A Political Soldier* (Oxford: Oxford University Press, 2006), p. 266.
33. Major General Sir Charles E. Callwell, *Field Marshall Sir Henry Wilson: His Life and Diaries, Volume II* (London: Cassels, 1927), p. 252.
34. Sir Henry Wilson, quoted in Callwell, *Sir Henry Wilson (II)*, p. 263.
35. Letter from Major General Radcliffe to Sir Henry Wilson, 23 September 1920, quoted in Townshend, *British Campaign in Ireland*, p. 119.
36. Townshend, *British Campaign in Ireland*, p. 120, p. 101.

37. Jonathan Evershed, *Ghosts of the Somme: Commemoration and Culture War in Northern Ireland* (Notre Dame, IN: University of Notre Dame Press, 2018).
38. Michael Farrell, *Arming the Protestants: The Formation of the Ulster Special Constabulary and the Royal Ulster Constabulary, 1920–27* (London: Pluto Press, 1983), pp. 7–29.
39. Sir Basil Brooke, quoted in Farrell, *Arming the Protestants*, p. 29.
40. Sir Henry Wilson quoted in Paul Bew, Peter Gibbon and Henry Patterson, *Northern Ireland 1921–1994: Political Forces and Social Classes* (London: Serif, 1995), p. 36; Callwell, *Sir Henry Wilson (II)*, p. 254.
41. Bew, Gibbon and Patterson, *Northern Ireland*, p. 35.
42. Ibid., p. 41.
43. Farrell, *Arming the Protestants*, p. 100.
44. Ibid., pp. 159–60.
45. Michael Farrell, *Northern Ireland: The Orange State* (London: Pluto Press, 1976); Michael Farrell, *Arming the Protestants*.
46. The 'B' Specials were one branch of the UCS when it was first created, the others were discontinued overtime.
47. Farrell, *The Orange State*, p. 96.
48. Laura K. Donohue, *Counter-terrorist Law an Emergency Powers in the United Kingdom, 1922–2000* (Dublin: Irish Academic Press, 2001), p. xxi.
49. Dermot Walsh, *Bloody Sunday and the Rule of Law in Northern Ireland* (Dublin: Gill and Macmillan, 2000), p. 28. See also Laura K. Donohue, *Counter-terrorist Law*; Laura K. Donohue, *The Cost of Counterterrorism: Power, Politics and Liberty* (Cambridge: Cambridge University Press, 2008).
50. Ronald Weitzer, *Policing Under Fire: Ethnic Conflict and Police–Community Relations in Northern Ireland* (Albany, NY: State University of New York Press, 1995), p. 42.
51. John McGuffin, *Internment* (Tralee: Anvil Books, 1973), p. 84.
52. Walsh, *Bloody Sunday and the Rule of Law*, p. 28.
53. Ibid., p. 29.
54. Graham Ellison and Jim Smyth, *The Crowned Harp: Policing in Northern Ireland* (London: Pluto Press, 2000) p. 42.
55. Ibid., p. 38; Mark Brogden and Graham Ellison, *Policing in an Age of Austerity: A Postcolonial Perspective* (Abingdon: Routledge, 2013), pp. 85–102.
56. Pat Finucane Centre, *The Hidden History of the UDR: The Secret Files Revealed* (Derry: Pat Finucane Centre, 2014); Margaret Urwin, *A State in Denial: British Collaboration with Loyalist Paramilitaries* (Cork: Mercier Press, 2016).
57. Ellison and Smyth, *Crowned Harp*, p. 138. See also Niall Ó Dochartaigh, *From Civil Rights to Armalites: Derry and the Birth of the Irish Troubles* (Basingstoke: Palgrave, 1997), p. 144.
58. Ministry of Defence, *Operation Banner: An Analysis of Military Operations in Northern Ireland, Army Code 71842* (London: MoD, 2006), pp. 3–6.

Operation Banner is the British Army's own strategic analysis of its 37-year campaign in Northern Ireland.
59. Ibid., p. 3–5, Ellison and Smyth, *Crowned Harp*, p. 73, Sir Michael Morland, *The Rosemary Nelson Inquiry Report* (London: HMSO, 2011), p. 179; CAIN, 'Security and Defence', available at: http://cain.ulst.ac.uk/ni/security.htm.
60. Ministry of Defence, *Operation Banner*, pp. 3–5, pp. 3–6.
61. SDLP report on the UDR, 1980, quoted in Chris Ryder, *The Ulster Defence Regiment: An Instrument of Peace* (London: Methuen, 1991), p. 199.
62. Pat Finucane Centre, *Hidden History of the UDR*.
63. Ellison and Smyth, *Crowned Harp*, pp. 139–40.
64. Ministry of Defence, *Operation Banner*, pp. 3–5.
65. Mark McGovern, 'Informers, agents and the liberal ideology of collusion in Northern Ireland', *Critical Studies on Terrorism*, 9:2 (2016), pp. 292–311, pp. 297–8. See also Ellison and Smyth, *Crowned Harp*, pp. 138–41; Pat Finucane Centre, *Hidden History of the UDR*; Relatives for Justice, *Loughinisland Massacre: Collusion, Cover-up* (Belfast: RFJ, 2012).
66. For a thorough and detailed analysis of the activities of the Glennane Gang see Anne Cadwallader, *Lethal Allies: British Collusion in Ireland* (Cork: Mercier Press, 2013). See also Michael Maguire, *The Murders at the Heights Bar, Loughinisland, 18 June 1994* (Belfast: PONI, 2016).
67. Joe Tiernan, *The Dublin and Monaghan Bombings* (Dublin: Joe Tiernan, 2006), p. 93. See also Denis Faul and Raymond Murray, *The Triangle of Death: Sectarian Assassinations in the Dungannon-Moy-Portadown Area* (Dungannon: Denis Faul and Raymond Murray, 1975); Raymond Murray, *The SAS in Ireland* (Dublin: Mercier Press, 1990).
68. Cadwallader, *Lethal Allies*, pp. 99–108, Don Mullan, *The Dublin and Monaghan Bombings* (Dublin: Merlin Publishing, 2000); Tiernan, *Dublin and Monaghan Bombings*; Stephen Travers and Neil Fetherstonhaugh, *The Miami Showband Massacre: A Survivors Search for Truth* (Dublin: Hodder Headline, 2007).
69. Among those attacked were McArdle's Bar (Crossmaglen), Donnelly's (Silverbridge), Kay's Tavern (Dundalk), Tully's Bar (Belleeks) and the Step Inn (Keady), leaving multiple deaths. See Cadwallader, *Lethal Allies*.
70. Susan McKay, 'Families of the Troubles' victims must learn the truth', *The Irish Times*, 13 June 2008.
71. Cadwallader, *Lethal Allies*, pp. 195–203.
72. Justice Henry Barron, *Interim Report on the Report of the Independent Commission of Inquiry into the Bombing of Kay's Tavern, Dundalk* (Dublin: Stationary Office, 2006), p. 134.
73. Doug Cassels, Suzie Kemp, Piers Pigou and Stephen Sawyer, *Report of the Independent International Panel on Alleged Collusion in Sectarian Killings in Northern Ireland* (Notre Dame IND: Centre for Civil and Human Rights, Notre Dame Law School, 2006).
74. Ibid.; Cadwallader, *Lethal Allies*; Tiernan, *Dublin and Monaghan Bombings*.

75. Liam Clarke, 'RUC men's secret war with the IRA', *Sunday Times*, 7 March 1999.
76. Lord Lowry judgement quoted in Cadwallader, *Lethal Allies*, pp. 306–7.
77. Graham Ellison and Jim Smyth, *The Crowned Harp: Policing in Northern Ireland* (London: Pluto Press, 2000) p. 134.
78. 'British Army Memo "UDR – membership of the UDA", 31 July 1972', available at: hwww.patfinucanecentre.org/sites/default/files/2016–11/1972_02.pdf; David McKittrick, Seamus Kelters, Brian Feeney and Chris Thornton, *Lost Lives: The Stories of the Men, Women and Children Who Died as a Result of the Northern Ireland Troubles* (Edinburgh: Mainstream Publishing, 1999), p. 1475.
79. Pat Finucane Centre, *Hidden History of the UDR*.
80. Urwin, *State in Denial*, p. 61, p. 63.
81. Murray, *SAS in Ireland*, pp. 91–3.
82. Owen Bowcott, 'Former general sued over death of Catholic minibus driver during Troubles', *The Guardian*, 27 April 2015. See also Justice Henry Barron, *Houses of the Oireachtas Joint Committee on Justice, Equality, Defence and Women's Rights Interim Report on the Report of the Independent Commission of Inquiry into the Dublin Bombings of 1972 and 1973* (Dublin: Stationary Office, 2004); Martin Dillon, *The Dirty War* (London: Arrow Books, 1991), pp. 264–77; Ken Livingstone, *Livingstone's Labour* (London: Harper Collins, 1989); Ed Moloney, *Voices from the Grave: Two Men's War in Ireland* (London: Faber and Faber, 2011, 2nd edn), p. 341.
83. Murray, *SAS in Ireland*, pp. 263–4, Urwin, *State in Denial*, pp. 198–9.
84. Mark McGovern, 'The dilemma of democracy: collusion and the state of exception', *Studies in Social Justice*, 5:2 (2011), pp. 213–30; Bill Rolston, '"An effective mask for terror": democracy, death squads and Northern Ireland', *Crime, Law and Social Change*, 44:2 (2005), pp. 181–203.
85. McKittrick et al., *Lost Lives*, pp. 793–9.
86. Ibid., pp. 779–80.
87. Margaret Thatcher, *Margaret Thatcher: The Downing Street Years* (London: HarperCollins, 1993), p. 414; McKittrick et al., *Lost Lives*, p. 799.
88. Prison uniforms for 'special category status' prisoners were introduced as part of a wider criminalisation policy in 1976. Republican prisoners who refused to wear the uniform were given nothing but a blanket to cover themselves. They were also denied prison visits and remission of their sentences, and were subject to beatings and forced body searches. After being confined to their cells for 24 hours a day, and then refusing to leave them to be cleaned, having been beaten when they did, the campaign of the 'blanketmen' escalated to the 'no wash' protest in 1978. This involved those 'on the banket' smearing their own excrement on the walls of their prison cells. The five-year protest campaign only ended with the hunger strike of 1981. David Beresford, *Ten Men Dead: The Story of the 1981 Hunger Strike* (London: Grafton Books, 1987); Brian Campbell, Laurence McKeown and Felim O'Hagan, *Nor Meekly Serve My Time: The H-Block Struggle 1976–1981* (Belfast: Beyond the Pale Publications, 1994); Liam

Clarke, *Broadening the Battlefield: The H-Blocks and the Rise of Sinn Fein* (Dublin: Gill and Macmillan, 1987); Tim Pat Coogan, *On the Blanket: The H-Block Story* (Swords: Ward River Press, 1980).
89. Clarke, *Broadening the Battlefield*; Coogan, *On the Blanket*.
90. Murray, *SAS in Ireland*, pp. 259–60, Urwin, *State in Denial*, pp. 192–5.
91. Murray, *SAS in Ireland*, p. 260; Urwin, *State in Denial*, pp. 195–6.
92. Urwin, *State in Denial*, p. 195.
93. Interview with Suzanne Bunting, 25 June 2013.
94. Ibid.
95. Ibid.
96. Connla Young, 'Claims that RUC were watching house where two INLA men were shot dead', *Irish News*, 28 May 2016.
97. Suzanne Bunting interview.
98. Suzanne Bunting quoted in Jack Holland and Henry McDonald, *INLA: Deadly Divisions* (Dublin: Torc, 1994), p. 159.

Chapter 3

1. Judge Peter Cory, *Cory Collusion Inquiry Report: Patrick Finucane* (London: HMSO, 2004), p. 96. See also Justin O'Brien, *Killing Finucane: Murder in Defence of the Realm* (Dublin: Gill and Macmillan, 2005), pp. 16–17.
2. 'Minutes of a meeting with senior RUC officers, 25 July 2012', quoted in Sir Desmond de Silva QC, *The Report of the Patrick Finucane Review: Volume I* (London: HMSO, 2012), p. 89.
3. Adrian Guelke, 'The Northern Ireland peace process and the War against Terrorism: conflicting conceptions?', *Government and Opposition*, 42:3 (2007), pp. 272–91.
4. Colm Campbell and Ita Connolly, 'A model for the "War against Terrorism"? Military intervention in Northern Ireland and the 1970 Falls curfew', *Journal of Law and Society*, 30:3 (2003), pp. 341–75; Fionnuala Ní Aoláin, *The Politics of Force: Conflict Management and State Violence in Northern Ireland* (Belfast: Blackstaff Press, 2000).
5. Liam O'Dowd, Bill Rolston and Mike Tomlinson, 'From Labour to the Tories: the ideology of containment in Northern Ireland', *Capital and Class*, 6:3 (1982), 72–90; Bill Rolston, 'Containment and its failure: the British State and the control of conflict in Northern Ireland', in *Western State Terrorism*, ed. by Alexander George (Cambridge: Polity Press, 1991), pp. 155–79.
6. Guelke, 'Northern Ireland peace process', p. 275.
7. Paul Bew and Henry Patterson, *The British State and the Ulster Crisis* (London: Verso, 1985); Michael J. Cunningham, *British Government Policy in Northern Ireland, 1969–1989* (Manchester: Manchester University Press, 1991); William Beattie Smith, *The British State and the Northern Ireland Crisis, 1969–73* (Washington, DC: United States Institute of Peace, 2011).

8. Freddie Cowper-Coles, '"Anxious for peace": the Provisional IRA in dialogue with the British government, 1972–75', *Irish Studies Review*, 20:3 (2012), pp. 223–42; Niall Ó Dochartaigh, '"Everyone trying", the IRA ceasefire, 1975: a missed opportunity for peace?', *Field Day Review*, 7 (2011), pp. 51–60.
9. Dermot Walsh, *Bloody Sunday and the Rule of Law in Northern Ireland* (Dublin: Gill and Macmillan, 2000).
10. Guelke, 'Northern Ireland peace process', p. 276.
11. Ní Aoláin, *Politics of Force*, pp. 29–71.
12. Ibid., p. 57.
13. Ibid., p. 58, p. 66.
14. Kevin Hearty, 'The political and military value of the "set-piece" killing tactic in east Tyrone 1983–1992', *State Crime*, 3:1 (2014), pp. 50–72.
15. David A. Charters, 'Counter-insurgency intelligence: the evolution of British theory and practice', *Journal of Conflict Studies*, 29 (2009), pp. 55–74.
16. Colonel Charles E. Callwell, *Small Wars: Their Principle and Practice* (Lincoln, NE: University of Nebraska Press, 1996, 3rd edn), p. 144.
17. Major-General Charles Gwynn, *Imperial Policing* (London: Macmillan, 1939, 3rd edn), p. 393.
18. Charters, 'Counter-insurgency intelligence'.
19. Ibid.
20. Tony Geraghty, *The Irish War: The Military History of a Domestic Conflict* (London: Harper Collins, 1998); Andrew Sanders, 'Northern Ireland: the intelligence war 1969–75', *British Journal of Politics and International Relations*, 13 (2011), pp. 230–48.
21. Jack Holland and Susan Phoenix, *Phoenix: Policing the Shadows* (London: Hodder and Stoughton, 1996), pp. 223–34.
22. Peter Taylor, *Beating the Terrorists: Interrogations in Omagh, Gough and Castlereagh* (London: Penguin, 1980).
23. Lawyers Committee for Human Rights, *Beyond Collusion: The UK Security Forces and the Murder of Pat Finucane* (New York: LCHR, 2002); Peter Taylor, *Brits: The War against the IRA* (London: Bloomsbury, 2001), p. 242.
24. Mark Urban, *Big Boys' Rules: The Secret Struggle Against the IRA* (London: Faber and Faber, 1992), p. 95.
25. Michael Kirk-Smith and James Dingley, 'Countering terrorism in Northern Ireland: the role of intelligence', *Small Wars and Insurgencies*, 20:3–4 (2009), pp. 551–73, p. 551; Jon Moran, 'Evaluating Special Branch and the use of informant intelligence in Northern Ireland', *Intelligence and National Security*, 25:1 (2010), pp. 1–23.
26. Bradley C. Bamford, 'The role and effectiveness of intelligence in Northern Ireland', *Intelligence and National Security*, 20:4 (2005), pp. 581–607.
27. Moran, 'Evaluating Special Branch', pp. 20–1.
28. Peter Neumann, 'The myth of Ulsterization in British security policy', *Studies in Conflict and Terrorism*, 26:5 (2003), pp. 365–77.

29. William Matchett, *Secret Victory: The Intelligence War that Beat the IRA* (Belfast: Matchett, 2016), p. 169.
30. Paddy Hillyard, 'Perfidious Albion: collusion and cover-up in Northern Ireland', *Statewatch*, 22:4 (2013), pp. 1–14, p. 2.
31. Christopher Andrew, *The Defence of the Realm: The Authorised History of MI5* (London: Allen Lane, 2009), p. 561; Walker report quoted in O'Brien, *Killing Finucane*, appendix 1, p. 150; Patrick Walker, *Towards Independence in Africa: A District Officer in Uganda at the End of Empire* (London: I.B. Tauris, 2009).
32. Walker, *Towards Independence in Africa*.
33. Ibid., p. 204.
34. Hillyard, *Perfidious Albion*, p. 2. See also Andrew, *Defence of the Realm*, pp. 699–700. The existence of the Walker Report was only revealed by a BBC Northern Ireland *Insight* programme in 2001. See BBC, 'Policing the police: force within a force', *Insight*, first aired 17 April 2001; O'Brien, *Killing Finucane*, p. 6.
35. Walker Report, quoted in O'Brien, *Killing Finucane*, appendix 1, p. 153.
36. Ibid., p. 153, p. 156.
37. Ibid., pp. 151–2.
38. Interview with Sir Ronnie Flanagan, *UTV Live*, 4 May 2001.
39. De Silva, *Patrick Finucane Review (I)*, p. 252.
40. Ibid., p. 251.
41. Ibid., pp. 254–5.
42. 'Security forces compendium of leaks, 1989', quoted in ibid., p. 255.
43. 'Security Service Loose Minute', quoted in ibid., p. 324.
44. De Silva, *Patrick Finucane Review (I)*, pp. 257–9.
45. 'Security Service, HAG to Director and Co-ordinator of Intelligence (DCI), 29 September 1989', quoted in ibid., pp. 253–5.
46. De Silva, *Patrick Finucane Review (I)*, p. 255, p. 260.
47. Ibid., p. 253.
48. Urban, *Big Boys' Rules*, p. 108; Geraghty, *Irish War*, p. 155.
49. Geraghty, *Irish War*, p. 155.
50. De Silva, *Patrick Finucane Review (I)*, p. 61.
51. Ibid., pp. 118–19.
52. Ibid., pp. 119–21.
53. Ibid., p. 124.
54. 'Gordon Kerr, prepared statement to Stevens Investigation, 2 December 2002', quoted in ibid., p. 109.
55. De Silva, *Patrick Finucane Review (I)*, p. 128.
56. Colin Crawford, *Inside the UDA: Volunteers and Violence* (London: Pluto Press, 2003), p. 44; John Ware, BBC Transcript from *Panorama*, 'A Licence to kill'. First broadcast 19 June 2002.
57. De Silva, *Patrick Finucane Review (I)*, p. 253.
58. Paul Foot, 'Brian Nelson', *The Guardian*, 17 April 2003.

59. See for example Steve Bruce, *The Red Hand: Protestant Paramilitaries in Northern Ireland* (Oxford: Oxford University Press, 1992); Moran, 'Evaluating Special Branch'.
60. Nuala O'Loan, *Statement by the Police Ombudsman for Northern Ireland on Her Investigation into the Circumstances Surrounding the Death of Raymond McCord Jnr and Related Matters* (Belfast: PONI, 2007).
61. Laleh Khalili, *Time in the Shadows: Confinement in Counterinsurgencies* (Stanford CA: Stanford University Press, 2013), p. 46.
62. Stephen Dorril, *The Silent Conspiracy: Inside the Intelligence Services in the 1990s* (London: William Heinemann, 1993), p. 202.
63. 'DPP note 18 October 1990', quoted in de Silva, *Patrick Finucane Review (I)*, p. 70.
64. 'RUC commentary on the *Home Office Guidelines on the Use of Informants*, 11 February 1988', quoted in de Silva, *Patrick Finucane Review (I)*, p. 71.
65. De Silva, *Patrick Finucane Review (I)*, p. 72.
66. Urban, *Big Boys' Rules*, p. 88, p. 112.
67. 'Instructions for source control and handling', quoted in de Silva, *Patrick Finucane Review (I)*, p. 72.
68. De Silva, *Patrick Finucane Review (I)*, pp. 75–88.
69. Ibid., p. 90.
70. 'Commentary on *Home Office Guidelines on the Use of Informants*, by ACC Monahan, 11 February 1988', quoted in ibid., p. 77; 'Loose minute, ACC Blair Wallace to Chief Constable, 27 June 1989', quoted in ibid., p. 80.
71. 'NIO notes for record of RUC-NIO meeting, 13 March 1987', quoted in ibid., p. 76; 'Letter from NIO to RUC, 22 April 1988', quoted in ibid., p. 78.
72. 'Loose minute, ACC Blair Wallace to Chief Constable, 27 June 1989', quoted in ibid., p. 80.
73. De Silva, *Patrick Finucane Review (I)*, p. 89.
74. 'Handwritten note, Solicitor General, 11 August, 1992', quoted in ibid., p. 81.
75. 'MI5 on hunger strike', *Bobby Sands Trust*, 19 March 2009.
76. 'Minute, Security Service Legal Adviser, 25 March 1992', quoted in de Silva, *Patrick Finucane Review (I)*, p. 83.
77. David McKittrick, 'IRA ceasefire: unhappy unionists left outflanked', *Independent*, 1 September 1994; 'Briefing note on agent handling, 1 September 1994', quoted in de Silva, *Patrick Finucane Review (I)*, p. 87.
78. Ibid.
79. Cabinet Office, *Lessons Learnt by Government Departments from Sir Desmond de Silva's Report of the Patrick Finucane Review: A Report by the Cabinet Secretary, the Secretary of State for Defence and the Secretary of State for Northern Ireland* (London: HMSO, 2015).
80. De Silva, *Patrick Finucane Review (I)*, p. 69.
81. Desmond de Silva quoted in John Ware, 'De Silva Report on Finucane case turns spotlight on MI5', *BBC News*, 13 December 2012.
82. 'Anonymous Senior RUC Officer (R/15)', quoted in de Silva, *Patrick Finucane Review (I)*, p. 88.

83. 'Minutes of a meeting with senior RUC officers, 25 July 2012', quoted in ibid., p. 89. R/15 has since been identified as Raymond White, a former Head of RUC Special Branch and latterly the lead on legacy issues for the Northern Ireland Retired Police Officers Association. See Deborah McAleese, 'RTE documentary uncovers Government collusion with loyalist paramilitaries', *Belfast Telegraph*, 12 June 2015.
84. 'NIO record of meeting, 13 March 1987', quoted in ibid., pp. 76–8; Anthony Jennings, 'Shoot to kill: the final courts of justice', in *Justice Under Fire: The Abuse of Civil Liberties in Northern Ireland*, ed. by Anthony Jennings (London: Pluto Press 1990), pp. 104–30, p. 118.
85. 'Submission of John Chilcot to the Secretary of State, 14 July 1993', quoted in de Silva, *Patrick Finucane Review (I)*, p. 86.
86. Consultative Group on the Past, *Report of the Consultative Group on the Past* (London: HMSO 2009), p. 68. See also Cheryl Lawther, 'Denial, silence and the politics of the past: unpicking the opposition to truth recovery in Northern Ireland', *International Journal of Transitional Justice*, 7:1 (2013), pp. 157–77; Cheryl Lawther, 'Securing the past: policing and the contest over truth in Northern Ireland', *British Journal of Criminology*, 50:3 (2010), pp. 455–73; Patricia Lundy and Mark McGovern, 'A Trojan horse: unionism, trust and truth-telling in Northern Ireland', *International Journal of Transitional Justice*, 2:1 (2008d), pp. 42–62.
87. 'A/05, statement to Stevens III Investigation, 2002', quoted in de Silva, *Patrick Finucane Review (I)*, p. 88.
88. Deputy Chief Constable John Stevens, *Report*, 1990; Sir Peter Brooke, 'Northern Ireland (Stevens Report)', *Hansard*, HC Deb, 17 May 1990, vol. 172 cc. 1027–37.
89. David McKittrick, Seamus Kelters, Brian Feeney and Chris Thornton, *Lost Lives: The Stories of the Men, Women and Children Who Died as a Result of the Northern Ireland Troubles* (Edinburgh: Mainstream Publishing, 1999), p. 1176. See also Amnesty International, *Political Killings in Northern Ireland* (London: Amnesty International British Section, 1994), p. 14; O'Brien, *Killing Finucane*, p. 106.
90. Stevens, *Report*, 1990, p. 6.
91. Sir Peter Brooke, HC Deb 17 May 1990 Vol. 172, cc. 1027–8.
92. Amnesty International, *Political Killings*, p. 34; Cory, *Patrick Finucane Report*, p. 95.
93. 'RUC Chief Constable Public Statement, 17 May 1990', quoted in de Silva, *Patrick Finucane Review (I)*, p. 265.
94. 'Lord Stevens of Kirkwhelpington to Rt Hon Sir Desmond de Silva, 4 October 2012', quoted in de Silva, *Patrick Finucane Review (I)*, p. 266.
95. Sir John Stevens, *Stevens Enquiry 3: Overview and Recommendations*, 17 April 2003, p. 13.
96. De Silva, *Patrick Finucane Review (I)*, pp. 467–8; Stevens, *Stevens Inquiry 3*, p. 13.
97. British-Irish Rights Watch, *Deadly Intelligence: State Involvement in Loyalist Murder in Northern Ireland* (London: BIRW, 1999), p. 5.

98. Stevens, *Stevens Inquiry 3*, p. 13, de Silva, *Patrick Finucane Review (I)*, p. 468.
99. De Silva, *Patrick Finucane Review (I)*, p. 468.
100. Ibid., p. 457–60; de Silva, *Patrick Finucane Review (II)*, pp. 308–12.
101. De Silva, *Patrick Finucane Review (I)*, p. 469.
102. Cory, *Patrick Finucane Report*, p. 96. See also O'Brien, *Killing Finucane*, pp. 16–17.
103. Geraghty, *Irish War*, p. 231.
104. Peter Gill and Mark Phythian, *Intelligence in an Insecure World* (Cambridge: Polity Press, 2012); Steve Hewitt, *Snitch! A History of the Modern Intelligence Informer* (London: Continuum, 2010).
105. David Luban, 'Liberalism, torture and the ticking bomb', *Virginia Law Review*, 91 (2005), pp. 1425–61, pp. 1430–8.
106. Luban, 'Liberalism, torture and the ticking bomb', p. 1427. See also Bob Brecher, *Torture and the Ticking Bomb* (Oxford: Blackwell, 2007); David Luban, *Torture, Power and Law* (Cambridge: Cambridge University Press, 2014); David Luban, 'Military necessity and the cultures of military law', *Leiden Journal of International Law*, 26:2 (2013), pp. 315–49.
107. Luban, 'Liberalism, torture and the ticking bomb', p. 1436.
108. Ibid., p. 1439.
109. Ibid., p. 1446.
110. Mark McGovern, 'State violence and the colonial roots of collusion', *Race and Class*, 57:2 (2015), pp. 3–23.
111. Stan Cohen, *States of Denial: Knowing about Atrocities and Suffering* (Cambridge: Polity Press, 2001).
112. B.W. Morgan and M.L.R. Smith, 'Northern Ireland and minimum force: the refutation of a concept?', *Small Wars and Insurgencies*, 27:1 (2016), pp. 81–105.
113. Giorgio Agamben, *State of Exception* (Chicago, IL: University of Chicago Press, 2005), p. 30.

Chapter 4

1. Jim Cusack and Henry McDonald, *UVF* (Dublin: Poolbeg Press, 2000, 2nd edn), pp. 220–5; Peter Taylor, *Loyalists* (London: Bloomsbury, 2000), pp. 188–95.
2. See Cusack and McDonald, *UVF*, pp. 220–5; Taylor, *Loyalists*, pp. 188–95.
3. Taylor, *Loyalists*, pp. 190–1. As a result the weapons are referred to by some authors as the 'Lebanon shipment'.
4. Michael Maguire, *The Murders at the Heights Bar, Loughinisland, 18 June 1994* (Belfast: PONI, 2016), p. 19.
5. Jeffrey A. Sluka, '"For God and Ulster": the culture of terror and loyalist death squads in Northern Ireland', in *Death Squad: The Anthropology of State Terror*, ed. by Jeffrey A. Sluka (Philadelphia, PA: University of Pennsylvania Press, 2000), pp. 127–57, p. 139; Relatives for Justice, *Collusion*

1990-1994: Loyalist Paramilitary Murders in North of Ireland (Belfast: Relatives for Justice, 1995), p. 3.
6. British-Irish Rights Watch, *Deadly Intelligence: State Involvement in Loyalist Murder in Northern Ireland* (London: BIRW, 1999); BBC, 'The Dirty War', *Panorama*, 8 June 1992; Relatives for Justice, *Collusion* (Belfast: RFJ, 2002); Relatives for Justice, *Collusion 1990-1994*; Sinn Fein, *An Appalling Vista: Collusion, British Military Intelligence and Brian Nelson* (Dublin: Sinn Fein, 1997).
7. See Cusack and McDonald, *UVF*, p. 221, Taylor, *Loyalists*, p. 188.
8. Taylor, *Loyalists*, pp. 189-90.
9. Sir Desmond de Silva QC, *The Report of the Patrick Finucane Review: Vol. I* (London: HMSO, 2012), p. 107.
10. Ibid., pp. 96-7.
11. Peter Madden, 'The de Silva Report', *Collusion: From Downing Street to Fortwilliam Drive: Pat Finucane Anniversary Talk*, Belfast, 12 February 2015.
12. Maguire, *Loughinisland*, p. 27.
13. Ibid., p. 34.
14. Ibid.
15. Ibid., p. 37.
16. Ibid., p. 35.
17. Ibid., p. 8, p. 134.
18. Cusack and McDonald, *UVF*, p. 223.
19. Ibid., p. 224.
20. De Silva, *Patrick Finucane Review (I)*, p. 107.
21. Gregory Campbell quoted in Taylor, *Loyalists*, p. 187, p. 190; David McKittrick, 'Citizens' force set up with backing of loyalist politicians and businessmen, "Independent", 24 April, 1989', in *Despatches from Belfast* (Belfast: Blackstaff Press, 1989), pp. 170-2. See also Arthur Aughey, *Under Siege: Ulster Unionism and the Anglo-Irish Agreement* (Belfast: Blackstaff Press, 1989), p. 75; Steve Bruce, *The Red Hand: Protestant Paramilitaries in Northern Ireland* (Oxford: Oxford University Press, 1992), p. 169; Fearghal Cochrane, *Unionist Politics and the Politics of Unionism Since the Anglo-Irish Agreement* (Cork: Cork University Press, 1997), p. 161.
22. Taylor, *Loyalists*, p. 185; Aughey, *Under Siege*, p. 76.
23. Cochrane, *Unionist Politics*, p. 161.
24. Taylor, *Loyalists*, pp. 193-4; 'Man on arms charges jailed', *Irish Times*, 20 January 1990.
25. Cusack and McDonald, *UVF*, p. 221; Taylor, *Loyalists*, p. 188.
26. Martin Dillon, *The Trigger Men* (Edinburgh: Mainstream Publishing, 2004, 2nd edn), pp. 253-4.
27. Taylor, *Loyalists*, pp. 193-5. See also 'The South African connection: guns for arms', *BBC NI: Spotlight*, 27 April 1989.
28. David McKittrick, 'Arms from Africa fuel paramilitary terror in Northern Ireland', *Independent*, 29 October 1991; Taylor, *Loyalists*, pp. 193-4.

29. Ian Cobain, 'Northern Ireland loyalist shootings: one night of carnage, 18 years of silence', *The Guardian*, 15 October 2012.
30. Chris Anderson, *The Billy Boy: The Life and Death of LVF Leader Billy Wright* (Edinburgh: Mainstream Publishing, 2002); Anne Cadwallader, *Lethal Allies: British Collusion in Ireland* (Cork: Mercier Press, 2013).
31. Cusack and McDonald, *UVF*, p. 271.
32. Ed Moloney, *Voices from the Grave: Two Men's War in Ireland* (London: Faber and Faber, 2011, 2nd edn), p. 414.
33. Colin Crawford, *Inside the UDA: Volunteers and Violence* (London: Pluto Press, 2003), pp. 154–64.
34. Jim Cusack and Max Taylor, 'Resurgence of a terrorist organisation: part 1: the UDA, a case study', *Terrorism and Political Violence*, 5:3 (1993), pp. 1–27, p. 5.
35. Cusack and Taylor, 'UDA, a case study', p. 24, p. 26.
36. Bruce, *Red Hand*, pp. 224–5.
37. Jon Moran, 'Evaluating Special Branch and the use of informant intelligence in Northern Ireland', *Intelligence and National Security*, 25:1 (2010), pp. 1–23, p. 23.
38. Moloney, *Voices from the Grave*, p. 418. See also Cobain, 'One Night of Carnage'; Relatives for Justice, *Loughinisland Massacre: Collusion, Cover-up* (Belfast: RFJ, 2012); Nuala O'Loan, *Statement by the Police Ombudsman for Northern Ireland on Her Investigation into the Circumstances Surrounding the Death of Raymond McCord Jnr and Related Matters* (Belfast: PONI, 2007).
39. Taylor, *Loyalists*, p. 192.
40. Jack Holland and Susan Phoenix, *Phoenix: Policing the Shadows* (London: Hodder and Stoughton, 1996), p. 237.
41. Taylor, *Loyalists*, p. 192. The senior UDA figure was Davy Payne, a former British Army paratrooper involved in some of the most horrendous and savage sectarian killings of Catholics during the conflict, often torturing his victims before their death.
42. Holland and Phoenix, *Policing the Shadows*.
43. When young, Phoenix had served in an SAS-led covert unit in Borneo. This often lionized, secret cross-border counterinsurgency campaign dovetailed with US and British destabilisation efforts in Indonesia that would ultimately collaborate with the Indonesian military in the massacre of some half a million people. See Holland and Phoenix, *Policing the Shadows*, p. 30. See also Newsinger, *The Blood Never Dried: A People's History of the British Empire* (London: Bookmarks, 2010, 2nd edn), pp. 212–13.
44. Holland and Phoenix, *Policing the Shadows*, p. 192.
45. Ibid., p. 218.
46. In 1994 Ian Phoenix was one of the 25 senior police, military and intelligence figures, many intimately involved in running covert operations in the North, killed in the Chinook helicopter crash on the Mull of Kintyre.
47. Maguire, *Loughinisland*, p. 39.

48. Ibid., pp. 41–7.
49. Justice Henry Barron, *Interim Report on the Report of the Independent Commission of Inquiry into the Dublin and Monaghan Bombings* (Dublin: Stationary Office, 2003).
50. Cadwallader, *Lethal Allies*, p. 194.
51. Maguire, *Loughinisland*, p. 44.
52. Susan McKay, 'Families of the Troubles victims' must learn the truth', *Irish Times*, 13 June 2008.
53. Cadwallader, *Lethal Allies*, pp. 306–9.
54. Maguire, *Loughinisland*, p. 62, p. 145.
55. Ibid., p. 49.
56. Ibid., p. 59.
57. Ibid., p. 50.
58. Ibid., p. 55, p. 59. See also Holland and Phoenix, *Policing the Shadows*, p. 237.
59. Maguire, *Loughinisland*, p. 62.
60. 'PSNI, Submission to the Review, 6 September 2012, p. 9', quoted in de Silva, *Patrick Finucane Review (I)*, p. 96; Holland and Phoenix, *Policing the Shadows*, p. 237.
61. 'Daily Telegraph, 24 April, 1989', quoted in Taylor, *Loyalists*, p. 194.
62. 'Man on arms charges jailed'.
63. Joe Tiernan, *The Dublin and Monaghan Bombings* (Dublin: Joe Tiernan, 2006), p. 94.
64. 'Colin Wallace, "Irish Independent", 4 June 1998', quoted in Cadwallader, *Lethal Allies*, p. 330.
65. Justice Henry Barron, *Interim Report on the Report of the Independent Commission of Inquiry into the Bombing of Kay's Tavern, Dundalk* (Dublin: Stationary Office), 2006, p. 135.
66. David McKittrick, Seamus Kelters, Brian Feeney and Chris Thornton, *Lost Lives: The Stories of the Men, Women and Children Who Died as a Result of the Northern Ireland Troubles* (Edinburgh: Mainstream Publishing, 1999), p. 724.

Chapter 5

1. Ministry of Defence, *Operation Banner: An Analysis of Military Operations in Northern Ireland, Army Code 71842* (London: MoD, 2006), p. 242, pp. 2–15.
2. 'John Stalker, "The Times", February 1988', quoted in European Court of Human Rights, *McKerr v United Kingdom: Final Judgement*, 4 August 2001, (Application no. 28883/95), p. 10.
3. General Sir John Waters, General Officer Commanding Northern Ireland, June 1989, quoted in Brian Brady, 'Pursuit of terrorists is "like a tiger hunt", said British General', *Independent*, 18 March 2012.
4. Tim Pat Coogan, *The Troubles: Ireland's Ordeal 1966-1995 and the Search for Peace* (London: Hutchinson, 1995), p. 290; David McKittrick, Seamus

Kelters, Brian Feeney and Chris Thornton, *Lost Lives: The Stories of the Men, Women and Children Who Died as a Result of the Northern Ireland Troubles* (Edinburgh: Mainstream Publishing, 1999), p. 1080; Mark Urban, *Big Boys' Rules: The Secret Struggle Against the IRA* (London: Faber and Faber, 1992), pp. 227–37; William Matchett, *Secret Victory: The Intelligence War that Beat the IRA* (Belfast: Matchett, 2016). The eight IRA members killed were: Declan Arthurs, Seamus Donnelly, Michael Gormley, Eugene Kelly, Patrick Kelly, James Lynagh, Padraig McKearney and Gerard O'Callaghan. The Catholic civilian killed was Anthony Hughes.
5. Peter Taylor, *Provos: The IRA and Sinn Fein* (London: Bloomsbury, 1997), p. 277.
6. Kevin Hearty, 'The political and military value of the "set-piece" killing tactic in east Tyrone 1983–1992', *State Crime*, 3:1 (2014), pp. 50–72, pp. 54–5; Richard English, *Armed Struggle: A History of the IRA* (London: Macmillan, 2003); Ed Moloney, *A Secret History of the IRA* (Harmondsworth: Penguin, 2007, 2nd edn), pp. 311–16; Urban, *Big Boys' Rules*.
7. The two police officers killed at Loughgall in the 1985 attack were Reserve Constable William Clements and Constable George Gilliland. See Bill Rolston, *Unfinished Business: State Killings and the Quest for Truth* (Belfast: Beyond the Pale Publications, 2000), p. 128.
8. English, *Armed Struggle*, p. 254; Moloney, *Secret History of the IRA*, p. 314.
9. Kevin Toolis, *Rebel Hearts: Journey's Within the IRA's Soul* (London: Picador, 1995), p. 53.
10. Moloney, *Secret History of the IRA*, p. 314.
11. McKittrick et al., *Lost Lives*, pp. 1214–15. The British soldiers killed were Lance-Corporal Stephen Burrows and Kingsmen Stephen Beacham, Vincent Scott, David Sweeney and Paul Worrall. On the same night a member of the Royal Irish Rangers (Cyril Smith) was also killed by a proxy bomb attack on an army checkpoint near Newry, Co. Down. See McKittrick et al., *Lost Lives*, p. 1216.
12. Ibid., p. 1269. The men killed were David Harkness, William Bleeks, Cecil Caldwell, Robert Dunseith, John McConnell, Nigel McKee, Robert Irons and Oswald Gilchrist. See also Brendan O'Brien, *The Long War: The IRA and Sinn Fein 1985 to Today* (Dublin: O'Brien Press, 1993), pp. 219–21.
13. McKittrick et al., *Lost Lives*, pp. 1273–7. The RUC officer was Allen Moore. The men he killed were Sinn Fein members Pat McBride, Paddy Loughran and Michael O'Dwyer.
14. Relatives for Justice, *Sean Graham Bookmakers Atrocity: Wednesday 5 February 1992* (Belfast: RFJ, 2012).
15. Matchett, *Secret Victory*, p. 23.
16. Fionnuala Ní Aoláin, *The Politics of Force: Conflict Management and State Violence in Northern Ireland* (Belfast: Blackstaff Press, 2000); pp. 5–6.
17. Matchett, *Secret Victory*, pp. 16–19.
18. Hearty, '"Set-piece" killing', p. 59.
19. Ministry of Defence, *Operation Banner*, p. 242, pp. 2–15.
20. Ibid., pp. 243–4, pp. 2–15.

21. Ibid., p. 244, pp. 2–15.
22. Dermot Walsh, 'The Royal Ulster Constabulary: a law unto themselves?', in *Whose Law and Order? Aspects of Crime and Social Control in Irish Society*, ed. by Mike Tomlinson, Tony Varley and Ciaran McCullagh (Belfast: Sociological Association of Ireland, 1988), pp. 92–108, p. 95.
23. Ní Aoláin, *Politics of Force*, pp. 29–71.
24. Ibid., p. 63.
25. Marie-Therese Fay, Mike Morrissey and Marie Smyth, *Northern Ireland's Troubles: The Human Costs* (London: Pluto Press, 1999), p. 159, p. 137. See also Michael McKeown, *Two Seven Six Three: An Analysis of Fatalities Attributable to Civil Disturbances in Northern Ireland in the Twenty Years Between July 13, 1969 and July 12, 1989* (Lucan: Murlough Press, 1989); Malcolm Sutton, *Bear in Mind These Dead: An Index of Deaths from the Conflict in Ireland, 1969–1993* (Belfast: Beyond the Pale Publications, 1994).
26. McKittrick et al., *Lost Lives*, p. 1473.
27. Anthony Jennings, 'Shoot to kill: the final courts of justice', in *Justice Under Fire: The Abuse of Civil Liberties in Northern Ireland*, ed. by Anthony Jennings (London: Pluto Press 1990), pp. 104–30.
28. Ministry of Defence, *Operation Banner*, p. 244, 2–15.
29. Hearty, '"Set-piece" killing', p. 64.
30. Ní Aoláin, *Politics of Force*, p. 62.
31. Ministry of Defence, *Operation Banner*, 2–14.
32. Brian Robinson was killed by undercover soldiers in North Belfast on 2 September 1989 minutes after he had shot dead a Catholic man, Paddy McKenna, from Ardoyne. See Ardoyne Commemoration Project, *Ardoyne: The Untold Truth* (Belfast: Beyond the Pale Publications, 2002), pp. 451–3; McKittrick et al., *Lost Lives*, pp. 1176–8.
33. William Millar, a member of the UVF, was shot dead in South Belfast in 1983. See McKittrick et al., *Lost Lives*, p. 940. Keith White, the only Protestant killed by a plastic bullet throughout the conflict, was shot during an Apprentice Boys parade in Portadown in 1986. See McKittrick et al., *Lost Lives*, p. 1035; Relatives for Justice, *Ambush, Assassination and Impunity: The Killings of Kevin Barry O'Donnell, Patrick Vincent, Peter Clancy and Sean O'Farrell* (Belfast: Relatives for Justice, 2012), pp. 19–21.
34. Urban, *Big Boys' Rules*, p. 239.
35. Matchett, *Secret Victory*.
36. Ken Connor, *Ghost Force: The Secret History of the SAS* (London: Cassels, 2006 2nd edn), p. 288.
37. Jennings, *Shoot to Kill*, p. 113; Raymond Murray, *The SAS in Ireland* (Dublin: Mercier Press, 1990), pp. 185–269.
38. Connor, *Ghost Force*, p. 287.
39. Mark Urban, *UK Eyes Alpha: The Inside Story of British Intelligence* (London: Faber and Faber, 1997, 2nd edn), p. 92.
40. Connor, *Ghost Force*, p. 288.
41. Quoted in Urban, *UK Eyes Alpha*, p. 92.

42. Brady, 'Pursuit of terrorists'.
43. Sir Desmond de Silva QC, *The Report of the Patrick Finucane Review: Volume I* (London: HMSO, 2012), pp. 456–60.
44. Major-General Charles Guthrie, later to become Chief of the Army General Staff, quoted in Brady, 'Pursuit of terrorists'.
45. See David Murphy, *The Stalker Affair and the Press* (London: Unwin Hyman, 1991); John Stalker, *Stalker* (London: Harrap, 1988); Peter Taylor, *Stalker: The Search for Truth* (London: Faber and Faber, 1987).
46. 'John Stalker, "Times", 9 February 1988', quoted in ECHR, *McKerr v UK*, p. 10.
47. Urban, *Big Boys' Rules*, pp. 91–2.
48. Hearty, '"Set-piece" killing', p. 62.
49. Ibid., pp. 52–3; Oren Gross and Fionnuala Ní Aoláin, *Law in Times of Crisis: Emergency Powers in Theory and Practice* (Cambridge: Cambridge University Press, 2002); Jennings, *Shoot to Kill*; Mark McGovern, 'Ignatieff, Ireland and the lesser evil', in *Discourses and Practices of Terrorism: Interrogating Terror*, ed. by Bob Brecher, Mark Devenney and Aaron Winter (London: Routledge, 2010), pp. 135–55; Ní Aoláin, *Politics of Forces*; Dermot Walsh, *Bloody Sunday and the Rule of Law in Northern Ireland* (Dublin: Gill and Macmillan, 2000).
50. Jennings, *Shoot to Kill*; Patricia Lundy, *Research Brief: Assessment of HET Review Processes and Procedures in Royal Military Police Investigations* (2012); Barry McCaffrey, 'Declassified documents reveal army lobbied Attorney General not to prosecute soldiers', *The Detail*, 15 April 2013.
51. Amnesty International, *Northern Ireland: Killings by Security Forces and 'Supergrass' Trials* (London: Amnesty International, 1988); Stephen Greer, 'The Supergrass system', in *Justice Under Fire: The Abuse of Civil Liberties in Northern Ireland*, ed. by Anthony Jennings (London: Pluto, 1990), pp. 73–103.
52. David A. Charters, 'From Palestine to Northern Ireland: British adaptation to low-intensity operations', in *Armies in Low-Intensity Conflict: A Comparative Analysis*, ed. by David Charters and Maurice Tugwell (London: Brassey's Defence Publishers, 1989), pp. 169–249, p. 209; Keith Jeffrey, 'Security policy in Northern Ireland: some reflections on the management of violent conflict', *Terrorism and Political Violence*, 2:1 (1990), pp. 21–31.
53. Jennings, *Shoot to Kill*, pp. 107–10; Ní Aoláin, *Politics of Force*, pp. 104–5; Walsh, *Bloody Sunday and the Rule of Law*, pp. 173–80.
54. Walsh, *Bloody Sunday and the Rule of Law*, p. 174.
55. 'Attorney General for Northern Ireland's Reference [1976] NI, 169, 193', quoted in Jennings, *Shoot to Kill*, pp. 108–9.
56. 'Attorney General for Northern Ireland's Reference [1977] AC 105', quoted in Walsh, *Bloody Sunday and the Rule of Law*, p. 178.
57. Jennings, *Shoot to Kill*, p. 112. See also Judge Peter Cory, *Cory Collusion Inquiry Report: Lord Justice Gibson and Lady Gibson* (London: HMSO, 2003).

58. Jennings, *Shoot to Kill*, p. 116; McKittrick et al., *Lost Lives*, p. 920; Taylor, *Stalker*, p. 33. See also ECHR, *McKerr v. UK*.
59. Urban, *UK Eyes Alpha*, p. 92.
60. Ibid., pp. 92–3.
61. Ibid., p. 76.
62. Ní Aoláin, *Politics of Force*, pp. 135–81. See also Committee on the Administration of Justice, *Inquests and Disputed Killings in Northern Ireland* (Belfast: CAJ, 1992).
63. Committee on the Administration of Justice, *Inquests and Disputed Killings*, p. 5.
64. Hearty, '"Set-piece" killing', p. 57; Relatives for Justice, *Ambush, Assassination and Impunity*. See also, Ní Aoláin, *Politics of Force*, p. 68.
65. Relatives for Justice, *Ambush, Assassination and Impunity*. See also McKittrick et al., *Lost Lives*, pp. 1238–9, pp. 1280–1. Those killed in Coagh were Lawrence McNally, Pete Ryan and Tony Doris and in Clonoe, Barry O'Donnell, Sean O'Farrell, Peter Clancy and Patrick Vincent.
66. High Court of Justice Northern Ireland, 'Judge finds shooting by undercover army unit not justified', *McKeever v. Ministry of Defence*, 7 October 2011.
67. 'Republican Roll of Honour, 1969–2012', *An Phoblacht/Republican News* (2012); Gerard Magee, *Tyrone's Struggle for Irish Freedom* (Dublin: Tyrone Sinn Fein Commemoration Committee, 2011); McKittrick et al., *Lost Lives*. The first such victim was Eugene Devlin, shot by members of a British Army foot patrol in Strabane, 27 December 1972. See also Raymond Murray, *The SAS in Ireland* (Dublin: Mercier Press, 1990), pp. 201–7.
68. Murray, *SAS in Ireland*, pp. 297–304.
69. The victim was Antoin Mac Giolla Bríde, killed on 2 December 1984. See Murray, *SAS in Ireland*, pp. 320–8.
70. Hearty, '"Set-piece" killing', p. 61.
71. Ibid., p. 60.
72. An Phoblacht/Republican News, *Republican Roll of Honour*; McKittrick et al., *Lost Lives*.
73. Murray, *SAS in Ireland*, pp. 289–97. See also Hearty, '"Set-piece" killing', p. 50; McKittrick et al., *Lost Lives*, p. 965; Urban, *Big Boys' Rules*, pp. 173–7.
74. 'Statement of Soldier B', quoted in Murray, *SAS in Ireland*, p. 291.
75. Murray, *SAS in Ireland*, p. 290.
76. 'Republican statement', quoted in ibid.
77. 'Soldier's Statement', quoted in ibid., p. 309. See also McKittrick et al., *Lost Lives*, p. 990.
78. 'Republican statement', quoted in Murray, *SAS in Ireland*, p. 306.
79. Murray, *SAS in Ireland*, pp. 348–65; 'Statement of Soldier A', quoted in ibid., p. 353.
80. Murray, *SAS in Ireland*, p. 356.
81. Hearty, '"Set-piece" killing'; Jack Holland and Susan Phoenix, *Phoenix: Policing the Shadows* (London: Hodder and Stoughton, 1996), pp. 205–18;

McKittrick et al., *Lost Lives*, pp. 1077-80; Ed Moloney, *Voices from the Grave: Two Men's War in Ireland* (London: Faber and Faber, 2011, 2nd edn), pp. 104-18; Murray, *SAS in Ireland*, pp. 376-96; Ní Aoláin, *Politics of Force*, pp. 66-8; Urban, *Big Boys' Rules*, pp. 227-37.
82. Moloney *Voices from the Grave*, p. 305.
83. Murray, *SAS in Ireland*, p. 380.
84. Hearty, '"Set-piece" killing', p. 58, Moloney, *Voices from the Grave*, p. 306.
85. Urban, *Big Boys' Rules*, p. 229.
86. Moloney, *Voices from the Grave*, p. 305; Ní Aoláin, *Politics of Force*, p. 66.
87. Henry McDonald, 'True tale of IRA martyrs revealed', *The Observer*, 29 September 2002.
88. High Court of Justice NI, *McKeever v. MoD (2011)*, p. 2. See also 'Judge rules getaway driver shooting "not justified"', *BBC News*, 7 October 2011; Relatives for Justice, *Ambush, Assassination and Impunity*, pp. 12-13.
89. High Court of Justice NI, *McKeever v. MoD (2011)*.
90. Ibid., p. 5.
91. Ibid.
92. Ibid., p. 4.
93. Ní Aoláin, *Politics of Force*, p. 69.
94. Michael Stohl, 'The state as terrorist: insight and implications', *Democracy and Security*, 2:1 (2006), pp. 1-25.
95. Stan Cohen, *States of Denial: Knowing about Atrocities and Suffering* (Cambridge: Polity Press, 2001), p. 19.
96. English, *Armed Struggle*, p. 238.
97. Walsh, *Bloody Sunday and the Rule of Law*, pp. 215-6.
98. Interview with Una Casey, 18 July 2013.
99. 'Rasharkin murder inquest adjourned: Death of IRA man – security force link alleged' (on file with Relatives for Justice).
100. Una Casey interview.
101. 'Rasharkin murder inquest adjourned'.
102. Una Casey quoted in 'Instructions taken from Una Casey by Fearghál Shiels, Madden and Finucane Solicitors, 26 February 2002' (on file with Relatives for Justice).
103. 'Security forces linked with murder – Fr. Faul' (on file with Relatives for Justice).
104. 'Rasharkin murder work of loyalist gang – Farren', *Antrim Guardian*, 6 April 1989; 'Loyalist hit squad fears', *Ballymoney and Moyle Times*, 4 April 1989.
105. 'Inquest reinforces collusion suspicion', *An Phoblacht/Republican News*, 2 November 1989, 'Rasharkin murder inquest adjourned'.
106. 'Rasharkin murder work of loyalist gang'.
107. 'Interview with Rev. Ian Paisley MP', *BBC NI News: Inside Ulster*, 4 April 1989.
108. 'IRA man perished by the sword' (on file with Relatives for Justice).
109. 'Interview with Sir John Herman, Chief Constable of the RUC', *BBC NI News: Inside Ulster*, 6 April 1989.

110. McKittrick et al., *Lost Lives*, p. 1168. Sutton, *Bear in Mind These Dead*, p. 168, p. viii, merely ascribes responsibility to a 'non-specific loyalist group'.
111. 'Rasharkin murder inquest adjourned'.
112. Una Casey interview.
113. Una Casey quoted in 'Instructions taken from Una Casey'.
114. Una Casey interview.
115. Ibid.; 'Rasharkin murder inquest adjourned'; 'Death of IRA man'; 'Security forces linked with murder'.
116. Alex Maskey quoted in 'Rasharkin IRA' (on file with Relatives for Justice).
117. In May 1987 and July 1988. See de Silva, *Patrick Finucane Review (I)*, p. 163.
118. Ibid., p. 164.
119. Ibid.
120. 'Trial transcript, R v. Brian Nelson, 22 January 1992, p. 17', quoted in Ibid., p. 164.
121. Nicholas Davies, *Ten-Thirty Three: The Inside Story of Britain's Secret Killing Machine in Northern Ireland* (Edinburgh: Mainstream Publishing, 2007, 2nd edn), p. 106.
122. Alex Maskey, quoted in 'Rasharkin IRA' (on file with Relatives for Justice); in 'Tyrone shooting exposes crown forces collusion', *An Phoblacht/Republican News*, 7 December 1989; in 'Security tight at incident free IRA funeral' (on file with Relatives for Justice); 'Funeral of Vol. Gerry Casey: His memory will live', *An Phoblacht/Republican News*, 13 April 1989.
123. Una Casey interview; quoted in 'Gerard Casey unpublished case notes' (on file with Relatives for Justice); Una Casey quoted in 'Instructions taken from Una Casey'.
124. 'Rasharkin murder inquest adjourned'; 'Gerard Casey unpublished case notes'.
125. Una Casey cited in 'Affidavit in the application by Tara Marie Casey for leave to apply for judicial review, November 2003' (on file with Relatives for Justice).
126. 'Rasharkin murder inquest adjourned'.
127. Una Casey quoted in 'Instructions taken from Una Casey'.
128. Murray, *SAS in Ireland*, p. 449, Martin Ingram and Greg Harkin, *Stakeknife: Britain's Secret Agents in Ireland* (Dublin: O'Brien Press, 2004), p. 186; McKittrick et al., *Lost Lives*, pp. 1171–2.
129. Davies, *Ten-Thirty Three*, pp. 191–2.
130. *Queen v. Browne (2008) NILST 11*, 1. All three were released on licence under the terms of the Good Friday Agreement. In 2008 the former soldier was returned to prison having broken the terms of his licence.
131. Murray, *SAS in Ireland*, p. 449; McKittrick et al., *Lost Lives*, p. 1172.
132. De Silva, *Patrick Finucane Review (I)*, p. 453.
133. 'FRU contact form, 26 November 1988', quoted in ibid., p. 454.
134. 'MISR, 6 December 1988', quoted in ibid., p. 454.

135. 'Statement of Stevens Office 7 February 1990', 'Chief of G2 statement, 18 October 1990' and 'Record of the meeting between Sir John Stevens and Army Officers, 20 September 1990', quoted in de Silva, *Patrick Finucane Review (I)*, pp. 460–1.
136. 'FRU MISR 6 September 1989', quoted in de Silva, *Patrick Finucane Review (I)*, p. 461.
137. 'FRU contact form, 22 September 1989', 'FRU contact form, 12 October 1989', 'A/02 statement to Stevens I investigation, 5 December 1990', quoted in de Silva, *Patrick Finucane Review (I)*, p. 455.
138. Gerard Casey's brother-in-law, 'Relatives for Justice interview with Ann Hassan and husband, 24 May 2002' (on file with Relatives for Justice).
139. Una Casey interview.
140. Ibid.
141. 'Rasharkin murder inquest adjourned'.
142. Ibid.; 'Inquest raises serious questions', *An Phoblacht/Republican News* (on file with Relatives for Justice).
143. 'Inquest reinforces collusion suspicion', *An Phoblacht/Republican News*, 2 November 1989; 'Inquest raises serious questions'.
144. Una Casey quoted in 'Instructions taken from Una Casey'.
145. 'Rasharkin murder inquest adjourned'; 'Letter from Madden and Finucane Solicitors to Coroner's Branch of the Northern Ireland Court Service, 13 June 2002' (on file with Relatives for Justice).
146. Una Casey quoted in 'Instructions taken from Una Casey'; 'Rasharkin murder inquest adjourned'.
147. 'Inquest sham grieves widow', *An Phoblacht/Republican News* (on file with Relatives for Justice).
148. Una Casey interview; 'Instructions taken from Una Casey'.
149. Una Casey interview.
150. Magee, *Tyrone's Struggle*; Moloney, *Secret History*, p. 313, p. 316.
151. *BBC NI News: Inside Ulster*, 30 November 1989.
152. 'Tyrone shooting exposes crown forces collusion', *An Phoblacht/Republican News*, 7 December 1989.
153. Interview with Eugene Ryan, 16 January 2014.
154. Interview with Helen Ryan, 16 January 2014.
155. Ibid.
156. In October 1993 the UFF killed eight people at the Rising Sun bar in Greysteel, Co. Derry, and in June 1994 the UVF massacred six men in the Heights bar in the small townland of Loughinisland, Co. Down.
157. Interview with Councillor John Haughey, SDLP, *UTV News*, 30 November 1989.
158. *BBC NI News: Inside Ulster*, 30 November 1989; interview with Anthony Ryan, 16 January 2014.
159. Interview with anonymous eyewitness, *BBC NI News: Inside Ulster*, 30 November 1989.
160. Helen Ryan interview.
161. *BBC NI News: Inside Ulster*, 30 November 1989.

162. Eyewitnesses quoted in McKittrick et al., *Lost Lives*, p. 1186.
163. Helen Ryan interview.
164. Eugene Ryan interview.
165. Helen Ryan interview.
166. Councillor Francie McNally, Sinn Fein, quoted in *BBC NI News: Inside Ulster*, 30 November 1989.
167. Magee, *Tyrone's Struggle*, p. 459; Murray, *SAS in Ireland*, p. 450.
168. Interview with the Ryan family, 16 January 2014.
169. Helen Ryan interview.
170. Eugene Ryan interview.
171. Murray, *SAS in Ireland*, p. 449.
172. Magee, *Tyrone's Struggle*, p. 459.
173. Ibid.; Anthony Ryan interview.
174. *BBC NI News: Inside Ulster*, 30 November 1989.
175. Murray, *SAS in Ireland*, p. 450; Anthony Ryan interview.
176. McKittrick et al., *Lost Lives*, p. 1186.
177. Helen Ryan interview.
178. Ryan family interview.
179. Helen Ryan interview; Magee, *Tyrone's Struggle*, p. 459.
180. Councillor Francie McNally, Sinn Fein, quoted in *BBC NI News: Inside Ulster*, 30 November 1989; 'Victims of loyalists using two VZ58 assault rifles', *Irish News*, 5 May 2014.
181. Magee, *Tyrone's Struggle*; Moloney, *Secret History*, p. 323.
182. Interview with Sean McGuckin, brother-in-law of Michael Devlin, *BBC NI News: Inside Ulster*, 30 November 1989.
183. See CAIN, 'IRA Memorial (Cappagh)'.
184. Bernadette McAliskey, quoted in 'British Army terrorises Irish town', *Green Left Weekly*, 1 July 1992; interview with Bernadette McAliskey, 24 November 2011; 'Paratroopers in Coalisland', *UTV: Counterpoint*, 27 May 1992.
185. Michael Mates MP quoted in 'Paratroopers in Coalisland'; David McKittrick, 'Coalisland "soldiers not entirely innocent": five paratroopers bound over by the court', *Independent*, 18 May 1993. Unusually the commanding officer was however relieved of his command.
186. Peter Taylor, *Loyalists* (London: Bloomsbury, 2000), p. 214.
187. The pamphlet was written by Fr Denis Faul and Fr Raymond Murray, see Murray, *SAS in Ireland*, p. 122. See also Cadwallader, *Lethal Allies*, pp. 99–108; Don Mullan, *The Dublin and Monaghan Bombings* (Dublin: Merlin Publishing, 2000), pp. 52–3; Magee, *Tyrone's Struggle*, p. 416; McKittrick et al., *Lost Lives*, p. 416.
188. McKittrick et al., *Lost Lives*, pp. 555–6.
189. John Weir, quoted in Liam Clarke 'RUC men's secret war with the IRA', *Sunday Times*, 7 March 1999.
190. Justice Henry Barron, *Interim Report on the Report of the Independent Commission of Inquiry into the Dublin and Monaghan Bombings* (Dublin: Stationary Office, 2003).

191. Ann Cadwallader, *Lethal Allies*, p. 53.
192. Ibid., pp. 32–3; McKittrick et al., *Lost Lives*, pp. 381–2.
193. Cadwallader, *Lethal Allies*, pp. 151–8.
194. Magee, *Tyrone's Struggle*, p. 416.
195. See CAIN, 'Cappagh Memorial Cross'; Relatives for Justice, *Collusion in Cappagh: State Sponsored Murder at Boyle's Bar, Cappagh, Sunday 3rd March 1991* (Belfast: RFJ, 2016).
196. Interview with Michael Armstrong, 13 October 2011.
197. Martin Hurson was the fifth hunger striker to die after his 46th day on the 1981 republican hunger strike. The Loughgall attack referred to is that of May 1987.
198. Interview with Siobhan Nugent, 13 October 2011.
199. Interview with Briege O'Donnell, 13 October 2011.
200. Interview with Poilin Quinn, 9 November 2011.
201. Magee, *Tyrone's Struggle*, p. 440.
202. Siobhan Nugent interview.
203. Poilin Quinn interview.
204. Ibid.
205. Malachy Rafferty quoted in McKittrick et al., *Lost Lives*, pp. 1227–8.
206. Magee, *Tyrone's Struggle*, p. 417; McKittrick et al., *Lost Lives*, p. 1228; Sean McPhilemy, *The Committee: Political Assassination in Northern Ireland* (Niwot COL: Roberts Rhinehart, 1998), pp. 54–5.
207. McPhilemy, *The Committee*, pp. 53–5.
208. Poilin Quinn interview.
209. See for example Jim Cusack and Henry McDonald, *UVF* (Dublin: Poolbeg Press, 2000, 2nd edn), pp. 220–5; Peter Taylor, *Loyalists* (London: Bloomsbury, 2000), p. 270.
210. *UTV News: Tonight*, 4 March 1991.
211. Briege O'Donnell interview.
212. Interview with Michael Armstrong, 13 October 2011.
213. Account from an eyewitness, *UTV News*, 4 March 1991.
214. Taylor, *Loyalists*, p. 214.
215. Ibid.
216. Michael Armstrong interview.
217. Siobhan Nugent interview.
218. Paul Larkin, *A Very British Jihad: Collusion, Conspiracy and Cover-up in Northern Ireland* (Belfast: Beyond the Pale Publications, 2004), p. 231.
219. Siobhan Nugent interview.
220. Briege O'Donnell interview.
221. Poilin Quinn interview; McKittrick et al., *Lost Lives*, p. 1229.
222. Michael Armstrong interview.
223. Siobhan Nugent interview.
224. Michael Armstrong interview.
225. Briege O'Donnell interview.
226. *UTV News: Tonight*, 4 March 1991.
227. Billy Wright in the 'Guardian', quoted in Larkin, *Very British Jihad*, p. 231.

228. McPhilemy, *The Committee*, pp. 53–5; 'The Committee', *Channel 4: Dispatches*, 2 October 1991; Taylor, *Loyalists*, p. 212.
229. Larkin, *Very British Jihad*, p. 231. *UTV News: Tonight*, 5 March 1991.
230. Briege O'Donnell interview.
231. Sinn Fein Statement, quoted in *UTV News*, 5 March 1991.
232. *UTV News*, 4 March 1991.
233. Interview with Fr Denis Faul, ibid.
234. SDLP Councillor, quoted in McKittrick et al., *Lost Lives*, p. 1228.
235. Ibid.
236. *UTV News: Tonight*, 5 March 1991.
237. Michael Armstrong interview.
238. Briege O'Donnell interview.
239. McKittrick et al., *Lost Lives*, p. 1228.
240. Poilin Quinn interview.
241. Briege O'Donnell interview.
242. Siobhan Nugent interview.
243. Michael Armstrong interview.
244. Poilin Quinn interview.

Chapter 6

1. John Davey is sometimes referred to as 'John Joe', a name never used by his family. It apparently originates with the security forces; interview with Pauline Davey-Kennedy, 23 November 2011.
2. Sir John Stevens, *Stevens Enquiry 3: Overview and Recommendations*, 17 April 2003, p. 11; Sir Desmond de Silva QC, *The Report of the Patrick Finucane Review: Volume 1* (London: HMSO, 2012), p. 292; *Hansard*, HC 'Standing Committee B', 17 January 1989, Douglas Hogg MP, cc. 508, Seamus Mallon MP, cc. 519.
3. 'Northern Ireland Act 1974 (Interim Period) Extension Order, 1988', *Hansard*, HC Deb, 29 June 1988, Vol. 136, cc. 438; David McKittrick, Seamus Kelters, Brian Feeney and Chris Thornton, *Lost Lives: The Stories of the Men, Women and Children Who Died as a Result of the Northern Ireland Troubles* (Edinburgh: Mainstream Publishing, 1999), p. 1053. Not the intended target, Kenneth Johnston was shot dead by the IRA in Magherafelt. The IRA were trying to kill a civilian connected with a local building firm that worked on security force installations.
4. Pauline Davey-Kennedy interview.
5. Mary Davey, quoted in 'John Davey: a man of commitment', *An Phoblacht/Republican News*, 11 February 1999.
6. Pauline Davey-Kennedy interview.
7. Colin Crawford, *Inside the UDA: Volunteers and Violence* (London: Pluto Press, 2003).
8. 'Republican Roll of Honour, 1969–2012', *An Phoblacht/Republican News* (2012), available at: www.anphoblacht.com/roll-of-honour.

9. John Davey near his home in Gulladuff; Tommy Donaghy and Danny Cassidy in Kilrea; Bernard O'Hagan outside his workplace in Magherafelt and Malachy Carey from Loughgeil was shot dead in nearby Ballymoney, Co. Antrim.
10. *BBC NI News: Inside Ulster*, 14 February 1989.
11. Ibid.
12. Jon Bew and Martyn Frampton, 'Debating the stalemate: a response to Dr Dixon', *Political Quarterly*, 83:2 (2012), pp. 277–82; Jon Bew, Martyn Frampton and Inigo Gurruchaga, *Talking to Terrorists: Making Peace in Northern Ireland and the Basque Country* (London: Hurst, 2009); Paul Dixon, 'Was the IRA defeated? Neo-conservative propaganda as history', *Journal of Imperial and Commonwealth History*, 2:1 (2012), pp. 303–20; Paul Dixon, 'Guns first, talks later: neoconservatives and the Northern Ireland peace process', *Journal of Imperial and Commonwealth History*, 39:4 (2011), pp. 649–76; Martyn Frampton, *The Long March: The Political Strategy of Sinn Fein, 1981–2007* (Basingstoke: Palgrave Macmillan, 2009).
13. William Matchett, *Secret Victory: The Intelligence War that Beat the IRA* (Belfast: Matchett, 2016).
14. Anthony McIntyre, 'Modern Irish republicanism: the product of British state strategies', *Irish Political Studies*, 10:1 (1995), pp. 97–122.
15. Brigadier Gavin Bulloch, 'Military doctrine and counter-insurgency: a British perspective', *Parameters: US Army War College Quarterly*, Summer (1996), pp. 4–16, p. 5.
16. Kevin Bean, *The New Politics of Sinn Féin* (Liverpool: Liverpool University Press, 2007), pp. 62–6. See also Agnés Maillot, *New Sinn Féin: Irish Republicanism in the Twenty-First Century* (London: Routledge, 2005).
17. Mark McGovern and Peter Shirlow, 'Language, discourse and dialogue: Sinn Fein and the Irish peace process', *Political Geography*, 17:2 (1999), pp. 171–86; Tommy McKearney, *The Provisional IRA: From Insurrection to Parliament* (London: Pluto Press, 2011). See also Eamonn Mallie and David McKittrick, *The Fight for Peace: The Secret Story behind the Irish Peace Process* (London: Heinemann, 1996); Brian Rowan, *Behind the Headlines: The Story of the IRA and Loyalist Ceasefires* (Belfast: Blackstaff Press, 1995).
18. Mark McGovern, 'Unity in diversity: the SDLP and the peace process', in *Peace or War? Understanding the Peace Process in Northern Ireland*, ed. by Chris Gilligan and Jon Tonge (Aldershot: Ashgate, 1997), pp. 54–71.
19. Henry Patterson, *Ireland Since 1939: The Persistence of Conflict* (London: Penguin, 2007). See also Arthur Aughey, *Under Siege: Ulster Unionism and the Anglo-Irish Agreement* (Belfast: Blackstaff Press, 1989), pp. 62–98; Jonathan Bardon, *A History of Ulster* (Belfast: Blackstaff, 1992), pp. 758–68.
20. McKittrick et al., *Lost Lives*, p. 1475; Malcolm Sutton, *Bear in Mind These Dead: An Index of Deaths from the Conflict in Ireland, 1969–1993* (Belfast: Beyond the Pale Publications, 1994), p. 206.
21. Crawford, *Inside the UDA*, p. 45.

22. Jeffrey A. Sluka, '"For God and Ulster": the culture of terror and loyalist death squads in Northern Ireland', in *Death Squad: The Anthropology of State Terror*, ed. by Jeffrey A. Sluka (Philadelphia, PA: University of Pennsylvania Press, 2000), pp. 127–57, pp. 144–6.
23. Richard English, *Armed Struggle: A History of the IRA* (London: Macmillan, 2003), p. 241; Margaret Thatcher, *Margaret Thatcher: The Downing Street Years* (London: Harper Collins, 1993), p. 385, p. 396; Nicholas Watt, 'Thatcher suggested "Cromwell solution" for Northern Ireland', *The Guardian*, 16 June 2001.
24. Andrew Mumford, 'Covert peacemaking: clandestine negotiations and backchannels with the Provisional IRA during the early "Troubles"', *Journal of Imperial and Commonwealth History*, 39:4 (2011), pp. 633–48; Niall Ó Dochartaigh, 'The longest negotiation: British policy, IRA strategy and the making of the Northern Ireland peace settlement' *Political Studies*, 63 (2015), pp. 202–20.
25. Michael Gove, *The Price of Peace: An Analysis of British Policy in Northern Ireland* (London: Centre for Policy Studies, 2000), pp. 12–13.
26. Paul Dixon, 'In defence of politics: interpreting the peace process and the future of Northern Ireland', *Political Quarterly*, 83:2 (2012), pp. 265–76, p. 265. For a debate on neo-conservative historians and the peace process see also, Bew and Frampton, *Debating the Stalemate*; Dixon, *Was the IRA Defeated*; Dixon, *Guns First, Talks Later*.
27. English, *Armed Struggle*, p. 266; Thatcher, *Downing Street Years*, p. 414.
28. Brendan Murtagh, 'Community, conflict and rural planning in Northern Ireland', *Journal of Rural Studies*, 14:2 (1998), pp. 221–31, p. 228.
29. Henry Patterson, 'Sectarianism revisited: the Provisional IRA campaign in a border region of Northern Ireland', *Terrorism and Political Violence*, 22:3 (2010), pp. 337–56.
30. Martin Flannery MP (Labour, Sheffield Hillsborough) and Claire Short MP (Labour, Birmingham Ladywood), *Hansard*, HC Deb, 29 June 1988, vol. 136 cc. 451, cc. 464.
31. *Hansard*, HC Deb, 29 June 1988, vol. 136 cc. 438; McKittrick et al., *Lost Lives*, p. 1053; Adrian Rutherford, 'State papers: DUP MP William McCrea wanted air strikes launched on the Republic in the 1980s', *Belfast Telegraph*, 29 December 2014.
32. William McCrea, HC Deb, 29 June 1988, vol. 136 cc. 440–1.
33. Ibid., cc. 441–2.
34. Rev. Ian Paisley, ibid., cc. 406.
35. William McCrea, ibid., cc. 438.
36. Ibid., cc. 439.
37. Jim Marshall MP (Labour, Leicester South) HC Deb, 29 June 1988, vol. 136 cc. 469.
38. Pauline Davey-Kennedy interview.
39. McKittrick et al., *Lost Lives*, pp. 1110–11. See also *BBC NI News: Inside Ulster*, 14 February 1989.
40. Pauline Davey-Kennedy interview.

41. Tim Pat Coogan, *The Troubles: Ireland's Ordeal 1966–1995 and the Search for Peace* (London: Hutchinson, 1995), p. 202.
42. *BBC NI News: Inside Ulster*, 16 August 1991.
43. McKittrick et al., *Lost Lives*, pp. 1242–54.
44. Jim Carson, killed at his shop on the junction of the Falls and Donegall Roads, West Belfast, 10 August 1991, and Lawrence Murchan shot dead near his shop, West Belfast, 28 September 1991. See ibid., p. 1244, p. 1250.
45. 'Eddie Fullerton', *RTE*, 5 March 2005.
46. Pauline Davey-Kennedy interview. See also Liz Curtis and Mike Jempson, *Interference on the Airwaves: Ireland, the Media and the Broadcasting Ban* (London: National Union of Journalists, 1993); Ed Moloney, 'Closing down the airwaves: the story of the broadcasting ban', in *The Media and Northern Ireland: Covering the Troubles*, ed. by Bill Rolston (Macmillan: London, 1991), pp. 8–50.
47. 'Elected Authorities (Northern Ireland) Act 1989', pp. 1–3.
48. 'Statement of John O'Hagan in relation to the murder of Bernard O'Hagan', submitted to the Office of the Police Ombudsman of Northern Ireland (PONI), 2007 (on file with Relatives for Justice), p. 5; 'Row flares in district council chamber', *Mid-Ulster Mail* (on file with Relatives for Justice).
49. Pauline Davey-Kennedy interview.
50. Ibid.
51. Michael Stone, *None Shall Divide Us* (London: John Blake Publishing, 2003), p. 111; Martin Dillon, *The Trigger Men* (Edinburgh: Mainstream Publishing, 2004, 2nd edn), p. 206.
52. Stone, *None Shall Divide Us*, p. 60.
53. Ibid., p. 112.
54. Martin Dillon, *Stone Cold: The True Story of Michael Stone and the Milltown Massacre* (London: Hutchinson, 1992), p. 132.
55. Ibid., p. 133; Stone, *None Shall Divide Us*, p. 113. Stone's description of this event and much else surrounding it does, though, bear considerable resemblance to the earlier account provided by Martin Dillon.
56. Pauline Davey-Kennedy interview.
57. John Davey quoted in Dillon, *Stone Cold*, p. 135; Pauline Davey-Kennedy interview. See also Crawford, *Inside the UDA*, pp. 150–1. Stone would later state that this was the sound of a signal to his getaway driver.
58. Pauline Davey-Kennedy interview.
59. Dillon, *Stone Cold*, pp. 135–40; Stone, *None Shall Divide Us*, pp. 113–14.
60. Stone, *None Shall Divide Us*, pp. 119–20.
61. Dillon, *Stone Cold*, pp. 160–3; Dillon, *Trigger Men*, pp. 207–9.
62. Dillon, *Trigger Men*, pp. 206–7.
63. 'Witness Statements of Mary Davey, Francis Fitzsimmon and John Corey, 11 December 1991', submitted to HM Coroner for East Tyrone and Magherafelt (on file with Relatives for Justice).
64. Downtown Radio, 15 February 1989; Pauline Davey-Kennedy interview.

65. Witness Statements of Francis Fitzsimons and Joseph O'Neill, 11 December 1991, submitted to HM Coroner for East Tyrone and Magherafelt (on file with Relatives for Justice).
66. 'Witness Statement, Chief Inspector Michael Brown, RUC, 11 December 1991', submitted to HM Coroner for East Tyrone and Magherafelt (on file with Relatives for Justice); Pauline Davey Kennedy interview.
67. Pauline Davey-Kennedy interview.
68. 'Witness Statements, RUC, 11 December 1991', submitted to HM Coroner for East Tyrone and Magherafelt (on file with Relatives for Justice).
69. Pauline Davey-Kennedy interview.
70. The other turned up burnt out near Greysteel.
71. 'Witness Statements, Fredrick Matthews and Sergeant Ian Mapp, RAOC, 11 December 1991', submitted to HM Coroner for East Tyrone and Magherafelt (on file with Relatives for Justice).
72. Pauline Davey-Kennedy interview.
73. McKittrick et al., *Lost Lives*, p. 1162.
74. Pauline Davey-Kennedy interview.
75. Ed Moloney, *A Secret History of the IRA* (Harmondsworth: Penguin, 2007, 2nd edn), p. 322.
76. 'The killing of Eddie Fullerton: many unanswered question, the family demands public inquiry', *An Phoblacht/Republican News*, 8 February 2001.
77. Interview with John O'Hagan, 3 July 2013.
78. Ibid.; 'Statement of John O'Hagan', p. 1.
79. 'Statement of John O'Hagan', p. 2; 'RUC letter from Detective Chief Superintendent McIvor 23rd February 1990', quoted in 'Statement of John O'Hagan', p. 3; 'John J. McNally and Co. Solicitors letter 15th March 1990', quoted in 'Statement of John O'Hagan', p. 3.
80. 'Statement of John O'Hagan', p. 4.
81. Ibid., p. 4; John O'Hagan interview.
82. Pauline Davey-Kennedy interview.
83. 'Statement of John O'Hagan', p. 6; John O'Hagan interview.
84. John O'Hagan interview.
85. 'Witness Statements of Orla Moore and Roisin Horner, 25 May 1994', submitted to HM Coroner for East Tyrone and Magherafelt (on file with Relatives for Justice); John O'Hagan interview.
86. 'Autopsy report for Bernard O'Hagan, 16 September 1991' (on file with Relatives for Justice).
87. John O'Hagan interview.
88. 'Statement of John O'Hagan', p. 7.
89. 'Autopsy report for Bernard O'Hagan'.
90. John O'Hagan interview.
91. 'Statement of John O'Hagan', p. 8.
92. *BBC NI News: Inside Ulster*, 16 September 1991.
93. 'Adams claims British directed murder attack', *Irish News*, 17 September 1991.

94. *BBC NI News: Inside Ulster*, 16 September 1991; 'Nationalists condemn councillor's murder as McCrea lashes out' (on file with Relatives for Justice).
95. DUP Councillor Sammy Wilson quoted in 'Sammy Wilson in row over SF murder', *Irish News*, 17 September 1991.
96. McKittrick et al., *Lost Lives*, p. 1249; 'Statement of John O'Hagan', p. 11. A motion of condolence was eventually passed by the council in April 1992.
97. 'Loyalists plan mass protest over Magherafelt commemoration plaques', *Mid-Ulster Mail*, 20 February 2014.
98. 'Letter from John Madden to Chief Constable 16 September 1992', 'Letter from Assistant Chief Constable W. M. Johnston, 26 October 1992', quoted in 'Statement of John O'Hagan', p. 9.
99. John O'Hagan interview.
100. Ibid.
101. 'Witness Statements of Orla Moore and Roisin Horner'; John O'Hagan interview.
102. John O'Hagan interview; 'Statement of John O'Hagan', p. 11.
103. John O'Hagan interview.
104. 'PSNI Letter to Janet McGrail, 6 September 2004' (on file with Relatives for Justice); 'Sinn Fein activist shot dead', *An Phoblacht/Republican News*, 1 November 1990. See also Gerard Magee, *Tyrone's Struggle for Irish Freedom* (Dublin: Tyrone Sinn Fein Commemoration Committee, 2011), p. 569.
105. Interview with Janet McGrail, 12 July 2012.
106. Interview with Fran Casey, 12 July 2012.
107. 'Sinn Fein activist shot dead'.
108. 'Sinn Fein councillors are "targets for assassination"', *Mid-Ulster Observer*, 27 September 1990.
109. Ibid.
110. Ibid.
111. Ibid.
112. Janet McGrail interview.
113. 'SF Man was "in wrong place at wrong time"', *Mid-Ulster Mail*, 1 November 1990.
114. 'Autopsy report for Thomas Henry Casey, 27 October 1990', submitted to HM Coroner for East Tyrone and Magherafelt (on file with Relatives for Justice); Relatives for Justice, *Collusion 1990–1994: Loyalist Paramilitary Murders in North of Ireland* (Belfast: Relatives for Justice, 1995), p. 11.
115. 'Murdered painter was shot 11 times', *Mid-Ulster Mail*, 9 June 1994.
116. 'Sinn Fein activist shot dead'. See also 'Witness statement of Kathleen Casey, 9 October 1991', submitted to HM Coroner for East Tyrone and Magherafelt (on file with Relatives for Justice).
117. 'Witness Statement of Karen Mulgrew, 27 October 1990', submitted to HM Coroner for East Tyrone and Magherafelt (on file with Relatives for Justice). See also 'Murdered painter was shot 11 times'.
118. Fran Casey interview.
119. Interview with Colette Casey, 12 July 2012.

120. Janet McGrail interview.
121. 'IRA vows to avenge SF man's murder', *Irish News*, 29 October 1990; *BBC NI News: Inside Ulster*, 29 October 1990.
122. 'Witness statements of Kathleen Casey and Karen Mulgrew, 27 October 1990'. See also 'Murdered painter was shot 11 times'.
123. 'SF man was in "wrong place at wrong time"'.
124. 'Witness statement of Kathleen Casey'.
125. Connla Young, 'Four UDR members arrested following sectarian attack', *Irish News*, 17 April 2017.
126. McKittrick et al., *Lost Lives*, pp. 1216–17.
127. Sean Anderson was shot on 25 October 1991, see ibid., p. 1254.
128. 'Murdered painter was shot 11 times'.
129. Janet McGrail interview.
130. 'Tommy Casey honoured', *An Phoblacht/Republican News* (on file with Relatives for Justice).
131. Sean McPhilemy, *The Committee: Political Assassination in Northern Ireland* (Niwot, COL: Roberts Rhinehart, 1998), pp. 125–6; Anne Cadwallader, *Lethal Allies: British Collusion in Ireland* (Cork: Mercier Press, 2013), pp. 326–30. See also Paul Larkin, *A Very British Jihad: Collusion, Conspiracy and Cover-up in Northern Ireland* (Belfast: Beyond the Pale Publications, 2004), p. 183.
132. 'Loyalist murder victims' family to sue Matt Baggott', *Irish News*, 12 May 2014.
133. Casey family interview, 12 July 2012; Relatives for Justice, *Collusion, 1990–1994*, p. 11.
134. 'IRA vows to avenge SF man's murder'.
135. McKittrick et al., *Lost Lives*, p. 1217.
136. Ibid., p. 1218.
137. 'Inquest system fails families', *Mid-Ulster Mail*, 9 June 1994.
138. Coroner Roger McLernon, quoted in 'Murdered painter was shot 11 times'.
139. Janet McGrail interview.
140. Young, 'Four UDR members arrested'.
141. 'Witness Statements of Detective Inspector Millar Farr and Constable Johnston Leslie Cairns, RUC, 6 June 1994', submitted to HM Coroner for East Tyrone and Magherafelt (on file with Relatives for Justice).
142. Young, 'Four UDR members arrested'.
143. Connla Young, 'Republicans' secret Tyrone meeting with loyalists halted UVF gang's murder spree', *Irish News*, 17 April 2017.
144. Interview with the Shanaghan family, 27 October 2011.
145. Castlederg/Aghyaran Justice Group (CAJG), *Report of the Public Inquiry into the Killing of Patrick Shanaghan, held in Aghyaran GAA Centre, Castlederg, Co. Tyrone on 17th, 18th and 19th September 1996* (Castlederg/Aghyaran Justice Group, 1996), p. 8.
146. Interview with Anna Shanaghan, 27 October 2011.
147. Interview with Mary Bogues, 27 October 2011.
148. Anna Shanaghan interview.

149. Mary Bogues interview.
150. Shanaghan family interview.
151. Interview with Martin Bogues, 27 October 2011.
152. Relatives for Justice, *Collusion, 1990–1994*, p. 16.
153. 'Evidence of RUC Inspector to Inquest', quoted in CAJG, *Shanaghan Inquiry*, p. 102.
154. 'Letter to the Inquiry of Doctor W. A. Stewart', in CAJG, *Shanaghan Inquiry*, p. 33.
155. 'Deposition of Delia Margaret Hogg to Inquest', quoted in Human Rights Watch/Helsinki, *To Serve Without Favour: Policing, Human Rights and Accountability in Northern Ireland* (London: Human Rights Watch, 1997), p. 83.
156. Human Rights Watch/Helsinki, *To Serve Without Favour*, p. 83.
157. 'Letter to Inquiry of Dr James Garvey', in CAJG, *Shanaghan Inquiry*, p. 33.
158. Martin Bogues interview.
159. McPhilemy, *The Committee*, p. 331; Shanaghan Family interview.
160. Martin Bogues interview.
161. Mary Bogues interview.
162. Human Rights Watch/Helsinki, *To Serve Without Favour*, p. 84.
163. Martin Bogues interview.
164. Martin Bogues quoted in CAJG, *Shanaghan Inquiry*, p. 27.
165. Mary Bogues interview.
166. Mary Bogues, quoted in CAJG, *Shanaghan Inquiry*, p. 24.
167. Mary Shanaghan, quoted in ibid., p. 22.
168. European Court of Human Rights (ECHR), *Shanaghan v. The United Kingdom*, (Application no. 37715/97), Judgement, 4 May 2001, p. 4; Shanaghan family interview.
169. Mary Bogues interview.
170. Mary Shanaghan, quoted in CAJG, *Patrick Shanaghan Inquiry*, p. 21.
171. ECHR, *Shanaghan v. UK*, p. 3. See also CAJG, *Shanaghan Inquiry*.
172. Mary Shanaghan, quoted in CAJG, *Shanaghan Inquiry*, p. 22.
173. ECHR, *Shanaghan v. UK*, p. 3.
174. CAJG, *Shanaghan Inquiry*, pp. 90–100.
175. Ibid., p. 97.
176. Ibid.
177. Sean McPeake, quoted in ibid., p. 46.
178. Declan Gormley, quoted in ibid., p. 38.
179. Mary Bogues interview.
180. Mary Bogues interview.
181. Shanaghan family interview.
182. Gerry Keenan, quoted in CAJG, *Shanaghan Inquiry*, p. 45.
183. Human Rights Watch/Helsinki, *To Serve Without Favour*, p. 82.
184. Mary Bogues interview.
185. CAJG, *Shanaghan Inquiry*, p. 35; 'Three accuse police after interrogation', *The Ulster Herald*, 24 February 1990, quoted in CAJG, *Shanaghan Inquiry*, p. 110.

186. Mary Bogues interview.
187. ECHR, *Shanaghan v. UK*, p. 3.
188. Ibid., p. 4. See also CAJG, *Shanaghan Inquiry*, pp. 86–8.
189. ECHR, *Shanaghan v. UK*, p. 4.
190. Ibid., p. 31.
191. Ibid., p. 4.
192. British-Irish Rights Watch, *Alleged Collusion and the RUC* (London: BIRW, 1996), p. 7.
193. Martin Bogues interview.
194. Committee on the Administration of Justice, *Inquests and Disputed Killings in Northern Ireland* (Belfast: CAJ, 1992); Fionnuala Ní Aoláin, *The Politics of Force: Conflict Management and State Violence in Northern Ireland* (Belfast: Blackstaff Press, 2000), pp. 135–81.
195. *BBC NI News: Inside Ulster*, 12 August 1991; Martin Bogues interview.
196. ECHR, *Shanaghan v. UK*, p. 6; Mary Bogues interview.
197. The High Court of Justice in Northern Ireland, 'An application by the Chief Constable of the Royal Ulster Constabulary for judicial review in the matter of Patrick Shanaghan, KERK2136.T. 3–4,18 June 1996', quoted in ECHR, *Shanaghan v. UK*, pp. 6–7; Human Rights Watch/Helsinki, *To Serve without Favour*, p. 87.
198. Anna Shanaghan interview.
199. Human Rights Watch/Helsinki, *To Serve without Favour*, p. 86.
200. Mary Bogues interview.
201. Committee on the Administration of Justice, *Cause for Complaint: The System of Dealing with Complaints Against the Police in Northern Ireland*, Pamphlet No. 16. (Belfast: CAJ, 1990), p. iv.
202. Ronald Weitzer, *Policing Under Fire: Ethnic Conflict and Police-Community Relations in Northern Ireland* (Albany, NY: State University of New York Press, 1995), p. 198.
203. ECHR, *Shanaghan v. UK*, pp. 7–8.
204. Anna Shanaghan interview.
205. Honourable Judge Andrew Somers, quoted in CAJG, *Shanaghan Inquiry*, p. 57.
206. Anna Shanaghan interview.
207. Interview with Johnny Donaghy, 16 January 2014.
208. Ibid.
209. McKittrick et al., *Lost Lives*, p. 1246.
210. Johnny Donaghy interview.
211. Ibid.
212. Ibid.
213. 'Autopsy report for Thomas Donaghy, 16 August 1991', submitted to the Coroner for East Tyrone and Magherafelt (on file with Relatives for Justice); 'Witness statement of John Bradley, 23 June 1994', submitted to the coroner for East Tyrone and Magherafelt (on file with Relatives for Justice).

214. 'Autopsy report for Thomas Donaghy'; 'Witness statement of John Bradley'; Johnny Donaghy interview.
215. Johnny Donaghy interview.
216. 'Witness statement of John Bradley'.
217. *BBC NI News: Inside Ulster*, 16 August 1991.
218. 'Witness statement of Inspector E. Colvin Burton, RUC, 23 June 1994', submitted to the coroner for East Tyrone and Magherafelt (on file with Relatives for Justice).
219. Johnny Donaghy interview.
220. Ibid.
221. Interview with Johnny Donaghy, *BBC NI News: Inside Ulster*, 16 August 1991.
222. 'Witness statement of Detective Inspector James Davison, Head of CID, Magherafelt, RUC, 23 June 1994', submitted to the coroner for East Tyrone and Magherafelt (on file with Relatives for Justice).
223. Johnny Donaghy interview.
224. Ibid.
225. Interview with Danny Carey, 23 July 2013.
226. 'Malachy Carey: solid and dependable', *An Phoblacht/Republican News*, 19 December 2002.
227. David Beresford, *Ten Men Dead: The Story of the 1981 Hunger Strike* (London: Grafton Books, 1987), p. 85; 'Malachy Carey', *An Phoblacht/Republican News*.
228. 'Malachy Carey', *An Phoblacht/Republican News*.
229. Danny Carey interview.
230. Sharon O'Neil, 'DUP selection of ex-UDA man "odd"', *Irish News*, 30 January 2004.
231. 'Statement of Emmanuelle Cassidy to Clara Reilly and Stephen McCloskey (RFJ), 23 June 2007' (on file with Relatives for Justice).
232. Ibid. See also Tony Gifford, *Supergrasses: Use of Accomplice Evidence in Northern Ireland* (London: Cobden Trust, 1984), p. 10.
233. Edward Daly, Bishop of Derry, *BBC NI News: Inside Ulster*, 6 April 1992.
234. John Dallat, SDLP Councillor, ibid.
235. 'Non-republican source', quoted in David McKittrick, 'RUC face collusion row over security leak', *Independent*, 3 September 1992.
236. McKittrick, 'RUC face security row'.
237. Statement of Emmanuelle Cassidy'.
238. Barry McCaffrey, 'Fullertons told UDA murder suspects cannot be charged', *Irish News*, 21 May 2007.
239. 'Eddie Fullerton', RTE, 5 March 2005.
240. Ibid.
241. 'The killing of Eddie Fullerton: many unanswered questions', *An Phoblacht/Republican News*, 8 February 2001; 'Death on the cards', *BBC Insight*, 29 May 2003; McCaffrey, 'UDA murder suspects'; 'Eddie Fullerton', RTE; McKittrick et al., *Lost Lives*, pp. 1236–7.
242. 'The killing of Eddie Fullerton'.

243. Diana Fullerton quoted in 'Eddie Fullerton', *RTE*.
244. Sammy Wilson, quoted in *Sunday World*, 15 June 1991; 'Sammy Wilson in row over SF murder', *Irish News*, 17 September 1991.
245. 'Eddie Fullerton', *RTE*.
246. McKittrick et al., *Lost Lives*, p. 1241, p. 1244; 'Death on the Cards'.
247. Journalist Chris Moore, 'Death on the Cards'.
248. Henry McDonald, 'The double agent who helped run terror cell', *Observer*, 20 April 2003; 'Eddie Fullerton', *RTE*.
249. McDonald, 'Double Agent'.
250. Former RUC Officer Jonty Brown quoted in 'Eddie Fullerton', *RTE*.
251. Solicitor Greg O'Neill quoted in ibid.
252. Fullerton family solicitor quoted in ibid.
253. McCaffrey, 'UDA murder suspects'.
254. Amanda Fullerton quoted in ibid.

Chapter 7

1. Interview with Siobhan Nugent, sister of Malcolm Nugent, 13 October 2011.
2. Aidan O'Toole, quoted in Ian Cobain, 'Northern Ireland loyalist shootings: one night of carnage, 18 years of silence', *The Guardian*, 15 October 2012.
3. The other victims were 54-year-old Dan McGregor, father-of-three Malcolm Jenkinson, 35-year-old Patsy O'Hare and 39-year-old Eamonn Byrne, a father of four, the youngest of whom was just three months old.
4. David McKittrick, Seamus Kelters, Brian Feeney and Chris Thornton, *Lost Lives: The Stories of the Men, Women and Children Who Died as a Result of the Northern Ireland Troubles* (Edinburgh: Mainstream Publishing, 1999), p. 1476. See also Jeffrey A. Sluka, '"For God and Ulster": the culture of terror and loyalist death squads in Northern Ireland', in Jeffrey A. Sluka (ed), *Death Squad: The Anthropology of State Terror* (Philadelphia, PA: University of Pennsylvania Press, 2000).
5. Michael Maguire, *The Murders at the Heights Bar, Loughinisland, 18 June 1994* (Belfast: PONI, 2016).
6. Ibid., p. 137.
7. Ibid., p. 146.
8. Ibid., p. 135.
9. Ibid., p. 64.
10. Ibid., p. 77.
11. Ibid., p. 78.
12. Ibid., pp. 67–8.
13. Ibid., p. 75.
14. Ibid., p. 78.
15. Ibid., pp. 85–127.
16. Ibid., p. 136.
17. Ibid., pp. 118–24.
18. Ibid., p. 121.

19. Ibid., p. 112. Most key suspects were only arrested after a holdall containing the clothing used by the killers, and nearby the automatic rifle, were found. See ibid., p. 121.
20. Ibid., p. 117.
21. Ibid.
22. For analyses of sectarianism in urban areas see, for example, F.W. Boal and J.N.H. Douglas (eds), *Integration and Division: Geographical Perspectives on the Northern Ireland Problem* (London: Academic Press, 1982); John Darby, *Intimidation and the Control of Conflict in Northern Ireland* (Syracuse, NY: Syracuse University Press, 1986); Peter Shirlow and Brendan Murtagh, *Belfast: Segregation, Violence and the City* (London: Pluto Press, 2006). For the nature of sectarianism see: John Brewer, 'Sectarianism and racism, and their parallels and differences', *Ethnic and Racial Studies*, 15:3 (1992), pp. 352–64; Frank Burton, *The Politics of Legitimacy: Struggles in a Belfast Community* (London: Routledge and Kegan Paul, 1978); Robbie McVeigh, 'Is sectarianism racism? Theorising the racism/sectarianism interface', in *Rethinking Northern Ireland: Culture, Ideology and Colonialism*, ed. by David Miller (London: Longman, 1998), pp. 179–98.
23. Andrew Hamilton, Clem McCartney, Tony Anderson and Ann Finn, *Violence and Communities* (Coleraine: University of Ulster, 1990); Brendan Murtagh, *Community and Conflict in Rural Ulster* (Coleraine: University of Ulster, 1999); Brendan Murtagh, 'Community, conflict and rural planning in Northern Ireland', *Journal of Rural Studies*, 14:2 (1998), pp. 221–31. On ethnographies of social divisions in rural Northern Ireland, see also Hastings Donnan and Graham MacFarlane, '"You get on better with your own": social continuity and change in rural Ireland', in *Ireland: A Sociological Profile*, ed. by Patrick Clancy, Sheelagh Drudy, Kathleen Lynch and Liam O'Dowd (Dublin: Institute of Public Administration, 1986), pp. 380–99; Rosemary Harris, *Prejudice and Tolerance in Ulster: A Study of Neighbours and 'Strangers' in a Border Community* (Manchester: Manchester University Press, 1972); Joan Vincent, 'Local knowledge and political violence in County Fermanagh', in *Ireland From Below: Social Change and Local Communities*, ed. by Chris Curtin and Thomas M. Wilson (Galway: Galway University Press, 1987), pp. 92–108.
24. Harris, *Prejudice and Tolerance*.
25. Jennifer Hamilton, Ulf Hansson, John Bell and Sarah Toucas, *Segregated Lives: Social Division, Sectarianism and Everyday Life in Northern Ireland* (Belfast: Institute for Conflict Research, 2008), p. 5.
26. Murtagh, *Community and Conflict*; Murtagh, 'Community, conflict and rural planning', pp. 227–8.
27. Interview with Bernadette McAliskey, 24 November 2011.
28. Elaine Scarry, *The Body in Pain: The Making and Unmaking of the World* (Oxford: Oxford University Press, 1985).
29. Robert Goodin, *What's Wrong with Terrorism?* (London: Polity, 2006).
30. Michael Stohl, 'The state as terrorist: insight and implications', *Democracy and Security*, 2:1 (2006), pp. 1–25, p. 6.

31. C.A.J. Coady, 'Defining terrorism', in *Terrorism: The Philosophical Issues*, ed. by Igor Primoratz (London: Palgrave, 2004), pp. 3–14; Goodin, *What's Wrong with Terrorism?*; Igor Primoratz, *Civilian Immunity in War* (Oxford: Oxford University Press, 2007).
32. *BBC NI News: Inside Ulster*, 9 August 1994.
33. McKittrick et al., *Lost Lives*, pp. 1373–4; interview with Sean McPeake, 22 July 2013.
34. Paddy O'Hagan, quoted in 'Jury hear details of O'Hagan family terror', *An Phoblacht/Republican News*, 3 July 1997.
35. Damian O'Hagan, quoted in 'Family of pregnant woman murdered by UVF in call for collusion inquiry', *Belfast Telegraph*, 18 July 2015; 'Son still seeking answers 20 years after mother's brutal murder', *Ulster Herald*, 1 August 2014.
36. Interview with Charity McPeake, 22 July 2013.
37. Interview with Sean and Charity McPeake, 22 July 2013.
38. 'O'Hagan family terror'.
39. Charity McPeake interview.
40. Sean McPeake interview.
41. Statement by Bernadette McKearney for Relatives for Justice (on file with Relatives for Justice).
42. Interview with Poilin Quinn, 9 November 2011.
43. Sean Brown, shot dead by the LVF, Moneyrick Road, near Randalstown, Co. Antrim, 12 May 1997.
44. Ed Moloney, *A Secret History of the IRA* (Harmondsworth: Penguin, 2007, 2nd edn), p. 321. See also Eamonn Mallie and David McKittrick, *The Fight for Peace: The Secret Story behind the Irish Peace Process* (London: Heinemann, 1996), pp. 57–60; McKittrick, *Lost Lives*, pp. 1094–8.
45. Senior IRA source quoted in Mallie and McKittrick, *Fight for Peace*, p. 59.
46. Interview with former Tyrone IRA member, quoted in Moloney, *Secret History*, p. 322.
47. 'Roseann Mallon murder: inquest shock as gun used by loyalists to kill pensioner linked with six other killings', *Belfast Telegraph*, 26 November 2013.
48. Interview with Siobhan Nugent, 13 October 2011.
49. 'Shooting victim', 1 December 1988 (on file with Relatives for Justice).
50. Interview with Henry McNally, 2 July 2013.
51. Gerard Magee, *Tyrone's Struggle for Irish Freedom* (Dublin: Tyrone Sinn Fein Commemoration Committee, 2011), p. 478.
52. McNally family interview, 2 July 2013.
53. McKittrick et al., *Lost Lives*, p. 1153; *UTV News*, 26 November 1988.
54. McKittrick et al., *Lost Lives*, p. 1125; 'Statement of Francis McNally, concerning the murder of Phelim McNally, Relatives for Justice, 23 June 2007' (on file with Relatives for Justice).
55. Henry McNally interview.
56. 'Statement of Francis McNally'.

57. Mary Campbell, 'New mum to bury murdered husband', *Irish News*, 26 November 1988; 'Statement of Francis McNally'.
58. Danny Morrison, Sinn Fein spokesperson, quoted in Campbell, 'New mum to bury murdered husband'; 'Shooting victim'.
59. 'Statement of Francis McNally'.
60. Francie McNally, quoted in Damien Gaffney, 'Born into a world of murder' (on file with Relatives for Justice).
61. '"End these things" plea at funeral', *Mid-Ulster Mail*, 1 December 1988; Henry McNally interview; 'Statement of Francis McNally'.
62. 'Statement of Francis McNally'; 'Witness statement of Francis McNally, 19 April 1990', submitted to HM Coroner for East Tyrone and Magherafelt (on file with Relatives for Justice).
63. Henry McNally interview.
64. Ibid.
65. Interview with Francie McNally, *UTV News*, 26 November 1988.
66. 'Statement of Francie McNally'.
67. 'Report of Autopsy of Phelim McNally, 25 November 1988', submitted to HM Coroner for East Tyrone and Magherafelt (on file with Relatives for Justice).
68. 'Witness statement of Dr Richard Gilfinnan, 19 April 1990', submitted to HM Coroner for East Tyrone and Magherafelt (on file with Relatives for Justice); 'I was the intended target – murdered man's brother', *Mid-Ulster Mail*, 26 April 1990; 'Statement of Francis McNally'.
69. Henry McNally interview, 2 July 2013.
70. 'Witness statement of Robert Armour, Holywell Hospital, 19 April 1990', submitted to HM Coroner for East Tyrone and Magherafelt (on file with Relatives for Justice).
71. 'Witness statement of Constable Stephen Dowie, RUC, Cookstown, County Tyrone, 25 November 1988' and 'Witness Statement of Sergeant Aaron Murphy, RUC, Coagh, County Tyrone, 19 April 1990', submitted to HM Coroner for East Tyrone and Magherafelt (on file with Relatives for Justice).
72. Interview with Kevin McNally, 2 July 2013.
73. 'Witness statement of Constable Russell Young, RUC Coagh, County Tyrone, 19 April 1990', submitted to HM Coroner for East Tyrone and Magherafelt (on file with Relatives for Justice).
74. Interview with Lawrence McNally, 2 July 2013.
75. Henry McNally interview.
76. 'Witness statement of Francis McNally'.
77. 'Witness statement of Daniel Costello, 19 April 1990', submitted to HM Coroner for East Tyrone and Magherafelt (on file with Relatives for Justice).
78. 'Witness statement of Sergeant Stewart McConnell, RUC, Coagh, County Tyrone, 19 April 1990', submitted to HM Coroner for East Tyrone and Magherafelt (on file with Relatives for Justice).
79. 'Father of six gunned down' (on file with Relatives for Justice).

80. 'Witness statement of Constable John Magee, RUC, Dungannon, County Tyrone, 19 April 1990', submitted to HM Coroner for East Tyrone and Magherafelt (on file with Relatives for Justice).
81. Kevin McNally interview.
82. 'I was the intended victim', *Mid-Ulster Mail*.
83. Anne Cadwallader, *Lethal Allies: British Collusion in Ireland* (Cork: Mercier Press, 2013); Paul Larkin, *A Very British Jihad: Collusion, Conspiracy and Cover-up in Northern Ireland* (Belfast: Beyond the Pale Publications, 2004), p. 167; Sean McPhilemy, *The Committee: Political Assassination in Northern Ireland* (Niwot COL: Roberts Rhinehart, 1998), pp. 1–5; Malcolm Sutton, *Bear in Mind These Dead: An Index of Deaths from the Conflict* in Ireland, 1969–1993 (Belfast: Beyond the Pale Publications, 1994), p. 172. p. 175, p. 177.
84. RUC Inspector quoted in 'I was the intended victim'; 'Witness statement of Detective Inspector James Davison, RUC, CID Southern Region, 19 April 1990', submitted to HM Coroner for East Tyrone and Magherafelt (on file with Relatives for Justice).
85. 'Verdict on Inquest in the death of Phelim McNally, 19 April 1990', John McLernon, Coroner for the district of East Tyrone and Magherafelt (on file with Relatives for Justice).
86. British Army and RUC spokespersons quoted in Campbell, 'New mum to bury murdered husband'.
87. Henry McNally interview.
88. Kevin McNally interview.
89. Campbell, 'New mum to bury murdered husband'; 'Dad dies as son is born', *Mid-Ulster Mail*, 1 December 1988.
90. Relative, quoted in ibid.
91. Magee, *Tyrone's Struggle*, p. 632.
92. Interview with Eileen Hughes, 5 December 2012.
93. Ibid.
94. On 27 December 1997, the night after Billy Wright was killed inside the Maze/Long Kesh prison, members of the LVF opened fire on the dance hall of the Glengannon Hotel. There were some 300–400 young people in the club at the time. Three civilians, including a 14-year-old boy, were injured. A former republican prisoner, Seamus Dillon, who was working as a doorman, was killed in the attack. See 'LVF claim County Tyrone murder', *BBC News*, 29 December 1997.
95. Historical Enquiries Team (HET), *Review Summary Report Concerning the Murder of Patrick Francis Hughes* (Lisburn: HET, 2009) (on file with Relatives for Justice), p. 8.
96. Eileen Hughes interview.
97. Sharon O'Neil, 'Tell truth about my father's murder probe, police urged', *Irish News*, 13 May 2004.
98. Relatives for Justice, *Report into the Circumstances of the Death of Frank Hughes* (2007) (on file with Relatives for Justice); HET, *Francis Hughes Report*, p. 36.

99. Eileen Hughes interview. Records show it was 3.20 am when the brothers reported their father missing; HET, *Francis Hughes Report*, p. 6.
100. Interview with Eamonn Hughes, in 'Solving the Past', *BBC Spotlight*, 9 November 2004.
101. Eileen Hughes interview.
102. HET, *Francis Hughes Report*, p. 7.
103. Ibid., pp. 6–7.
104. Ibid., p. 13; O'Neill, 'Tell truth about my father's murder'; Relatives for Justice, *Report on Frank Hughes*.
105. Eileen Hughes interview.
106. The victim was 53-year-old William Aitken, *BBC NI News: Inside Ulster*, 24 October 1990.
107. HET, *Francis Hughes Report*, p. 15.
108. McKittrick et al., *Lost Lives*, p. 1207, p. 1210; 'The Committee', *Channel 4: Dispatches*, 2 October 1991; McPhilemy, *The Committee*, pp. 4–5.
109. HET, *Francis Hughes Report*, p. 8, pp. 27–8.
110. Eileen Hughes interview.
111. Relatives for Justice, *Report on Francis Hughes*.
112. 'Witness Statement of Brian McDonald', quoted in HET, *Francis Hughes Report*, p. 9. See also 'Solving the Past', *BBC Spotlight*; Eileen Hughes interview; 'Letter to Nuala O'Loan, Police Ombudsman for NI, in the matter of the Death of Patrick Francis Hughes, 20 May 2006' (on file with Relatives for Justice).
113. HET, *Francis Hughes Report*, p. 35.
114. Ibid., p. 36.
115. Eileen Hughes interview; Relatives for Justice, *Report on Francis Hughes*.
116. HET, *Francis Hughes Report*, p. 38, pp. 41–2; Eileen Hughes interview.
117. HET, *Francis Hughes Report*, p. 29.
118. Ibid., p. 32.
119. Ibid., pp. 36–8.
120. Ibid., p. 11, pp. 25–6.
121. Ibid., p. 10.
122. Ibid., p. 11, p. 26.
123. Ibid., pp. 16–17; Former RUC Detective Superintendent Tim McGregor and interview with Eamonn Hughes, 'Solving the Past', *BBC Spotlight*.
124. HET, *Francis Hughes Report*, p. 18; Eileen Hughes interview; Relatives for Justice, *Report on Francis Hughes*.
125. HET, *Francis Hughes Report*, pp. 40–7.
126. Patrick Boyle, shot dead by the UVF at his home in Eglish Park, Annaghmore, Co. Armagh. See McKittrick et al., *Lost Lives*, p. 1201.
127. HET, *Francis Hughes Report*, p. 31.
128. 'Solving the Past', *BBC Spotlight*.
129. Relatives for Justice, *Report on Francis Hughes*.
130. Eamonn Hughes quoted in O'Neill, 'Tell truth about my father's murder'.
131. 'Man convicted of Eamonn Hughes birthday party murder', *BBC News*, 13 April 2011.

132. Eileen Hughes interview.
133. Interview with Tommy McKearney, 6 December 2012.
134. Graham Ellison and Jim Smyth, *The Crowned Harp: Policing in Northern Ireland* (London: Pluto Press, 2000) p. 42; Tommy McKearney interview.
135. Cadwallader, *Lethal Allies*, p. 34.
136. Fr Denis Faul and Fr Raymond Murray (1976) *The Triangle of Death*, quoted in ibid., p. 34.
137. Cadwallader, *Lethal Allies*, p. 129.
138. Ibid., p. 132; McKittrick et al., *Lost Lives*, p. 634.
139. Historical Enquiries Team, *Review Summary Report Concerning the Murders of Kevin Joseph McKearney and John Francis McKearney* (Lisburn: HET, 2012) (on file with Relatives for Justice), p. 74; McKittrick et al., *Lost Lives*, p. 588.
140. 'HET report on Moy murders slammed as "slovenly and speculative"', *Tyrone Times*, 13 October 2012.
141. McKittrick et al., *Lost Lives*, p. 101.
142. Ibid., p. 647, Cadwallader, *Lethal Allies*, pp. 172–82; Doug Cassels, Suzie Kemp, Piers Pigou and Stephen Sawyer, *Report of the Independent International Panel on Alleged Collusion in Sectarian Killings in Northern Ireland* (Notre Dame, IN: Centre for Civil and Human Rights, Notre Dame Law School, 2006), pp. 53–4; McKittrick et al., *Lost Lives*, p. 645. The attacks on the Eagle Bar and Clancy's Bar on 15 May 1976 resulted in the deaths of father-of-four Frederick McLoughlin, Felix (Vincy) Clancy, owner of Clancy's Bar, Sean O'Hagan, and Robert McCullough. One of the perpetrators was a serving RUC officer.
143. McKittrick et al., *Lost Lives*, pp. 805–6. A brother of Fred Irwin, Thomas, was also later shot dead by the IRA, see ibid., p. 1034.
144. Cadwallader, *Lethal Allies*, p. 57; McKittrick et al., *Lost Lives*, p. 831.
145. McKittrick et al., *Lost Lives*, pp. 854–5.
146. Ibid., p. 1263.
147. HET, *McKearneys Report*, p. 67, pp. 72–3, Cadwallader, *Lethal Allies*, p. 333.
148. HET, *McKearneys Report*, p. 74.
149. Richard English, *Armed Struggle: A History of the IRA* (London: Macmillan, 2003), p. 128; Peter Taylor, *Provos: The IRA and Sinn Fein* (London: Bloomsbury, 1997), pp. 100–2.
150. See Magee, *Tyrone's Struggle*, p. 198; McKittrick et al., *Lost Lives*, p. 446.
151. Magee, *Tyrone's Struggle*, p. 364; Moloney, *Secret History*, 307.
152. Tommy McKearney interview.
153. HET, *McKearneys Report*, p. 9, p. 12; 'McKearney murders – RUC "did not do enough to stop the shootings"', *BBC News*, 27 September 2012; Tommy McKearney interview.
154. Statement of Bernadette McKearney for Relatives for Justice (on file with Relatives for Justice).
155. HET, *McKearneys Report*, p. 40, p. 9.
156. Ibid., p. 59.

157. Sir Desmond de Silva QC, *The Report of the Patrick Finucane Review: Volume I* (London: HMSO, 2012), p. 244.
158. 'RUC Occurrence Book record for 31 December 1991', quoted in HET, *McKearneys Report*, p. 58.
159. HET, *McKearneys Report*, p. 41, p. 66.
160. Ibid., pp. 60–1.
161. The Historical Enquiries Team made just this mistake, see ibid., p. 8.
162. Tommy McKearney interview.
163. HET, *McKearneys Report*, p. 43. These included the killing of Frank Hughes in October 1990 and Patrick and Diarmuid Shields, shot dead by the UVF at Lisnagleer Crossroads, near Dungannon, 3 January 1993.
164. Ibid., p. 15; Tommy McKearney interview.
165. HET, *McKearneys Report*, p. 20.
166. Ibid., p. 17.
167. Tommy McKearney interview.
168. UVF statement, 4 January 1992, quoted in HET, *McKearneys Report*, p. 29; *UTV News*, 4 January 1992.
169. HET, *McKearneys Report*, pp. 25–6.
170. Tommy McKearney interview.
171. HET, *McKearneys Report*, p. 66, p. 78.
172. Tommy McKearney interview.
173. HET, *McKearneys Report*, p. 66.
174. Ibid., p. 37; McKittrick et al., *Lost Lives*, p. 1259. The three men, all married with children, were Desmond Rodgers, Fergus Magee and John Lavery. They were killed as they left a forklift truck factory where they all worked, on 14 November 1991.
175. HET, *McKearneys Report*, p. 37.
176. 'Police records destroyed in Armagh', *UTV Live News*, 12 September 2011; 'Number of files destroyed at Gough Barracks due to asbestos', *FOI Request to PSNI*, 2011, 2011F2011 03150.
177. HET, *McKearneys Report*, p. 55.
178. Ibid., p. 28, p. 49, p. 14, p. 15, p. 17.
179. Ibid., p. 56, p. 72, p. 77.
180. Ibid., pp. 77–8.
181. Tommy McKearney interview.
182. '"Special Branch in Moy at time of murders" – shocking new claims', *Tyrone Times*, 6 October 2012.
183. HET, *McKearneys Report*, p. 15, p. 17, p. 62.
184. Ibid., p. 20, p. 25, p. 76.
185. Ibid., p. 63.
186. Ibid., p. 18.
187. Tommy McKearney interview.
188. HET, *McKearneys Report*, p. 72.
189. Ibid., p. 78.

190. 'Maginnis challenges HET murder report', *Belfast Newsletter*, 29 September 2012; 'HET: RUC didn't do enough to prevent killings', *Irish News*, 28 September 2012.
191. Tommy McKearney interview.
192. Interview with Paddy Fox, 11 July 2012.
193. Laura K. Donohue, *Counter-terrorist Law and Emergency Powers in the United Kingdom, 1922-2000* (Dublin: Irish Academic Press, 2001), p. 87.
194. Paddy Fox interview.
195. Harris, *Prejudice and Tolerance*.
196. Paddy Fox interview.
197. Peter and Jenny McKearney were shot dead in their home by loyalists, near Moy, 23 October 1975. See Cadwallader, *Lethal Allies*, pp. 127-34; McKittrick et al., *Lost Lives*, pp. 588-9. Tommy Molloy was killed in 1993 by the UVF in front of his family as they sat watching TV in the living room of their home in Loughgall. He was allegedly mistaken as being related to local Sinn Fein representative (later MP for Mid-Ulster) Francie Molloy. See McKittrick et al., *Lost Lives*, p. 1311.
198. 'Statement of Bernadette McKearney'.
199. Historical Enquiries Team (HET), *Review of Summary Report Concerning the Murders of Charles Daniel Fox and Teresa Fox* (Lisburn: HET, 2012) (on file with Relatives for Justice), p. 6.
200. Ibid., p. 10; 'Statement of Bernadette McKearney'.
201. There was later suspicion the family dog ('a barker') had been run over deliberately days before so it would not raise the alarm, see HET, *Charlie and Teresa Fox Report*, p. 55.
202. 'Statement of Bernadette McKearney'; HET, *Charlie and Teresa Fox Report*, p. 46.
203. HET, *Charlie and Teresa Fox Report*, pp. 23-5.
204. Ibid., pp. 29-30.
205. Ibid., p. 7, p. 37. The three men were Laurence Maguire, Andrew King and Ralph Phillips. A fourth man was convicted in 1997.
206. McKittrick et al., *Lost Lives*, p. 1308.
207. HET, *Charlie and Teresa Fox Report*, p. 69.
208. Ibid., p. 53.
209. Ibid., pp. 51-2.
210. 'Children of murdered Moy couple Charlie and Tess Fox call for public inquiry', *Tyrone Times*, 23 June 2015; 'Legal bid over UVF shootings probe', *Belfast Telegraph*, 23 November 2014.
211. HET, *Charlie and Teresa Fox Report*, p. 58.
212. 'Army and Police Patrols for the Moy area between Sunday, August 23 and Monday, September 7, 1992', ibid., appendix A.
213. Laurence Maguire quoted in HET, *Charlie and Teresa Fox Report*, p. 69.
214. Ibid.
215. HET, *Charlie and Teresa Fox Report*, p. 58.
216. 'Fox family statement, 7 September 1992', quoted in ibid., p. 35.

217. Paddy Fox, letter to the *Irish News*, quoted in McKittrick et al., *Lost Lives*, p. 1296; interview with local republican, 11 July 2012.
218. Paddy Fox interview.
219. Bernie McKearney quoted in 'Preliminary hearing into couples' murder to open', *Irish News*, 5 May 2014.
220. HET, *Charlie and Teresa Fox Report*, p. 21.
221. Ibid., p. 59.
222. Paddy Fox interview.
223. Historical Enquiries Team (HET), *Review Summary Report Concerning the Death of Noel Daniel O'Kane, Died on Thursday, March 25, 1993* (Lisburn: HET, 2010) (on file with Relatives for Justice), p. 17.
224. Seamus Mallon MP, interviewed on *BBC NI News: Inside Ulster*, 25 March 1993.
225. *BBC NI News: Inside Ulster*, 25 March 1993; Casement/Highstead/Kelly Sinn Féin Cumann, *Óglach Jimmy Kelly, Assassinated at Castlerock Doire, 25 March 1993: Commemorative Booklet* (Dublin: Republican publications, 2013), p. 3; McKittrick et al., *Lost Lives*, pp. 1314–15.
226. McKittrick et al., *Lost Lives*, pp. 1314–15.
227. Ivan Little, 'My boy and Tim Parry died the same day, but nobody remembers Damian', *Belfast Telegraph*, 27 May 2017.
228. Relatives for Justice, *Damien Walsh, a Young Life Cut Short: Murdered by the UDA on the 25 March 1993* (Belfast: RFJ, 2018), p. 6.
229. 'Letter of Dr Sean McLoughlin', quoted in McKittrick et al., *Lost Lives*, p. 1317.
230. UFF spokesperson quoted in Jim Cusack and Gerry Moriarty, 'RUC question men about four Derry killings', *Irish Times*, 27 March 1993.
231. Interview with Neecie Kelly, 23 November 2011. See also Brendan Anderson, 'Father tells of earlier murder bid to murder IRA workman', *Irish News*, 27 March 1993.
232. 'Victim a Provo say police', *Belfast Newsletter*, 27 March 1993.
233. Neecie Kelly interview. See also, Cusack and Moriarty, 'RUC question men'.
234. Neecie Kelly interview.
235. Cusack and Moriarty, 'RUC question men'.
236. Interview with Gerry McEldowney, 14 November 2013.
237. Neecie Kelly interview. See also Anderson, 'Father tells of earlier murder bid'.
238. Alan Smith, shot dead along with John McCloy, Garvagh, 25 April 1994, see McKittrick et al., *Lost Lives*, pp. 1353–4.
239. Interview with Donna Martin, 1 July 2013.
240. 'Statement by Declan Mullan to Relatives for Justice, 3 July 2006' (on file with Relatives for Justice). See also 'Witness Statement of Gerard McEldowney, 2 April 1993', submitted to HM Coroner for North Antrim (on file with Relatives for Justice).
241. 'Statement by Gerry McEldowney to RFJ, 10 April 2006' (on file with Relatives for Justice).

242. 'Statement by Declan Mullan'; 'Witness Statement of Gerard McEldowney'; Gerry McEldowney interview; 'Statement by Gerry McEldowney'.
243. Gerry McEldowney interview.
244. 'Statement by Declan Mullan'.
245. Gerry McEldowney interview.
246. HET, *Noel O'Kane Report*, p. 7.
247. 'Statement by Declan Mullan'.
248. Gerry McEldowney interview.
249. Ibid.
250. Interview with Oonagh Martin, 1 July 2013.
251. Gerry McEldowney interview.
252. Laura Friel, 'Focus on collusion: County Derry, South East Antrim. Collusion victims' families demand truth', *Republican News/An Phoblacht*, 25 May 2006.
253. HET, *Noel O'Kane Report*, p. 7.
254. Quoted in Mallie and McKittrick, *Fight for Peace*, p. 204. See also McKittrick et al., *Lost Lives*, pp. 1335–7.
255. Knight was found guilty of an assault on two women in 2009, had his licence revoked and was returned to prison until his release in 2010.
256. David McKittrick, 'Was this loyalist murderer in the police's pay?', *Independent*, 18 February 2006. The HET wrongly assert this story was first 'revealed' in the republican newspaper *An Phoblacht/Republican News*, but this largely echoed the allegations made in McKittrick's *Independent* piece several days earlier. See HET, *Noel O'Kane Report*, p. 37.
257. HET, *Noel O'Kane Report*, p. 45.
258. Office of the Police Ombudsman for Northern Ireland, 'No evidence Greysteel could have been prevented: Nuala O'Loan', *PONI Public Statement* (16 October 2007).
259. McKittrick, 'Was this loyalist murderer in the police's pay?'.
260. Nuala O'Loan, *Statement by the Police Ombudsman for Northern Ireland on her Investigation into the Circumstances Surrounding the Death of Raymond McCord Jnr and Related Matters* (Belfast: PONI, 2007).
261. Barry McCaffrey, 'Fullertons told UDA murder suspects cannot be charged', *Irish News*, 21 May 2007.
262. HET, *Noel O'Kane Report*, p. 27, pp. 35–6.
263. Neecie Kelly interview.
264. Ibid.; John Cassidy, 'Fears of bloody war', *Belfast Telegraph*, 27 March 1993.
265. Gerry McEldowney interview.
266. Oonagh Martin interview.
267. Fr James Crowley, interview on *Inside Ulster: BBC News Northern Ireland*, 9 May 1994.
268. Interview with Martin Mallon, 11 October 2011.
269. Ibid.
270. Ibid.
271. Ibid.

272. Interview with Mark Thompson, 28 September 2011; 'Incident recalls murder of Roseann Mallon', *An Phoblacht/Republican News*, 27 August 2009.
273. Martin Mallon interview.
274. Larkin, *Very British Jihad*, p. 235.
275. Martin Mallon interview.
276. Ibid.
277. McKittrick et al., *Lost Lives*, p. 1358.
278. Cardinal Cahal Daly quoted in Laura Friel, 'The killing of Roseann Mallon', *Republican News/An Phoblacht*, 25 April 2002.
279. Larkin, *Very British Jihad*, p. 235.
280. McKittrick et al., *Lost Lives*, pp. 1358–9; 'Inside Ulster', *BBC News (Northern Ireland)*, 9 May 1994; 'Inside Ulster', *BBC News (Northern Ireland)*, 11 May 1994.
281. Larkin, *Very British Jihad*, p. 237.
282. Martin Mallon interview.
283. Ibid.
284. Friel, 'Killing of Roseann Mallon'.
285. Martin Mallon interview.
286. Ibid.
287. Ibid.
288. Ibid. See also Larkin, *Very British Jihad*, p. 237.
289. 'Forensic report delays Roseann Mallon inquest', *BBC News*, 13 November 2013; 'Roseann Mallon inquest told Army tapes were wiped after UVF murder', *BBC News*, 5 November 2013.
290. HET, *McKearney's Report*, p. 45, p. 52; Martin Mallon interview.
291. Mark Thompson, 'Mallon murder weapon linked to other collusion cases', *Relatives for Justice* (Belfast: RFJ, 2014), available at: https://relativesforjustice.com/mallon-murder-weapon-linked-to-other-collusion-cases/.
292. Martin Mallon interview.
293. Friel, 'Killing of Roseann Mallon'.
294. Martin Mallon interview.

Conclusion

1. Interview with Jeffrey Donaldson, DUP, 15 July 2013.
2. Interview with Martin Mallon, 11 October 2011.
3. Lord Mark Saville, *Report of the Bloody Sunday Inquiry* (London: HMSO, 2010); Peter Taylor, *Brits: The War Against the IRA* (London: Bloomsbury, 2001), p. 77.
4. General Sir Mike Jackson, *Soldier: The Autobiography of General Sir Mike Jackson* (London: Bantam Press, 2007), p. 71.
5. Jackson, *Soldier*, p. 67.
6. Thomas Harding, 'Bloody Sunday paras were a "jolly good" unit, says general', *Daily Telegraph*, 25 September 2002.

7. William Matchett, *Secret Victory: The Intelligence War that Beat the IRA* (Belfast: Matchett, 2016), p. 34.
8. Patricia Lundy, *Research Brief: Assessment of HET Review Processes and Procedures in Royal Military Police Investigations* (2012); Tom Newton Dunn and Matt Wilkinson, 'Bloody outrage: decision to investigate brave British soldiers over all the killings in Northern Ireland's 30 years of The Troubles branded "witch hunt"', *The Sun*, 7 December 2016.
9. Mark McGovern, 'Ignatieff, Ireland and the lesser evil', in *Discourses and Practices of Terrorism: Interrogating Terror*, ed. by Bob Brecher, Mark Devenney and Aaron Winter (London: Routledge, 2010), pp. 135–55, p. 145.
10. Matthew Hickley and David Williams, '17 years after killing two joyriders, Lee Clegg is back on the frontline', *Daily Mail*, 11 September 2007; Sean Rayment, '15 years after killing joyrider, Lee Clegg is put back in the line', *The Telegraph*, 23 October 2005.
11. Christine Bell, 'Dealing with the past in Northern Ireland', *Fordham International Law Journal*, 26:4 (2002), pp. 1095–147, pp. 1098; Patricia Lundy and Mark McGovern, 'Truth, justice and dealing with the legacy of the past in Northern Ireland', *Ethnopolitics*, 7:1 (2008), pp. 177–93.
12. 'Statutory Instrument 2006 No 2963 (N.I. 17)', quoted in Consultative Group on the Past, *Report of the Consultative Group on the Past* (London: HMSO 2009), p. 67. See also for example, 'DUP MP Jeffrey Donaldson backs new law on definition of a victim', *BBC News*, 23 October 2013.
13. Judith Butler, *Frames of War: When is Life Less Grievable?* (London: Verso, 2010).
14. Consultative Group on the Past, *Report*.
15. 'Northern Ireland Richard Haas talks end without deal', *BBC News*, 31 December 2013.
16. Northern Ireland Office, *The Stormont House Agreement* (NIO: Belfast, 23 December 2014).
17. Ibid., pp. 6–9.
18. UK Government and DUP, *UK Government Financial Support for Northern Ireland*, 26 June 2017.
19. *Draft Northern Ireland (Stormont House Agreement Bill); Addressing the Legacy of the Past: Consultation Paper*, May 2018.
20. See, for example, Colonel Tim Collins, 'Legacy scandal: "security forces must be protected from witch-hunt to appease IRA", says Tim Collins', *Belfast Newsletter*, 20 August 2018; William Matchett, 'Legacy scandal: "republican conspiracy nonsense has been indulged and the RUC trashed", says William Matchett', *Belfast Newsletter*, 21 August 2018.
21. See, for example, Michael Fallon, 'Allowing a one-sided witch hunt against British soldiers is a craven surrender to Sinn Fein', *The Telegraph*, 9 May 2018; David Willetts, 'End the vendetta: MPs sign damning letter to Theresa May pleading with her to end legal witch-hunt of army veterans', *The Sun*, 27 June 2018.

22. See, for example, House of Commons Defence Committee, *Investigations into Fatalities in Northern Ireland Involving British Military Personnel: Seventh Report of Session 2016-2017*, HC 1064, 26 April 2017, p. 16; 'Prime Minister Questions', *Hansard*, HC Deb, 12 September 2018, vol. 646, cc. 754; Secretary of State for Northern Ireland Karen Bradley MP, 'Northern Ireland Debate', *Hansard*, HC Deb, 9 May 2018, vol. 640, cc. 661.
23. See, for example, Vincent Kearney, 'Troubles legacy cases bias disputed by figures', *BBC News (Northern Ireland)*, 2 February 2017; PSNI Chief Constable George Hamilton, cited in Vincent Kearney, 'PSNI chief disputes PM's "terrorists" claim', *BBC News (Northern Ireland)*, 14 May 2018; Northern Ireland Victims' Commissioner Judith Thompson, cited in Stephen Walker, 'Victims' Commissioner says PM's facts "incorrect"', *BBC News (Northern Ireland)*, 14 May 2018.
24. Sir John Stevens, *Stevens Enquiry 3: Overview and Recommendations*, 17 April 2003, p. 16.
25. See, for example, Judge Peter Cory, *Cory Collusion Inquiry Report: Rosemary Nelson* (London: HMSO, 2004).
26. Sir Desmond de Silva QC, *The Report of the Patrick Finucane Review: Volumes I and II* (London: HMSO, 2012).
27. Mike Ritchie, 'Coroner lambasts PSNI approach to disclosure of information on pensioner's killing', *Relatives for Justice*, 17 June 2015.
28. Ed Moloney, *Voices from the Grave: Two Men's War in Ireland* (London: Faber and Faber, 2011, 2nd edn), p. 418; Ian Cobain, 'Northern Ireland loyalist shootings: one night of carnage, 18 years of silence', *The Guardian*, 15 October 2012; Relatives for Justice, *Loughinisland Massacre: Collusion, Cover-up* (Belfast: RFJ, 2012); Nuala O'Loan, *Statement by the Police Ombudsman for Northern Ireland on her Investigation into the Circumstances Surrounding the Death of Raymond McCord Jnr and Related Matters* (Belfast: PONI, 2007).
29. Mark McGovern, 'Inquiring into Collusion? Collusion, the state and the management of truth recovery in Northern Ireland', *State Crime*, 2:1 (2013), pp. 4–29. See also Committee on the Administration of Justice, *Human Rights and Dealing with Historic Cases: A Review of the Office of the Police Ombudsman for Northern Ireland* (Belfast: CAJ, 2011); Patricia Lundy, 'Can the past be policed? Lessons from the Historical Enquiries Team Northern Ireland', *Journal of Law and Social Challenges*, 11 (2009), pp. 109–56.
30. Michael Kirk-Smith and James Dingley, 'Countering terrorism in Northern Ireland: the role of intelligence', *Small Wars and Insurgencies*, 20:3–4 (2009), pp. 551–73, p. 568.
31. Ibid.
32. William Matchett, *Secret Victory: The Intelligence War that Beat the IRA* (Belfast: Matchett, 2016), pp. 244–5, p. 249.
33. Ibid., p. 97.
34. O'Loan, *Raymond McCord Jnr Report*.

35. Michael Maguire, *An Inspection into the Independence of the Office of the Police Ombudsman for Northern Ireland* (Belfast: CJINI, 2011).
36. Michael Maguire, *The Murders at the Heights Bar, Loughinisland, 18 June 1994* (Belfast: PONI, 2016).
37. Relative for Justice, 'Mallon murder weapon linked to other collusion cases', 25 November 2013; 'Forensic report delays Roseann Mallon inquest', *BBC News*, 13 November 2013.
38. 'Gun tampering claims at murder inquest', *UTV News*, 13 January 2015.
39. Lesley-Ann McKeown, 'Roseann Mallon murder gun "tampered with by RUC Special Branch"', *Belfast Telegraph*, 14 January 2015; forensic scientist Jonathan Greer, quoted in 'Roseann Mallon inquest: Special Branch "could have tampered with gun"', *BBC News*, 13 January 2015; 'Gun tampering claims'.
40. Col. Gordon Kerr quoted in Stephen Dorril, *The Silent Conspiracy: Inside the Intelligence Services in the 1990s* (London: William Heinemann, 1993), p. 202; 'Statement to Stevens III Inquiry, 2002', quoted in de Silva, *Patrick Finucane Review (I)*, p. 88, p. 499.
41. Sean Rayment, 'Top secret army cell recruiting Iraqi insurgent double agents', *Sunday Telegraph*, 4 February, 2007.
42. Patricia Lundy and Mark McGovern, 'Whose justice? Rethinking transitional justice from the bottom up', *Journal of Law and Society*, 35:2 (2008), pp. 265–92; Patricia Lundy and Mark McGovern, 'The role of community in participatory transitional justice', in *Transitional Justice from Below: Grassroots Activism and the Struggle for Change*, ed. by Kieran McEvoy and Lorna McGregor (Portland, OR: Hart Publishing, 2008), pp. 99–120; Patricia Lundy and Mark McGovern, 'Participation, truth and participatory action research: community-based truth-telling and post-conflict transition in Northern Ireland', *Sociology*, 40:1 (2006), pp. 71–88.
43. Martin Mallon interview.
44. Sir Reginald Weir, *Verdict on Inquest, Ref: WEI10818*, Delivered 7/1/2019.
45. Ibid., p. 19.
46. Ibid., p. 6.
47. Ibid., pp. 6–12.
48. Ibid., p.11.
49. Ibid., p. 18
50. Ibid., p. 13–14.
51. Ibid., pp. 14–15.
52. Ibid., pp. 2–3.
53. Ibid., p.14.
54. Ibid., p.17.
55. Ibid., p.18.
56. Ibid.
57. Ibid., p. 3.

Further Reading

Amnesty International, *Political Killings in Northern Ireland* (London: Amnesty International British Section, 1994).

Anderson, David, *Histories of the Hanged: Britain's Dirty War in Kenya and the End of Empire* (London: Weidenfeld and Nicholson, 2006).

Bamford, Bradley C., 'The role and effectiveness of intelligence in Northern Ireland', *Intelligence and National Security*, 20:4 (2005), pp. 581–607.

Branch, Daniel, *Defeating Mau Mau, Creating Kenya: Counterinsurgency, Civil War and Decolonization* (Cambridge: Cambridge University Press, 2009).

British-Irish Rights Watch, *Alleged Collusion and the RUC* (London: BIRW, 1996).

British-Irish Rights Watch, *Deadly Intelligence: State Involvement in Loyalist Murder in Northern Ireland* (London: BIRW, 1999).

Cadwallader, Anne, *Lethal Allies: British Collusion in Ireland* (Cork: Mercier Press, 2013).

Cassels, Doug, Kemp, Suzie, Pigou, Piers and Sawyer, Stephen, *Report of the Independent International Panel on Alleged Collusion in Sectarian Killings in Northern Ireland* (Notre Dame, IN: Centre for Civil and Human Rights, Notre Dame Law School, 2006).

Charters, David A., 'Counter-insurgency intelligence: the evolution of British theory and practice', *Journal of Conflict Studies*, 29 (2009), pp. 55–74.

Charters, David A., 'Professionalizing clandestine military intelligence in Northern Ireland: creating the Special Reconnaissance Unit', *Intelligence and National Security*, 33:1 (2018), pp. 130–8.

Cory, Judge Peter, *Cory Collusion Inquiry Report: Patrick Finucane* (London: HMSO, 2004).

Crawford, Colin, *Inside the UDA: Volunteers and Violence* (London: Pluto Press, 2003).

Cusack, Jim and McDonald, Henry, *UVF* (Dublin: Poolbeg Press, 2000, 2nd edn).

Davies, Nicholas, *Ten-Thirty Three: The Inside Story of Britain's Secret Killing Machine in Northern Ireland* (Edinburgh: Mainstream Publishing, 2007, 2nd edn).

De Silva, Sir Desmond, *The Report of the Patrick Finucane Review: Volumes I and II* (London: HMSO, 2012).

Dillon, Martin, *The Dirty War* (London: Arrow Books, 1991).

Dillon, Martin, *The Trigger Men* (Edinburgh: Mainstream Publishing, 2004, 2nd edn).

Dixon, Paul (ed.), *The British Approach to Counterinsurgency: From Malaya and Northern Ireland to Iraq and Afghanistan* (Basingstoke: Palgrave, 2012).

Ellison, Graham and Smyth, Jim, *The Crowned Harp: Policing in Northern Ireland* (London: Pluto Press, 2000).

English, Richard, *Armed Struggle: A History of the IRA* (London: Macmillan, 2003).

Faligot, Roger, *Britain's Military Strategy in Ireland: The Kitson Experiment* (London: Zed Books, 1983).

Farrell, Michael, *Arming the Protestants: The Formation of the Ulster Special Constabulary and the Royal Ulster Constabulary, 1920–27* (London: Pluto Press, 1983).

Faul, Denis and Murray, Raymond, *The Triangle of Death: Sectarian Assassinations in the Dungannon-Moy-Portadown Area* (Dungannon: Denis Faul and Raymond Murray, 1975).

French, David, *The British Way in Counter-Insurgency, 1945–1967* (Oxford: Oxford University Press, 2011).

Geraghty, Tony, *The Irish War: The Military History of a Domestic Conflict* (London: Harper Collins, 1998).

Hearty, Kevin, 'The political and military value of the "set-piece" killing tactic in east Tyrone 1983–1992', *State Crime*, 3:1 (2014), pp. 50–72.

Hewitt, Steve, *Snitch! A History of the Modern Intelligence Informer* (London: Continuum, 2010).

Hillyard, Paddy, 'Perfidious Albion: collusion and cover-up in Northern Ireland', *Statewatch*, 22:4 (2013), pp. 1–14.

Holland, Jack and Phoenix, Susan *Phoenix: Policing the Shadows* (London: Hodder and Stoughton, 1996).

Hughes, Matthew, *Britain's Pacification of Palestine: The British Army, the Colonial State and the Arab Revolt, 1936–39* (Cambridge: Cambridge University Press, 2018).

Human Rights Watch/Helsinki, *To Serve without Favour: Policing, Human Rights and Accountability in Northern Ireland* (London: Human Rights Watch, 1997).

Ingram, Martin and Harkin, Greg, *Stakeknife: Britain's Secret Agents in Ireland* (Dublin: O'Brien Press, 2004).

Jennings, Anthony (ed.), *Justice Under Fire: The Abuse of Civil Liberties in Northern Ireland* (London: Pluto Press, 1990).

Khalili, Laleh, *Time in the Shadows: Confinement in Counterinsurgencies* (Stanford, CA: Stanford University Press, 2013).

Kilcullen, David, *Counterinsurgency* (Oxford: Oxford University Press, 2010).

Kitson, Frank, *Bunch of Five* (London: Faber and Faber, 1977).

Kitson, Frank, *Low Intensity Operations: Subversion, Insurgency and Peacekeeping* (London: Faber and Faber, 1971).

Kitson, Frank, *Gangs and Counter-Gangs* (London: Barrie and Rockliff, 1960).

Larkin, Paul, *A Very British Jihad: Collusion, Conspiracy and Cover-up in Northern Ireland* (Belfast: Beyond the Pale Publications, 2004).

Lawther, Cheryl, *Truth, Denial and Transition: Northern Ireland and the Contested Past* (Abingdon: Oxford, 2014).

Lawyers Committee for Human Rights, *Beyond Collusion: The UK Security Forces and the Murder of Pat Finucane* (New York: LCHR, 2002).

Luban, David, *Torture, Power and Law* (Cambridge: Cambridge University Press, 2014).

Lundy, Patricia, 'Can the past be policed? Lessons from the Historical Enquiries Team Northern Ireland', *Journal of Law and Social Challenges*, 11 (2009), pp. 109–56.

Lundy, Patricia and McGovern, Mark, 'Whose justice? Rethinking transitional justice from the bottom up', *Journal of Law and Society*, 35:2 (2008), pp. 265–92.

Lundy, Patricia and McGovern, Mark, 'Participation, truth and participatory action research: community-based truth-telling and post-conflict transition in Northern Ireland', *Sociology*, 40:1 (2006), pp. 71–88.

MacAirt, Ciarán, *The McGurk's Bar Bombing: Collusion, Cover-up and a Campaign for Truth* (Edinburgh: Frontline Noir, 2012).

Magee, Gerard, *Tyrone's Struggle for Irish Freedom* (Dublin: Tyrone Sinn Fein Commemoration Committee, 2011).

Matchett, William, *Secret Victory: The Intelligence War that Beat the IRA* (Belfast: Matchett, 2016).

McGovern, Mark, 'See no evil collusion in Northern Ireland', *Race and Class*, 58:3 (2017), pp. 46–63.

McGovern, Mark , 'Inquiring into Collusion? Collusion, the state and the management of truth recovery in Northern Ireland', *State Crime*, 2:1 (2013), pp. 4–29.

McGovern, Mark, 'State violence and the colonial roots of collusion', *Race and Class*, 57:2 (2015), pp. 3–23.

McGovern, Mark, 'Informers, agents and the liberal ideology of collusion in Northern Ireland', *Critical Studies on Terrorism*, 9:2 (2016), pp. 292–311.

McKearney, Tommy, *The Provisional IRA: From Insurrection to Parliament* (London: Pluto Press, 2011).

McKittrick, David, Kelters, Seamus, Feeney, Brian and Thornton, Chris, *Lost Lives: The Stories of the Men, Women and Children Who Died as a Result of the Northern Ireland Troubles* (Edinburgh: Mainstream Publishing, 1999).

McPhilemy, Sean, *The Committee: Political Assassination in Northern Ireland* (Niwot COL: Roberts Rhinehart, 1998).

Moloney, Ed, *A Secret History of the IRA* (Harmondsworth: Penguin, 2007, 2nd edn).

Mullan, Don, *The Dublin and Monaghan Bombings* (Dublin: Merlin Publishing, 2000).

Mumford, Andrew and Reis, Bruno C. (eds), *The Theory and Practice of Counter-insurgency* (London: Routledge, 2013).

Murray, Raymond, *The SAS in Ireland* (Dublin: Mercier Press, 1990).

Newsinger, John, *The Blood Never Dried: A People's History of the British Empire* (London: Bookmarks, 2010, 2nd edn).

Newsinger, John, *British Counter-insurgency: From Palestine to Northern Ireland* (Basingstoke: Palgrave, 2002).

Ní Aoláin, Fionnuala, *The Politics of Force: Conflict Management and State Violence in Northern Ireland* (Belfast: Blackstaff Press, 2000).

O'Brien, Justin, *Killing Finucane: Murder in Defence of the Realm* (Dublin: Gill and Macmillan, 2005).
Owens, Patricia, *Economy of Force: Counterinsurgency and the Historical Rise of the Social* (Cambridge: Cambridge University Press, 2015).
Pat Finucane Centre, *The Hidden History of the UDR: The Secret Files Revealed* (Derry: Pat Finucane Centre, 2014).
Patterson, Henry, *Ireland's Violent Frontier: The Border and Anglo-Irish Relations during the Troubles* (Basingstoke: Palgrave, 2013).
Punch, Maurice, *State Violence, Collusion and the Troubles: Counter Insurgency, Government Deviance and Northern Ireland* (London: Pluto Press, 2012).
Relatives for Justice, *Collusion in Cappagh: State Sponsored Murder at Boyle's Bar, Cappagh, Sunday 3 March 1991* (Belfast: RFJ, 2016).
Relatives for Justice, *Loughinisland Massacre: Collusion, Cover-up* (Belfast: RFJ, 2012).
Relatives for Justice, *Ambush, Assassination and Impunity: The Killings of Kevin Barry O'Donnell, Patrick Vincent, Peter Clancy and Sean O'Farrell* (Belfast: RFJ, 2012).
Rich, Paul B. and Duyvesteyn, Isabelle, *The Routledge Handbook of Insurgency and Counterinsurgency* (Abingdon: Routledge, 2014).
Rolston, Bill, '"An effective mask for terror": democracy, death squads and Northern Ireland', *Crime, Law and Social Change*, 44:2 (2005), pp. 181–203.
Rolston, Bill, *Unfinished Business: State Killings and the Quest for Truth* (Belfast: Beyond the Pale Publications, 2000).
Ryder, Chris, *The Ulster Defence Regiment: An Instrument of Peace* (London: Methuen, 1991).
Sluka, Jeffrey A. (ed.), *Death Squad: The Anthropology of State Terror*, ed. by Jeffrey A. Sluka (Philadelphia, PA: University of Pennsylvania Press, 2000).
Stone, Michael, *None Shall Divide Us* (London: John Blake Publishing, 2003).
Taylor, Peter, *Brits: The War Against the IRA* (London: Bloomsbury, 2001).
Taylor, Peter, *Loyalists* (London: Bloomsbury, 2000).
Taylor, Peter, *Provos: The IRA and Sinn Fein* (London: Bloomsbury, 1997).
Tiernan, Joe, *The Dublin and Monaghan Bombings* (Dublin: Joe Tiernan, 2006).
Travers, Stephen and Fetherstonhaugh, Neil, *The Miami Showband Massacre: A Survivors Search for Truth* (Dublin: Hodder Headline, 2007).
Urban, Mark, *Big Boys' Rules: The Secret Struggle Against the IRA* (London: Faber and Faber, 1992).
Urwin, Margaret, *A State in Denial: British Collaboration with Loyalist Paramilitaries* (Cork: Mercier Press, 2016).
Walsh, Dermot, *Bloody Sunday and the Rule of Law in Northern Ireland* (Dublin: Gill and Macmillan, 2000).
Whittingham, Daniel, '"Savage warfare": C.E. Callwell, the roots of counter-insurgency and the nineteenth century context', *Small Wars and Insurgencies*, 23:4–5 (2012), pp. 591–607.
Woods, Ian, *Crimes of Loyalty: A History of the UDA* (Edinburgh: Edinburgh University Press, 2006).

Index

accommodation phase 36
Adams, Gerry 109, 110
Adams, Stanley 143–4
agents
   growing role of 30–1, 39, 44–5
   handling of 41–2, 45–51, 167
   see also Nelson, Brian
Aggressive Observation posts 70–1
Anderson, Sean 103, 112–13
Anglo-Irish Agreement 99–101
Arab Revolt (1936-9) 14–16
'armalite and ballot box' strategy 99
arms importations 7, 57–65, 170
Armscor 57, 60
Armstrong, Michael 90, 93, 94, 95
Armstrong, Thomas 90–2
army *see* British Army
arrest and imprisonment
   hunger strikes 32, 197n197
   informer recruitment and 42
   before killing targets 79–80, 115–16
   Kitson's doctrine and 19
   prison abuse 116
   uniforms for prisoners 179n88
attritional violence 10, 68, 74, 77, 87, 131–5

B Specials (Ulster Special
   Constabulary, USC) 25–7, 143
Baker, Albert 'Ginger' 30–1
Ballygawley RUC station 67
Barron, Henry 65
Battery Bar ambush 83–7, 113
Bernhardt, Douglas 57, 60
Birches RUC station 67
Black and Tans 15, 23
Blelloch, John 48
Bloody Sunday 37, 161–3
Bogues, Mary 115–17, 118
Boyle, Harris 89

Boyle, Patrick 141
Boyle's Bar 89, 91–5
Bradley, Francis 74, 75–5
Bradley, Karen 164
'breakfast table' collusion 131
British Army
   agents and informers, handling of 46–7
   civilian killings, involvement in (proven and alleged) 72–3, 86–9, 156–60, 161–2; Pat Finucane 7, 42, 44, 96, 165, 166
   collusion, cover-up of 52–3, 71
   as counterinsurgency army 10–11
   Counterinsurgency manual of 9, 16–17
   killings of soldiers by republicans 2, 5, 32, 67
   reprisal killings by 23–4
   republicans, killings of by (proven and alleged) 33–5, 68–9, 74, 93–5, 105, 117, 192n67
   role of 38
   shoot-to-kill policy and 68, 70–3, 74–5
   surveillance of loyalist targets by: Battery Bar area 86; Bernadette McAliskey's house 31; Boyle's Bar area 93; Buntings' neighbourhood 35; Damien Walsh's workplace 152; Foxes' neighbourhood 150; Glennane Gang 29; Jimmy Kelly's house 152; John Davey's house 105; Kathleen O'Hagan's neighbourhood 133; Patrick Shanaghan's house 115–16, 117; Roseann Mallon's house 1–2, 157, 158–60, 168–70; Tommy Donaghy's house 119–20
   see also specific unit

Brooke, Peter 52
Brown, Sean 134
builders, killings of 67
Bulloch, Gavin 10
Bunting, Ronald 33–5
Bunting, Ronnie 33–4
Bunting, Suzanne 34, 35
Burns, Sean 73

Callwell, Charles E. 12–13, 24, 38, 172n29
Campbell, Brian 75
Campbell, Pat 83, 84, 85
Cappagh killings 75, 87–95, 166
Carey, Malachy 97–8, 122
Casey, Gerard 75, 78–83
Casey, Tommy 67, 110–13
Cassidy, Danny 97, 123–4
Castlerock massacre 151–5
ceasefire, violence to encourage 134, 151, 160
Chilcot, John 48, 51
Churchill, Winston 24, 25
CID 41–2, 63, 111, 159
Clonoe ambush 74, 75, 76
Coagh ambush 74, 135
Coalisland 87
COIN (British Counterinsurgency tradition)
  collusion, cover-up of 51–3, 77
  founding contributors to 12–20
  liberal ideology and 54–6
  as long-term practice 8–9, 11
  phases of 36–9
  statutory framework, lack of 49–51
collusion
  definition and use of term 3–4, 8
  family and social networks and 130–1
  formal vs informal 30
  intelligence leaks as core of 42–3
  investigation of 164–70
  as part of counterinsurgency 68
colonialism 32, 37, 40, 167
The Committee 112, 140
construction workers, killings of 67

Conway, John and Gerard 22
Cooper, Albert 113
Cory, Peter 3–4, 53, 165
counter-gangs 17, 19–20
counterinsurgency
  definition and methods 9–16
  goal of 6, 131
  as long-term practice 8, 11
  see also COIN
Counterinsurgency manual 9, 16–17
courts 72–3
criminalisation phase 36–7

Dallat, John 123–4, 155
Dalrymple, Gerry 151, 152, 154
Daly, Cahal 149, 158
Daly, Edward 123
Daly, Miriam 33
Davey, John 82, 96–7, 103, 104–6, 198n1
Davey-Kennedy, Pauline 96, 103, 104, 105, 106, 107
de Silva, Desmond, and report of
  on arms importing 57–8, 59, 62
  on Brian Nelson 7, 44, 58–9
  on collusion 42, 43, 53, 165
  on handling of agents and informers 45–6, 47, 48–50
  on intelligence targeting of republicans 104
  on RUC ignoring loyalist threats 144
detention *see* arrest and imprisonment
Devlin, Eugene 192n67
Devlin, Michael 84, 85, 87, 113, 135
Dillon, Charles 123
Dillon, Martin 105
Dillon, Seamus 212n94
Diplock, William John Kenneth 72–3
DMSUs 123–4
Dobson, Thomas and Robert 143
Donaghy, Tommy 97, 103, 119–21, 155
Donaldson, Denis 4
Donnelly, Jack 143
Downing Street Declaration 102

Driscoll, Tony 111
Dublin bombing (1974) 28, 29, 63, 64
Duffy, Paul 74
DUP (Democratic Unionist Party) 59, 100, 164

East Tyrone, as centrepiece of shoot-to-kill 68, 74–5, 77, 134
Elliott, William 143
'emergencies' 20, 26, 53–6
Enniskillen bombing 134
Erwin, Fred 143
European Court of Human Rights 118
evidence *see* justice
expediency, vs the law 17–18

family members, killing of 142–7
   targeting of directly: Charlie and Teresa Fox 132–4, 160; Kathleen O'Hagan 132–4, 160; Roseann Mallon 1–2, 155–60, 165, 166, 167–8
   while targeting Republicans 132; Frank Hughes 67, 132, 138–41; Phelim McNally 86, 98, 132, 135–8
Farmer, Robin 143
Faul, Denis 79, 94, 142
Feeney, Brian 103–4
Finucane, Pat 7, 42, 44, 96, 165, 166
Flanagan, Ronnie 42
force, in counterinsurgency strategy 10, 13, 14
formal collusion 30
Fox, Charlie and Teresa 134, 147–51, 166
Fox, Paddy 148, 150
FRU (Force Research Unit)
   'armchair rules' for 167
   arms trade, role of in 57–8
   establishment and role of 43–4
   Judge Cory on 53
   loyalists, sharing of intelligence with 7, 44–5, 80–1, 104
   Milltown massacre and 105
   UDA and 126

Fullerton, Eddie 67, 103, 124–7, 155
Fulton, Mark "Swinger" 141, 149

Gardaí inquiry 127
Geraghty, Tony 53
Gibson, Maurice 73
Gibson, Ned 135–6
Gillespie, Patsy 67
Glennane farm 63–4
Glennane Gang 28–31, 138
Glenngannon Hotel attack 212n94
Glover, James 43
Good Friday Agreement 154
Gough Barracks 39, 81, 113, 136, 146, 149, 156, 169
Gow, Ian 32, 101–2
Greer, Ned 126
Grew, Dessie 74, 90
Greysteel massacre 154, 155, 195n156
Gwynn, Charles 13–16, 38, 173n44

H-Blocks 32, 197n197
Harte, Gerard and Martin 74
'hearts and minds' doctrine 8
Heenan, Paddy 31
Heights Bar *see* Loughinisland massacre
Hermon, John 40, 79
HET (Historical Enquiries Team) investigations
   Castlerock massacre 155
   Charlie and Teresa Fox killings 149–50
   Damien Walsh killing 152
   elimination of 163, 165
   Frank Hughes killing 140–1
   Kevin and Jack McKearney killings 146–7
   Roseann Mallon killing 159–60
Hillcrest Pub bombing 142–3
Hogan, Henry 74
Hogg, Douglas 96
Hughes, Daniel 89
Hughes, Eamonn 132, 138–42
Hughes, Frank 67, 132, 138–41
human assets *see* agents; informers

hunger strikes 32, 197n197
Hurson, Martin 90

ideology 36–7
Imperial Policing (Gwynn) 12, 13–16
imprisonment *see* arrest and imprisonment
impunity culture 71–3, 162, 164
Independent Commission for Police Complaints 118
Indonesia 187n43
informal collusion 30
informers
  growing role of 30–1, 39
  handling of 41–2, 45–51, 167
INLA (Irish National Liberation Army) 32, 143
inquests
  delays to 76, 117–18
  evidence repression in 113, 117–18, 121
  reduced power of 73
  reopening of 163
  usefulness of 166–7
institutional collusion 4, 8
insurgency, definition 9
intelligence
  centrality of to counterinsurgency 19
  as policing paradigm 41–2
international public enquiries 118
IRA (Irish Republican Army)
  destruction of as British aim 68–9
  killings by: of B Specials 25, 143; of British soldiers 2, 32, 67; of civilians 2, 32, 67, 135–6, 143, 152; Enniskillen bombing 134; of Henry Wilson 12; of judges 72; of politicians 32, 101–2; of RUC police 2, 67, 143; of UDA 126; of UDR 2, 27, 67, 113, 135–6, 143
  killings of: by British Army 68–9, 74, 192n67; by colluding forces 78–95, 112–13; Loughgall ambush 2, 62, 66, 68, 76, 189n7; by RUC 69, 120–2; by SAS 71–2, 73, 74–7, 93–5, 135; by UFF 151–5
  official blaming of for loyalist actions 21
  see also PIRA
IRSP (Irish Republican Socialist Party) 32, 33–4
Israeli Special Forces 15

Jackson, Mike 10–11, 161–2
Jackson, Robin 60–1, 64–5, 89, 112, 122
Jeapes, Tony 46
Johnston, Kenneth 198n3
justice
  blaming of IRA for loyalist actions 22
  freedom from, in collusion 3, 29–30, 77, 168–70
  permitting of violence 53–6, 71–3, 77–8, 162
  shoot-to-kill, non-prosecution of 77, 82–3, 86–8, 94–5, 106, 109–10, 112–13, 117–18, 124, 129–30, 138, 140–2, 149–50, 154–5, 160
  withholding/destruction of information 33, 113, 117–18, 146, 149, 155, 159, 166–70
  witness tampering and suppression 73, 94, 109, 117–18, 157, 169–70
  see also rule of law

Kelly, Jimmy 75, 132, 134, 151–5
Kelly, Patrick 76
Kenya 20, 38
Kerr, Gordon 44, 45, 46–7, 51, 55, 167
Kitson, Frank 12–13, 16–20, 38, 161–2
Knight, Torrens 154–5, 218n255

Larkin, Paul 158
Lavery, Barney 135–6
Lavery, John 215n174
legacy investigations 164–8
Leslie, Roy 143

liberal ideology 53–6
Libya, arms from 67
Lisburn Lie Machine 21
Little, Noel 60
Lloyd George, David 23, 24
Loughgall ambush 2, 62, 66, 68, 76, 189n7
Loughinisland massacre 58, 61, 64, 128–30, 195n156, 208n3
Loughinisland report 61, 128–9, 166
Lowry, Robert 29–30
loyalist groups (in general)
    exclusion from shoot-to-kill operations 69–70
    intelligence provision to 42–3
    killings by 2, 5, 78–95, 100, 103, 128–9
    see also specific group
LVF (Loyalist Volunteer Force) 212n94
Lynagh, Jim 76
Lynch, Gary 126
Lyttle, Noel 33–4

MacMahon, Owen, and sons 25
Magee, Fergus 215n174
Maginn, Loughlin 51–2, 81
Maginnis, Ken 144, 147
Maguire, Laurence 149, 150
Maguire, Michael 63, 64
Malachy's bar 90
Malaya (British) 17, 19
Mallon, Christie 1
Mallon, Martin 1, 169
Mallon, Roseann 1–2, 155–60, 165, 166, 167–70
Mallon, Seamus 151
Martin, Declan 74
Martin, Donna 153
Maskey, Alex 79
Mates, Michael 88
May, Teresa 164
McAliskey, Bernadette 31, 32, 33, 131
McClelland, William 33
McConnell, Eric 33
McConnell, Robert 33

McCrea, William 96, 102–3, 104, 109
McEldowney, Gerry 152, 153–4
McElhone, Patrick 72
McGaughey, Martin 74, 90
McGirr, Colm 75
McGurk's Bar bombing 21
McIvor, Malachy 113
McKearney, Bernie (Bernadette) 134, 144, 147, 148–9, 151
McKearney, Jack 145–7
McKearney, Kevin 144–7
McKearney, Margaret 143–4
McKearney, Padraig 143–4
McKearney, Peter and Jenny 142–3, 148, 216n197
McKearney, Sean 143–4
McKearney, Tommy 142, 143–4, 146, 147
McKee, Liam 81
McKeever, Aidan 76–7
McKenna, James 151, 152, 153, 154
McKenna, Paddy 190n32
McKerr, Gervais 73
McKnight, Cecil 126
McMichael, John 60, 104, 126
McNally, Francie 86–7, 135–8
McNally, Phelim 86, 98, 132, 135–8
McNeill, Tony 156
McPeake, Charity 133
McPeake, Sean 116, 133
McVeigh, Patrick 22
MI5 7, 41, 156–7
Miami Showband massacre 28, 29, 64, 88–9
Mid-Ulster
    as critical site of battle 66, 74–5, 97
    loyalism and 64–5
    overview of conflict in 2, 6, 132
    see also East Tyrone
militarisation phase 36–7
military, the *see* British Army; FRU; MRF; SAS
Millar, William 190n33
Milltown Cemetery attack 105
minimum force doctrine 8, 14
Mitchell, James 63–4

Molloy, Tommy 148, 216n197
Moloney, Ed 134
Monaghan bombing 28, 29, 63, 64
'moral force of civilisation' 13
Mountbatten, Louis, 1st Earl of 32
Moy killings 142–7
MRF (Military Reaction Force) 20–1, 22, 30–1, 175n9 see also FRU; SRU
Mullan, Declan 153–4
Mullan, Francis and Bernadette 89, 142
Mullin, Brian 74
murder triangle 2, 28–31, 88–9, 142, 148
Murray, Raymond 19, 142

Neave, Airey 32
'necessity' doctrine
  in counterinsurgency strategy 10, 14
  legal veneers and 15–16, 17–18
  liberal ideology and 54–6
  military impunity and 162
  rejection of law for 167
Nelson, Brian
  arms trading, role of in 57–8, 60
  arrest and conviction of 45, 48, 61
  collusion by 7, 43–5, 80–1, 104
Nelson, Rosemary 165, 166
Newsinger, John 16
Nicol, Raymond 113
NIO (Northern Ireland Office) 47–8, 103
non-combatant immunity 131–2
Nugent, Malcolm 90–2
Nugent, Siobhan 90, 93, 95, 135

Observation Post (OP/React) 70–1, 76
O'Donnell, Briege 90, 92, 93, 94, 95
O'Donnell, Dwayne 90–2
O'Hagan, Bernard 97, 103, 104, 107–10
O'Hagan, Fiona 109
O'Hagan, Kathleen 132–4, 160
O'Hagan, Paddy 133

O'Kane, Noel 151, 152, 154
O'Loan, Nuala 155
Ormeau Road massacre 67
O'Toole, Fran 89

Paisley, Ian 60, 79
Palestine 14–16
Parachute Regiment 87–8, 161–3
Pascoe, Robert 46
Payne, Davy 187n41
Petraeus, David 9
Phoenix, Ian 62, 187n43, 187n46
PIRA (Provisional IRA) 5, 66
police
  counterinsurgency as paradigm for 40, 41–2
  militarisation of 39–40
  see also B Specials; RUC
Police Ombudsman 2, 58, 63, 128–9, 150–1, 155, 163, 165–6
political solutions, state violence as preliminary to 98, 101, 134, 151
politicians, targeting of see Sinn Fein
politics, and counterinsurgency strategy 10, 36–7, 98
Price, William 75
prisons see arrest and imprisonment
prosecution see justice
Protestant Action Force 138 see also UVF
pseudo-gangs 20, 22, 28
PSNI (Police Service of Northern Ireland) 165–6
Public Interest Immunity Certificates 73

Quinn, John 90–2
Quinn, Poilin 91, 92, 134

racism 13
Rafferty, Malachy 91
'reasonable force' 72–3, 75, 77
reprisals
  Gwynn on 16
  as regular tactic 23–4, 25
RIC (Royal Irish Constabulary) 23–4

RIPA 2000 (Regulation of Investigatory Powers Act) 50
Rising Sun pub massacre 154, 155, 195n156
Robinson, Brian 190n32
Rodgers, Desmond 215n174
Rooney, Daniel 22
Royal Irish Regiment 5
Royal Ulster Rifles, in Palestine 15
RUC (Royal Ulster Constabulary)
    agents and informers, handling of 40–3, 46
    arms importations and 58–9, 61–4
    cover-up of collusion by 52–3
    establishment of 25–6
    intelligence sharing practices of 42
    IRA killings of 2, 67, 143
    killings, involvement in (proven and alleged): Battery Bar 85–7; Bernard O'Hagan 107–10; Charlie and Teresa Fox 149–51; civilians 1–2, 152–60; Danny Cassidy 123–4; Eddie Fullerton 127; Gerard Casey 78, 80–3; Jimmy Kelly 152–5; John Daly 106; Justice Gibson's commendation of 73; Kevin and Jack McKearney 144–7; Malachy Carey 122; Owen MacMahon 25; Patrick Shanaghan 115–18; shoot-to-kill policy and 68, 71, 73; support for SAS killings 62, 68; Tommy Casey 110–13; Tommy Donaghy 120–1
    loyalist paramilitary groups, collusion with 28–31, 33, 43, 62–4, 166
    as template for counterinsurgency 26
    threats and threatening behaviour by 82, 95, 97, 104, 110, 111, 115–17, 122, 123–4, 134, 141, 150, 152–3, 157
    total number officers killed 5
RUC Reserve 5
RUC Special Branch
    arms importations and 58–9, 62
    intelligence and 41–2
    Judge Cory on 53
    killings, involvement in (proven and alleged): Jimmy Kelly and civilians 154; Kevin and Jack McKearney 146–7; Loughlin Maginn 81; Pat Finucane 7, 42, 44, 96, 165, 166; Roseann Mallon 156–60, 169–70; Step Inn 29
    role of 40
rule of law
    adaptability of laws 17–18, 26, 72
    agents and informers and 46–53, 55
    in counterinsurgency strategy 10, 14
    expediency law vs 17–18
    impunity culture vs 71–2, 162
    impunity, enshrining of in 164
    myths about 8–9, 14
    state violence and 53–6, 72–3, 77–8, 131–2
    unnecessary, consideration of as 36
    veneer of 15–16, 17–18, 72
    see also justice
Rush, Johnny 98
Ryan, Liam 75, 83–7, 113, 135
Ryan, Michael 83

SAS
    killings, involvement in (proven and alleged): Bunting and Lyttle 33–5; in Cappagh 88–9; civilians 66; in East Tyrone 74–7; increasing number of 70; IRA members 71–2, 73, 74–7, 93–5, 135; John Turnley 33; Loughgall ambush 2, 62, 66, 68, 76, 189n7; Milltown Cemetery 105
    shoot-to-kill policy 40, 69, 70, 71
    SRU and 22
Saville Inquiry 160
Scarry, Elaine 131
SDLP 27, 99, 101, 151–2
secrecy 54–5
sectarianism, constructions of 26

security forces *see* British Army; FRU; MRF; RUC; SAS
segregation 130–1
'set-piece' killings 67–78
Shanaghan, Patrick 97, 103, 114–18
Shields, Pat and Diarmuid 149
shoot-to-kill
  emergence of as policy 6, 37–8, 50–1, 68–9
  increasing number of 70–1
  legality and 72–3, 77–8, 131–2
  non-prosecution of 77, 82–3, 86–8, 94–5, 106, 109–10, 112–13, 117–18, 124, 129–30, 138, 140–2, 149–50, 154–5, 160
  as part of counterinsurgency 68
  as underwritten understanding 66
Sinn Fein
  attempted exclusion of 101, 103–4, 109, 110
  on Boyle's Bar attack 94
  killings/attempted killings of 6, 80, 82, 96–8, 103–27, 151; Bernard O'Hagan 97, 103, 104, 107–10; Eddie Fullerton 67, 103, 124–7, 155; Francie/Phelim McNally 86–7, 98, 132, 135–8; John Davey 82, 96–7, 103, 104–6, 198n1; Malachy Carey 97–8, 122; Patrick Shanaghan 97, 103, 114–18; rise in 101, 102; Tommy Donaghy 97, 103, 119–21, 155
  political strategies of 99–100
Small Wars (Callwell) 12–13
soldiers *see* British Army
South Africa, arms from 57–8, 60, 64
Special Powers Act (SPA) 26, 148
Specials *see* B Specials
SRU 22 *see also* MRF
Stakeknife 4–5
Stalker inquiry 102
Stalker, John 71
state collusion
  definition 4
  goal and methods 6
state terror 20, 22–3, 131–2

Step Inn bombing 29
Stevens inquiries 51–3, 71, 164–5
Stone, Michael 104–5, 201n55, 201n57
Stormont House Agreement (SHA) 163–4
'sudden movement' justification 75
supergrass strategy 72

Taylor, Peter 92–3
TCGs (Tasking and Co-ordinating Groups) 38–9, 62, 158
Teebane massacre 133, 189n12
terror, by the state 20, 22–3, 131–2
Thatcher, Margaret 32, 49–50, 101
Third Force 100
Thompson, Robert 17
'tiger hunt' instructions 71
Toman, Eugene 73
torture 20, 39
torture culture 53–4
truth recovery processes 163–8
Tudor, Henry (Major General Sir) 23
Tugwell, Maurice 21
Turnley, John 32–3
Tyrone Protestant Action Force 139–40

UDA (Ulster Defence Association)
  arms acquisitions by 58–62
  collusion by 7, 30, 42–3, 44–5, 81, 104
  killings, involvement in (proven and alleged) 30–1, 32–3, 126–7, 138
Ulster Resistance and 59–61
UDR (Ulster Defence Regiment)
  establishment and role of 27
  intelligence sharing and 42–3, 81, 129
  IRA killings of 2, 27, 67, 113, 135–6, 143
  killings, involvement in (proven and alleged) 42–3; Bernard O'Hagan 109; Boyle's Bar (Cappagh) 93, 94; in Cappagh

88–9; as Glennane Gang 28–31; Hillcrest pub bombing 142–3; Jimmy Kelly and civilians 152–5; Miami Showband massacre 28, 29, 64, 88–9; Peter and Jenny McKearney 142–3; Phelim McNally 135–6; Tommy Casey 111–13; Tommy Donaghy 119–21
  threats and threatening behaviour by 82, 95, 97, 104, 107, 111, 113, 115–16, 134, 136, 150
  total number of soldiers killed 5, 27
UFF (Ulster Freedom Fighters) 67, 80–1
  intelligence sharing by 104
  killings, involvement in (proven and alleged): civilians 67, 100, 115–18, 123–4, 151–5, 195n156; politicians 80–1, 97–8, 104–5, 109, 125–7; republicans 103
Ulster Clubs 60, 100
Ulster Resistance 59–62, 64, 100, 104–5
'Ulsterisation of blame' 51, 165
uniforms for prisoners 179n88
Urban, Mark 70
US Army's counterinsurgency manual 9–10
USC (Ulster Special Constabulary) see B Specials
UVF (Ulster Volunteer Force)
  arms importing by 58, 60–2
  establishment and role of 24–5
  FRU collusion with 44
  killings, involvement in (proven and alleged): Boyle's Bar 91–5; Charlie and Teresa Fox 148–51; civilians 1–2, 132–4, 140–7, 155–60, 165–8, 215n174, 216n197; Frank Hughes 140–1; Kathleen O'Hagan 132–4, 160; Kevin and Jack McKearney 145–7; Loughinisland massacre 129–30, 195n156; Peter and Jenny McKearney 142–3; Phelim McNally 138; Roseann Mallon 1–2, 155–60, 165, 166, 167–8; Tommy Casey 111; total number (1988-94) 61

victim, contested definitions of 163
violence/destruction by state
  attritional violence 10, 68, 74, 77, 87, 131–5
  ceasefire, to encourage 134, 151, 160
  'exemplary'/'performative of power' 13, 24
  in Kenya 20
  legality and 53–6, 72–3, 77–8, 131–2
  liberal ideology and 54–6
  reprisals 23–4, 25
  role of in counterinsurgency strategy 10, 13

Walker, Patrick (and report of) 40–2, 182n34
Wallace, Colin 64–5
Walsh, Damien 152
war model see militarisation phase
Waters, John 52–3, 70–1
weapons importations 7, 57–65, 170
Weir, John 29, 63, 89, 168–70
White, Keith 190n33
Widgery Inquiry 160
Wilford, Derek 159
Wilson, Henry 12, 24, 25
Wilson, Sammy 109, 125
witness tampering and suppression 73, 94, 109, 117–18, 157
Wright, Billy
  allegations against concerning killings: Cappagh killings 91, 93, 94; Charlie and Teresa Fox 149; Eddie Fullerton 126; Frank Hughes 140, 141; Kevin and Jack McKearney 146; Roseann Mallon 156, 159–60, 165, 169; Tommy Casey 112
  arms trading and 60–1